Witnessing Made Easy

Yes, You Can
Make a Difference

Bishop Dale P. Combs
Lisa Combs
Jim Barbarossa
Carla Barbarossa
Donald Mitchell

Witnessing Made Easy
Yes, You Can Make a Difference

For information, contact:

Jubilee Worship Center Step by Step Press
415 North Hobart Road
Hobart, Indiana 46432
http://www.jubileeworshipcenter.com

Published in the United States of America.

ISBN: 1-4392-4950-4

This book is dedicated to:

† Jesus Christ

† Ray Moore,
who taught Jim Barbarossa to write and share his testimony,
forever changing Jim's life and the lives of thousands worldwide
who have been touched by Jim's teachings

† the members of Jubilee Worship Center,
who willingly accepted
the call of God to evangelize the world

Foreword

And Jesus came and spoke to them, saying,
"All authority has been given to Me in heaven and on earth.
Go therefore and make disciples of all the nations,
baptizing them in the name of
the Father and of the Son and of the Holy Spirit,
teaching them to observe all things
that I have commanded you;
and lo, I am with you always,
even to the end of the age." Amen.

— Matthew 28:18-20 (NKJV)

I feel that before I can effectively talk about this book and its content, I first must say a word about its primary author. Bishop Dale P. Combs is the senior pastor of the Jubilee Worship Center Church of God in Hobart, Indiana. This great church has been a lighthouse in Northwest Indiana for many years, none brighter than during the last 28 years that Bishop Dale P. Combs has served as senior pastor. This church directly reflects the pastor's heart in benevolent giving, world missions, and involvement in many causes that arise in a growing, thriving community. Jubilee Worship Center has set a standard of excellence that is an example to other churches in and out of our denomination. For this reason, Bishop Dale P. Combs has been elected to the highest administrative boards in the State of Indiana and has served on many select committees. He has also been a viable part of our Chaplains Ministry with his extensive background as a chaplain for the federal government as well as state institutions. But even these accolades do not adequately tell the whole story of the man and his personal commitment to his God. Only when you get close to a person under situations of duress can the true character be revealed. I am glad to say that under some of the most stressful situations and crisis conditions, I have found Bishop Dale P. Combs to be a man of integrity and genuine Christian character, exhibiting a quiet confidence in God and bringing a sense of God's peace to troubled people in their times of distress.

I am excited to recommend to you this new book, *Witnessing Made Easy.* As a pastor and administrator, I have always been on the lookout for new tools and resources to assist the Christian Church in fulfilling the Biblical mandate of spreading the Gospel of Jesus Christ to the whole world, and especially to my immediate neighborhood. In this book, you find an A to Z manuscript for teaching new and established Christians how to comfortably share their faith. It is a concise roadmap that takes you from the start line through to the finish line with much attention to detail by covering the educational, spiritual, and pro- motional aspects of engaging your church to win the lost. It includes resources such as Scriptural basis, testimonies, and case results that will inspire every individual to become more involved in the personal responsibility of sharing their experience with Christ. No matter where you are in your Christian walk, whether a new believer or a seasoned veteran of the faith, you will enjoy being able to glean growth nuggets from *Witnessing Made Easy.* It has the potential to impact and refresh your life and revolutionize your church and, more importantly, to alter the eternal destination of many people within our reach who have yet to hear, understand, and accept the Salvation message of Jesus Christ. Only when we become walking testimonies of His great plan can we accomplish this daily mandate.

Once you have completed this book and have found it to give you insight on sharing your faith, pass it on to another. Nothing this effec- tive should lie dormant on a shelf!

MARK S. ABBOTT
State Administrative Bishop
Church of God

Greenwood, Indiana
June 2009

Preface

A Christmas Gift for God:
Seeds of the Search for Better Ways
to Help Save More Souls

For I am not ashamed of the gospel of Christ,
for it is the power of God to salvation for everyone who believes, ...

— Romans 1:16 (NKJV)

Enlisted into My Special Task

"So shall My word be that goes forth from My mouth;
It shall not return to Me void,
But it shall accomplish what I please,
And it shall prosper in the thing for which I sent it."

— Isaiah 55:11 (NKJV)

In the summer of 2006, I began to see how the 400 Year Project that God had directed me to lead for demonstrating how improvements should be accelerated by 20 times from 2015 through 2035 could be brought to a successful conclusion (See *Adventures of an Optimist,* Mitchell and Company Press, 2007). Realizing that perhaps I had devoted too much of my attention to this one challenge, I sought ways to rebalance my life. One of those rebalancing methods was to spend more time communing with God through praying, studying Scripture, attending services, and listening to the still, small voice within.

For several years I had been enjoying the devotionals sent to me daily over the Internet by evangelist Bill Keller. I liked many of them so much that I asked Bill if I could copy them into my blog, and he kindly gave me permission. In those days, he didn't keep an online archive and I felt like many people would want to look up various subjects.

One of those devotionals speared me like an arrow that summer. The evangelist reminded his readers that our responsibility as believers is to share the Gospel with others through our example and our words. Not feeling well equipped to do more than try to be a good example, I began to pray about what else I should be doing.

The next day, my answer came: I was to launch a global contest to locate the most effective ways that souls were being saved and be sure that information was shared widely. This sharing of information about evangelism would be a blessing for those who wished to fulfill the Great Commission to spread the Good News about Jesus Christ. Fortunately, I had studied for several years how such contests had been run by secular organizations to generate improvements. I decided to announce the contest in my blog, http://www.livespirituallybetterthana billionaire.blogspot.com, on August 26, 2006.

I didn't want to presume that someone already had good answers or ways to find such answers: I decided to offer free e-books of *The 2,000 Percent Solution* (AMACOM, 1999) and *The 2,000 Percent Solution Workbook* (iUniverse, 2005) to anyone who enrolled in the contest. It occurred to me that this sharing might also stimulate some good ideas to arise sooner. In pursuing this task, I recalled many conversations with Peter Drucker, the founder of the academic discipline of management, about how sharing secular knowledge with pastors had been helpful to the development of some Protestant megachurches.

I also wanted to share whatever else I could to help make the contest a success. As a prize, I offered the chance to be included in one of two books about great ways to help more souls to accept the Lord as Savior. I would coauthor both books and cover the launch expenses, and the proceeds would go to support the best ideas. Presumably, winning such a contest might also help with getting publicity, attracting volunteers, and gaining donations. My assumption was that most people who have been helping lead souls to Him have been working on that rather than on writing about what they do and seeking publicity to alert others to the opportunity. My experience in writing, producing, and promoting books could possibly be of help to such effective leaders.

I doubt if many people could have been more daunted than I was by the task. I felt like my role, at best, was to be a conduit for God's will. At worst, I might insert myself in ways that harmed the process. I can't quote Scripture accurately, didn't attend a Bible college, and find myself with more to learn about my faith than what I understand. But I do have lots of faith and as a result felt confident that God would find a way for His will to succeed regardless of my blunders.

In fact, as people wrote to me concerning the contest I began to realize that my sense of inadequacy in sharing my faith was pretty normal and that I was actually better equipped to share my faith than I thought. I have read the Bible many times. I'm familiar with the sections of the Bible that call for witnessing our faith to others. I try to set a good example in everything I do. I have become comfortable with telling others that I am a Christian and inviting them to learn more. My suggestions had helped some people begin a search for God that led to them becoming Christians. I began to realize that God may have chosen me for this role of directing the contest in part because I felt inadequate in sharing His love.

Helping Hands

"And whatever you ask in My name, that I will do,
that the Father may be glorified in the Son."

— John 14:13 (NKJV)

Fortunately, my spirituality blog had developed a following before I announced the contest. Within just a few days of the announcement, people sent e-mails with observations and questions about the contest. I appreciated and benefited from all of the comments I received.

Some feared for my soul: To them, this contest looked like I wanted to substitute my own thoughts and actions for the Holy Spirit's guiding hand in leading souls to Salvation. Others were concerned that I was trying to buy my way into heaven. I took those concerns to heart and asked people to pray for me so that I wouldn't fall into such traps.

A few people sent me useful Bible verses that spoke about the proper ways that Salvation might be gained by unbelievers following activities done by believers. I learned from those references and paid careful attention to them.

Many people were concerned by what they saw as ineffective evangelical efforts in the United States. Many different descriptions expressed those concerns, but a fair paraphrase would be to say that too much evangelism was aimed at those who had accepted Christ and too little at those who aren't Christians. In particular, people were concerned that evangelism had become something mostly pursued by a few superstar pastors and ministers while the bulk of Christians did little in this regard.

Other people still saw the biggest opportunities for evangelism in places outside the United States where few had heard of Jesus. They told me fascinating stories about successful witnessing experiments in underdeveloped nations, including even hard-core Muslim countries where sharing God's Word could lead to death.

Occasionally, I was contacted by someone who seemed to know more about how to work with the Christian community than I did. Whenever that occurred, I asked how to attract more contest enrollees. The advice I received was to simply let Christian leaders know about the contest, and the leaders would pass along the information to their congregations and readers. That seemed to me like a suggestion easier said than done. However, I felt encouraged by all of the care, concern, and advice that I received.

A Christmas Gift for God

And when they had come into the house,
they saw the young Child with Mary His mother,
and fell down and worshiped Him.
And when they had opened their treasures,
they presented gifts to Him: gold, frankincense, and myrrh.

— Matthew 2:11 (NKJV)

Christmas can be a disturbing holiday as the challenges of gift giving, card sending, and entertaining weigh heavily on our time, our minds, and our bank accounts. It's easy to lose sight of the reason we celebrate Christmas: to honor the birth of our Lord and Savior, Jesus Christ. I find that if I'm not careful, my Bible reading time diminishes rather than increases just before Christmas, despite my desire to do the opposite. My only remedy has been to devote much of Christmas Day to reading Matthew, Mark, Luke, and John.

Passing one jammed shopping mall after another during the fall of 2006, I began to wonder why no one ever thinks of giving a gift to God for Christmas. After all, the three Magi had presented gifts to Jesus when He was born. Surely, we should continue to give gifts to Him. The more I thought about that omission, the more convinced I became that some people would welcome the idea of enrolling in the contest to lead more souls to the Lord as a Christmas gift to God.

Having had some success in the past with putting out press releases, I took this route to share my idea in the usual way. The response was muted. The secular press just didn't seem very interested, and the Christian media hadn't seemed to notice the release.

After that disappointing result, I did a little online research and found that there were outlets for press releases that go solely to Christian media. I rewrote the earlier press release a little and sent it out via some of those services. I was pleased to find out that it was much less expensive to send out such a release solely to Christian media than to all media.

The response was very encouraging this time. Many Christian news outlets briefly summarized the contest, and inquiries about the contest rapidly picked up. I was also interviewed for some printed articles and drive-time radio programs.

Because of the long lead times involved with some of the stories, I decided to extend the end date for entries from January 31, 2007, to Easter 2007. That also seemed like a logical ending time for finishing a commitment made to God as a Christmas gift in 2006.

I was delighted to find that not only had the quantity of contest inquiries increased, but the quality of the most recent ideas provided some real eye-openers, as well. I was equally impressed that the ideas didn't duplicate one another; people were finding vastly different, effective ways to reach those who didn't know and accept Jesus.

Not surprisingly, the tools of mass communication appealed to some. If you can televise programs around the world where no one is now seeing Christian messages, you can begin to create fertile furrows in unplowed fields. One evangelist shared that by spending $110 in Kenya to televise an hour-long DVD, eleven people reported that they were saved and five others volunteered to work as evangelists. That apparently low cost per person contrasted with some e-mails I received that estimated a cost of more than $10,000 per person saved for some major evangelical events in the United States.

Radio was also described as a possible answer. One man reported that he had found a way to establish Christian radio stations for less than 1 percent of the usual cost. He had several stations operating in Canada and planned to expand to about a hundred more around the world. He reported that relatively few of his listeners had ever heard a Christian message before.

One man wanted to tap into the tremendous flows of tourists who seek entertainment. His idea was to build a Christian-themed multimedia experience in Branson, Missouri, where believers could bring their friends to learn about God's promises.

But most people had the opposite feeling about employing mass media: They saw energizing the vast numbers of Christians as the best way to help lead more souls to Him. After all, if each Christian would speak to just a few non-Christians, the potential for Him to open unsaved hearts would be tremendous.

As you can imagine, there are some amazing individual evangelists: They can walk up to anyone, quickly establish powerful rapport, and talk easily about becoming saved after just a few general sentences. Some of these people contacted me and shared their testimonies. One man even sent a book describing his methods. His approach was so well thought out that it could have been a role model for recruiting sergeants trying to find the next 100,000 U.S. Army troops.

Gradually, I began to hear from people who had focused on taking insecure believers and turning them into effective witnesses. What was the lesson? Directing Christians to help lead more souls to Him is an ongoing educational task of the church that deserves to be part of every worship service. Yes, that's right. People need to be reminded to share their faith during each service and to receive practical training in doing so.

What's the biggest hurdle to getting Christians to share their faith? Many Christians are delighted to be saved, but they don't feel like they have an obligation to help anyone else become saved. Without the desire to help the unsaved, there's little benefit gained by instructing people in how to accomplish that task.

Taking It Step by Step

Then he dreamed, and behold, a ladder was *set up on the earth,*
and its top reached to heaven;
and there the angels of God were ascending and descending on it.

— Genesis 28:12 (NKJV)

One day I was contacted by a pastor's wife, coauthor Lisa Combs, who had read about the contest in the *Church of God Faith News Network* (see http://www.churchofgod.org/), a resource that encourages spreading the Gospel and sharing useful methods for reaching lost people. Lisa told me that their church was very involved in evangelism and that she would pass along the information to the church's evangelists, coauthors Jim and Carla Barbarossa. I soon heard from Jim by e-mail, and I began to learn a lot from Jim and Carla.

While many people who contacted me focused on one evangelism approach or another, I was impressed to learn about Jim's bigger vision as an Ephesians 4 evangelist at Jubilee Worship Center in Hobart, Indiana (http://www.jubileeworshipcenter.com), and head of Step by Step Ministries in Porter, Indiana (http://www.step-by-step.org). Jim had developed a process for energizing and directing a church's congregation toward local, national, and international evangelism while serving as an example that other churches can emulate.

Jim's background was in business before finding Jesus later in life. Once having been saved, Jim heard a sermon only three days later by a layman, Ray Moore, sharing a message that the congregation could reach lost people by simply writing out their testimonies, printing up copies, and giving away those testimonies wherever they went. That teaching changed Jim's life forever and has since informed his vision and actions that affect lives all over the Earth.

On fire with this message, Jim immediately began witnessing enthusiastically with others. He passed out his testimony wherever he went. Six months later he unknowingly put his testimony under the windshield wiper of the car belonging to the pastor who headed Portage Christian Fellowship. Pastor Baker immediately prayed to God to send someone like the person who passed out the testimony to be in his church.

Eighteen months after that, Jim and Carla were looking for a new church. Ray Moore recommended his church, Portage Christian Fellowship. Pastor Baker quickly identified Jim's anointing as an evangelist.

Ray next told Jim that Ray had for a time taken five minutes in each service to talk about evangelism, but the encouragement to share their faith had never taken off in the congregation there. Ray mentioned to Pastor Baker and to Jim that Jim should take up this activity again. Both agreed, and Jim provided five minute exhortations to testify for the next two years until Pastor Baker was called to be with the Lord. At that point, Jim and Carla changed churches, and coauthor Bishop Dale P. Combs invited Jim and Carla to become evangelists at Jubilee Worship Center. If you ever get a chance to meet Jim, you'll see that he's a natural for his spiritual calling.

At the time I met Jim, here's how the step-by-step evangelism process worked. Jim had signed on with his wife, Carla, as an evangelist for Jubilee Worship Center. Now, if you are like me, you probably haven't ever been to a church with evangelists for the congregation on staff. Jim's view is that the first full-time pastoral employee a congregation should hire after a pastor or minister is an evangelist. This step should occur when the church has around seventy members.

Why does such a small church need an evangelist? Jim's view is that most ministers and pastors are overwhelmed with other responsibilities, especially if the church is just starting up and growing. In such circumstances, evangelism is usually limited to altar calls among the mostly saved congregation.

Jim's pastor, Bishop Dale P. Combs, wanted to do more and felt called to add an evangelist for his congregation. (See the Pastor's Prologue to learn more about witnessing from a pastor's point of view.) Bishop Combs asked Jim what resources Jim needed to succeed. Jim asked for five minutes out of every service; otherwise, he felt that he wouldn't be able to make steady-enough progress. At first, this time was devoted to creating a desire to witness. Church members were initially very resistant. However, Bishop Combs and Jim were firm in their commitment, and progress was slowly made in creating a desire to witness among the congregation.

Yet, even after creating a desire among congregants to witness, many admitted that they felt afraid to do so. Some were concerned about saying the wrong thing and harming someone. Others didn't want to face rejection. How could those fears be overcome?

Then Jim was inspired to ask each person in the congregation to provide a written personal testimony that could be combined into a book. Editors and typists helped parishioners with this writing. In many of the testimonies, people describe their lives before they accepted Jesus as their Savior and go on to explain how much better life has been since then. The stories are very powerful and interesting to read. I suspect that the members of many churches don't know what good works God has done within their congregations. Certainly, those who haven't been saved don't know what a wonderful experience receiving Salvation is. Each person also provided a photograph for the cover. Over time, most church members chose to share their testimonies in a book entitled *Real Life Stories*.

Each person in the church was then asked to take seven copies of *Real Life Stories* (you can read excerpts from the current version of the book in Appendix C) a week and to hand them out to friends, neighbors, strangers, bank tellers, grocery clerks, waitstaff, and anyone else it occurred to the church member to talk to. The books don't look "churchy" in Jim's view, and recipients are impressed to receive a book from an author whose picture appears on the cover. Church members are encouraged to inscribe the books to the recipient as though performing a formal signing at a major bookstore, noting on what page their testimony falls. Not surprisingly, many people took the books, looked at the one- or two-page testimony of the giver ... and kept reading.

This approach meant that congregants could be sure the right message was being shared and the perceived personal risk from their offer to witness was minimal. When a conversation ensued, the witness could fall back on describing a well-prepared personal testimony that would be interesting to most people.

In quantities of many thousands, these paperback books are inexpensive to print and bind. Where do the funds for producing the books come from? The church has a special box on the floor near the altar where members are asked to drop extra donations (above their normal tithes and offerings) for the purpose of evangelism.

As a result of continuing with the book program, about 40 percent of the church's members are out sharing the Gospel every week through handing out these books or tracts based on the testimonies. To me, that percentage was very impressive.

Before the church had these books containing members' testimonies, Jim had a few tracts printed up that contained practical messages about peoples' problems and how Jesus could be the answer. The tracts concluded the last page with the sinner's prayer and a way to contact Step by Step Ministries for discipleship. From the beginning, the most enthusiastic church members used the tracts to introduce people to Jesus.

Soon, Jim and Carla were hearing about copies of the tracts and books that had reached people all over the United States and in dozens of countries around the world. Jim began to think about what else might be done.

He decided to add audio tapes that could be shared. The power of the voice is often greater than the printed word, and such tapes are also helpful to people who cannot or don't have the time to read but want to learn about God.

In the system to provide these simple messages (via tracts, tapes, and books), Jim also realized that his evangelistic efforts could support foreign missions without the substantial expense involved of sending missionaries from the United States. Instead, Christians in foreign nations who wanted to share God's love could use Step by Step tracts, tapes, and books to do so. In many cases, the unsaved said they wouldn't read or listen to the material when offered, but took the materials anyway and later read or listened to them. After the tapes, tracts, and the books are provided by a volunteer, the idea is to visit again in three days to see if the recipient wants to talk about the material.

After a large-enough new congregation is established in a foreign land, local versions of the testimony books can be created from that congregation's experiences. In addition, it was often cheaper to translate and print the tracts and books or duplicate the tapes in underdeveloped countries than in the United States. By seeding these non-U.S. Christians with the tools and the witnessing process, the foreign Christians were able to save many souls and create communities of believers who can hopefully raise enough funds to become financially self-sufficient in their evangelism.

For months, one of my daily pleasures was to receive e-mails from Jim that contained reports of evangelical efforts in various countries. The most exciting of these reports would show dozens of individual photographs of smiling new Christians after emerging from their water baptisms. Other e-mails contained the happy testimonies of these excited new members of the faith.

In 2006, Jim and Carla realized that they could teach others to play the evangelist roles in their churches, and a conference was organized to provide this education. Plans are underway to do this again. DVDs of this conference are available and are sent to foreign nations to train church-connected evangelists in those countries.

I look forward to keeping in touch with Jim and Carla and their Bishop, Dale P. Combs, and Dale's wife, Lisa, to learn what steps they will add to further improve this process. If you pay attention to the steps you take to serve God, each single step can take you further toward God's will for your life and our world.

The biggest surprise of all was to realize that by God directing Jim to me through Lisa I had uncovered a 2,000 percent squared solution (two complementary ways of accomplishing twenty times as much with the same time, effort, and resources that permit benefits to increase by four hundred times over normal efforts). Here's what I mean: This approach used by Jubilee Worship Center and Step by Step Ministries to sharing the Gospel involves a twenty-times higher level of congregational witnessing than the typical church, and support for foreign witnessing has cost a mere 25 cents per person saved, way less than 4 percent of what traditional methods cost. As a result, one church is helping more than 400 times more people gain Salvation than would normally occur.

Hearing the Call to Discipleship

... as you know how we exhorted, and comforted, and charged every one of you,
as a father does his own children,
that you would walk worthy of God
who calls you into His own kingdom and glory.

— 1 Thessalonians 2:11-12 (NKJV)

New Christians often need a lot of support after accepting the Lord Jesus as their Savior and repenting their sins. Many converts don't yet know what it fully means to be a Christian, and most will want to learn more. For that reason, those who come to an altar call in church are usually given briefing materials and encouraged to take classes to pursue their new faith.

Many people asked me what would come next after the contest was over and the books were published. Some suggested that perhaps the contest could be repeated from time to time (much like Carol Coles, Robert Metz, and I encourage people to repeat the 2,000 percent solution process on the same issue).

I don't know if that's the right approach or not, but it may well be. Recently my mind has been very focused on concern about what could happen to lots of new believers if they aren't discipled well by more experienced Christians to learn more about their faith. I suspect that the numbers of people who have paid a lot of attention to what to do after Salvation are much larger than the people who have looked for more effective ways to share their faith about Jesus and Salvation. Is discipleship an area where there should be another contest? Or should some other activity be initiated?

I'm sure that what to do next will be much clearer after the books are written about the winners of the contest to identify and publicize ways to help lead more souls to accept Jesus Christ as Lord and Savior. Naturally, if God wants me to do something else, He'll let me know.

Please realize that the full story of this contest about helping lost people find and accept Salvation won't be written and understood for several years. Time is needed for the ripples of this contest to move forward in my life and across the lives of others to do God's will. God knows where it's all going, but I don't.

DONALD MITCHELL

Weston, Massachusetts
May 2008

Pastor's Prologue

The Pastor and
the in-Congregation Evangelist:
A Team for Leading More Souls to Christ

Now when they drew near Jerusalem,
and came to Bethphage, at the Mount of Olives,
then Jesus sent two disciples, ...

— Matthew 21:1 (NKJV)

The call to evangelize the world is something that every pastor has heard in one form or another. The words of Jesus speak to us louder than ever in our day and time. With so much happening on a global scale as well as in our own back yards, never has it been more urgent for pastors and church leaders to fulfill the commission of Christ to "Go therefore and make disciples of all the nations, baptizing them in the name of the Father and of the Son and of the Holy Spirit, ..." (Matthew 28:19, NKJV).

Pastors around the world have read this verse over and over again. Most all have preached from the text; they can quote it forward and backward, yet that does not change the fact that many pastors, especially in America, struggle to bring their congregations to fulfill this mandate of Christ to the lost world.

Check Your Beliefs

You say to God, "My beliefs are flawless and I am pure in your sight."

— Job 11:4 (NIV)

The challenge of leading a congregation to obey these words of Christ can be partly due to two incorrect beliefs. First, according to a survey taken in 2005 and published in January 2006 by the Barna Group, Protestant pastors usually believe that well more than half of the adults in their churches put their faith in God above all other priorities. (See the press release about this survey entitled, "Surveys Show Pastors Claim Congregants Are Deeply Committed to God, But Congregants Deny It!" at http://www.barna.org/FlexPage.aspx?Page=BarnaUpdate &BarnaUpdateID=215/.) Unfortunately, another 2005 survey conducted by the same organization and reported in the same press release noted that only 23 percent of adults in Protestant congregations put their faith first. Second, the Protestant pastors surveyed most often believed (54 percent) that church-related volunteer activity is the best means to measure the spiritual health of a congregation, while only 13 percent of congregants viewed witnessing as a measure of spiritual health.

I believe that most pastors view volunteerism as a measure of spiritual health because most pastors are overworked and they welcome any and all assistance to their ever-increasing schedules. The majority of ministry is done by what many in the church call the "paid professional," better known as the clergy. If someone is sick, call the pastor; if someone needs a visit, call the pastor; if someone is in the hospital, call the pastor; if your sink is plugged, call the pastor; if you need a ride somewhere, call the pastor; if someone needs to receive Salvation, CALL THE PASTOR!

The congregation seems to believe that it is the responsibility of the pastor to do all the church's ministry. The comment heard from many parishioners is, "That is why we pay him!"

Fifteen hundred pastors leave the ministry each month according to the 1998 report by Focus on the Family, but that's not the worst news. The stress of doing ministry for many pastors has become so overbearing that as many as 50 percent would leave the ministry if they could, but don't only because they know of no other way of making a living (according to a survey taken in 2005 and 2006 by the Francis A. Schaeffer Institute of Church Leadership Development and reported in an article, "Statistics on Pastors" by Dr. Richard A. Krejcir available at http://www.intothyword.org/apps/articles/default.asp?artic leid=36562&columnid=3958).

Too much work isn't the only problem plaguing pastors: As reported by Dr. Gary J. Oliver and Dr. Greg Smalley in "Enriching Relationships for a Lifetime," which can be read at www.liferelation ships.com/cri/, many say that the hardest thing about ministry is dealing with problem people, such as disgruntled elders, deacons, worship leaders, worship teams, board members, and associate pastors.

Ask the Lord for Help

I can do all things through Christ who strengthens me.

— Philippians 4:13 (NKJV)

Pastors always face challenges, but with Christ's help they can succeed. With so many deciding to quit and others discouraged, it may be that many pastors are not being persistent and patient in asking for the Lord's help. Consider this evidence: Eighty percent of pastors said they spend less than fifteen minutes a day in prayer (as reported in 2002 by Maranatha Life, "Statistics About Pastors," located at www.maranathalife.com/lifeline/stats.htm), and according to Dr. Krejcir's surveys, 70 percent reported that the only time they spend studying the Word is when they are preparing their sermons.

With only 20 percent of pastors spending significant time in daily prayer, is it any wonder those who don't pray much have such a distorted view of how to lead their congregations? As a pastor, I can relate to this. When I spend little time praying, I see the church through clouded eyes. My vision narrows and the church looks different to me: I have little compassion for hurting people; I start feeling overwhelmed; and, like Elijah, I begin to think I am the only one doing anything for the Kingdom of God.

Do not misunderstand what I am saying. I love the ministry and I love God's people: But when you are spiritually, emotionally, and physically depleted, it is easier to quit than to fix what needs fixing. It is not long before you find yourself on a slippery slope downward, and you justify your actions by measuring what you are doing outwardly rather than by what the Holy Spirit and the Scriptures tell you.

It is hard for me to imagine being called of God to do ministry and waking up one day no longer having a passion or desire to continue on. I am convinced that I do not have to be part of these statistics. Having a passion for ministry, loving the ministry, and enjoying the blessings of the ministry can be a reality.

Pastors need to reassess their calls to serve, repent before God of their lack of prayer, stay on their faces until they have a genuine encounter with the Holy Spirit, allowing Him to anoint their eyes with eye salve so they can see again (Revelation 3:18), and understand the Biblical principle for ministry in the local church by realizing that the real measure of ministry is being a witness and making disciples. That was the commission of Jesus to the church. That is what the early church was all about.

Accept Christ's Gifts

Therefore you do not lack any spiritual gift
as you eagerly wait for our Lord Jesus Christ to be revealed.

— 1 Corinthians 1:7 (NIV)

How should pastors refocus their congregations on witnessing? The answer lies in understanding Ephesians 4:11-12 (KJV): "And he gave some, apostles; and some, prophets; and some, evangelists; and some, pastors and teachers; For the perfecting of the saints, for the work of the ministry, for the edifying of the body of Christ: ...."

A quick look at these verses reveals five important gifts: Christ gave to the church body apostles, prophets, evangelists, pastors, and teachers. Each gift is given for the perfecting of the saints, for the work of the ministry, and the edifying of the body of Christ. How amazing is this?

As a pastor I am only one gift to the church. If I want to reach the world with the Gospel as I am called to do, I must allow Christ to give to the congregation the other gifts necessary to complete the task.

This view goes contrary to what many pastors do: When they want to extend ministry, they look for another pastor to assist them. For example, if a pastor sees the need to reach young people, he hires a youth pastor. If there is a need to reach those over 55, he hires a pastor for seniors. If he is having trouble staying in touch with all the new families visiting his church, he hires a visitation pastor. On and on the list goes, with very little thought about Ephesians 4:11-12.

Please do not misunderstand what I am saying: I think there is a need for youth pastors and visitation pastors and so on. It is essential to be sure that the other four gifts are available to the congregation.

To properly equip my congregation to witness, I had to realize that I am not an evangelist, not a prophet, and, at this point, not an apostle. I am a pastor-teacher. To help Christians witness, I have to expose them to the other three gifts of Christ that assist in doing so.

Accomplish More As a Pastor

Return to your rest, O my soul,
For the LORD has dealt bountifully with you.

— Psalm 116:7 (NKJV)

The mission of the church to this world has not changed. Christ is calling fallen humanity back to Him. As a pastor I realize I cannot do it all: I cannot preach every sermon, visit every home, care for every individual who walks through the door of the church, train and encourage every person in witnessing, organize lots of outreach to the lost, and support many foreign missions.

Thankfully I don't have to. Christ gave gifts in the offices of the apostle, the prophet, the evangelist, the pastor, and the teacher. When these gifts are employed for the congregation, more of the responsibility of reaching the world will be fulfilled by building on special talents granted by God. Let me share what I mean.

Since I was a child, I have always been a witness for Christ. While I was young, I gathered the kids on our block to preach to them. During my nonpastoral jobs, I talked to friends at work during lunch breaks. As a pastor, I realized that I spend much of my time talking with the already convinced, people who have already made commitments to Christ.

After a season of prayer twelve years ago, I decided that I needed to expand my contacts with unsaved people. To do this, I became a law enforcement chaplain. This work enabled me to spend time with both saved and unsaved people: I have witnessed to police officers as well as victims of crime and domestic violence; I have been on suicide calls; and I ministered Christ to a family that had lost a six-year-old girl in an abduction and murder case. Other opportunities to be a witness for Christ came in a variety of ways such as by joining the local YMCA to broaden my outreach. I realized that what I was doing other pastors could do but many do not for lack of time. The reason I had the time was because I allowed the gift of the evangelist to join the ministry of our Church.

I know what many of you pastors are thinking, "I can do that teaching and encouraging of the congregation myself!" Yes, you can, and so can I; however, evangelists offer an element to the message that I cannot give: They have a passion and ability to share Christ and to teach others how to witness that yield greater fruit than I can.

It is true I can preach and practice witnessing. I am a witness for Christ, but my gifts are as pastor and teacher, not as an evangelist. That seems natural to me when I study the Word: It makes no sense for the Apostle Paul under the inspiration of the Holy Spirit to say that Christ gave to the church both the gift of evangelist and the gift of the pastor. The logical conclusion from Ephesians 4 is that pastors are not called to be evangelists and evangelists are not called to be pastors.

Jim and Carla Barbarossa came to Jubilee Worship Center some years ago. After spending time with them and sensing their hearts for teaching and encouraging witnesses, I knew that it was a God-sent gift to partner with them: They are true evangelists of the sort Paul wrote about in Ephesians 4. They are not what you would term traditional, itinerate evangelists. Rather they have the ability to teach and encourage members of the congregation to be witnesses for Christ.

There is a difference in the gifts, and I can see it in the ministry of Jim and Carla. While I tried to play both roles through living and preaching evangelism to the Jubilee congregation, the congregation was not as active in witnessing. Today, there are many more people sharing their faith and in more ways than before Jim and Carla joined us.

If a pastor truly wants to see his congregation actively involved in evangelism, he must be open to the possibility that within his congregation the gift of evangelist resides. The pastor must not feel threatened by this person.

A pastor must know his calling. He cannot feel that when an evangelist comes along that he or she is there to steal his sheep. If the evangelist is a true one, she or he will not desire to pastor the church and will faithfully come under your authority.

As a pastor, I feel no threat of losing the congregation nor do I have an issue with the evangelists winning more to Christ than I do. This is not a contest. Our gifts are different but the benefits of having the evangelist far outweigh any of the negative things the enemy would try to plant within the congregation to subvert God's plan for His church.

When a church has an evangelist training and encouraging the congregation to be witnesses, the pastor can focus on the things that are important to the health and well-being of the body: He can be the man of prayer; he can train leaders for ministry; he will see more opportunities for personal witnessing; and the body of Christ will be edified for the glory of God. When a pastor realizes that the evangelist is a gift to the church in the same way the pastor is a gift to the church, he will no longer feel the threat over his territory or the ministry. He can focus his attention on meaningful ways to build the body of Christ, and the pastor and evangelist together can stir the congregation to fulfill the call to go into all the world and preach the Gospel.

BISHOP DALE P. COMBS

Hobart, Indiana
June 2008

Acknowledgments

Oh, give thanks to the LORD!
Call upon His name;
Make known His deeds among the peoples!

— 1 Chronicles 16:8 (NKJV)

Bishop Dale P. Combs

I would like to thank my parents Dr. Philip and Gillian Combs for being Godly examples and true witnesses of Christ to me as I grew up. It is because of my Godly heritage that I am who I am today.

Most of all, I want to thank my wife Lisa; she has been a stable force of prayer and a wonderful wife and mother to our children. She is truly a woman of God. God has used her to teach me, encourage me and keep me on track. Her honesty, love and support have been a constant strength in my life. Her beauty inside and out is enough to inspire me to be more then I see in myself.

Lisa Combs

My deepest admiration to ...

> My Pastor, Bishop Dale P. Combs, you truly do have the heart of a Pastor who has an earnest desire for the many souls who have yet to come to know Christ. I admire you for allowing our Ephesians 4 Evangelists to breathe into our congregation the craving to witness for our Lord and Savior Jesus Christ.

> Evangelists, Jim and Carla Barbarossa, the two of you have inspired me as I have had the privilege to journey with you and experience two true hearts beating for the purpose of reaching the lost for Christ. You truly are a "gift" from above that has given determinedly to the Body of Christ.

Jubilee Worship Center, of whom you have tread fearlessly where others may never go. I stand at awe of you and consider myself privileged to serve with you and strive with you as we see our harvest gathered.

Don Mitchell, for such a time as this our paths have crossed and together He has a plan and purpose. Thank you for such an awesome opportunity. Thank you for your patience as we traveled new paths in this endeavor.

Most important, how do I attempt to verbally express my gratefulness to our Lord and Savior, Jesus Christ? Words simply do not exist; however, He knows what resides deep within my heart.

Jim Barbarossa

Thanks to all the leaders and all the workers who have field tested the teachings found in this book and over the last three years used them to reach over 500,000 souls for Jesus.

Thanks Pastor Dale and Lisa for wanting and allowing the gift of the equipping evangelist to operate in the local church and for providing the necessary platform by giving the house evangelists 5 minutes of every service. Thanks to all that answered God's call to become JWC in-house evangelists. We would not be where we are without you.

Carla Barbarossa

Lisa Combs for seeing that contest on How To Win Souls and suggesting that Jim Barbarossa enter it. Mona Hursey for helping to get people to complete their surveys and helping to e-mail corrections back and forth. Everyone who was faithful to pray for Don Mitchell and his work in getting this book completed. Don Mitchell for his faithfulness to persevere through the many long hours and trying storms. I know it was laborious, but anything that is going to produce good lasting fruit always comes with a price.

Donald Mitchell

I would like to thank God for creating the universe and all the people on the Earth, our Lord, Jesus Christ, for providing the way for us to gain Salvation, and the Holy Spirit for guiding our daily paths towards righteousness. I also humbly acknowledge the perfect guidance I received from God to conduct a contest to help more people decide to accept Jesus Christ as Lord and Savior.

I thank Bill Keller for his many devotionals that made me realize that I needed to do more to share my faith and for helping us test potential titles with the many pastors who assist him.

I acknowledge and appreciate all those who helped publicize the contest and the many Godly people who entered the contest and shared their experiences with being witnesses for Him.

I am very grateful to my four coauthors who generously and kindly shared their knowledge, experiences, and encouragement to make the wonderful advice in this book possible. These are outstanding people of God, and it has been a continual inspiration to work with them.

Let me mention some of the wonderful things each coauthor did. Bishop Dale P. Combs did an outstanding job of checking the text for Biblical accuracy. Lisa Combs introduced me to Jubilee Worship Center and Step by Step Ministries, and provided wonderful insights into what it's like to live in a pastor's family and to be a pastor's wife. Jim Barbarossa sent me over a thousand e-mails filled with fascinating details of evangelism at work and devoted countless hours to the book's research. Carla Barbarossa provided many excellent improvements to the text and often provided good solutions to writing problems.

On behalf of all the coauthors, I would like to thank Bishop Abbott for providing a foreword for the book, Aaron Wentz for sharing his sermon on the importance of the resurrection as an appendix to the book, and the many members of the congregation at Jubilee Worship Center (JWC) and supporters of Step by Step Ministries who answered questions and shared experiences that allowed us to show God's glorious deeds in so many memorable ways. I am also humbled by and thankful for the many prayers that contributors made in asking God to bless the writing of this book.

Mona Hursey deserves special thanks for her endless enthusiasm and support of the information gathering from the congregation at JWC and for coordinating the corrections to the text.

I would like to express my gratitude to my family for allowing me the time and peace to work on such a huge and awe-inspiring project for God. They made many sacrifices without complaining and were a continual inspiration.

I appreciate my many clients who held off on their demands for my help so that this project could receive the attention it required over more than three years. Their financial support also made it possible for me to give this time to the Lord and invest in the expenses required to make this book available.

Finally, I am most appreciative of the many fine improvements that our editor, Bernice Pettinato, made in the text. This is the eighth book where she has helped me to make the messages clearer and more pleasant to read. As always, she was a delight to work with.

Introduction

Here's a story we learned of recently that may help you appreciate how much good God can do through one Salvation. Two boys were best friends. Sam had Christian parents, dedicated his life to the Lord at age 10, and began sharing his faith with his friends. His best friend, John, didn't want to hear about it.

John told Sam, "I'm just like everybody else, and I want to be like the crowd." John was embarrassed when Sam spoke about Jesus, especially during classroom reports.

One night at age 17 John began to think that there must be a God beyond all those stars and a Savior of the world. He began to wonder what had happened to those who had seen the stars before him and were now dead.

A few weeks later, John showed up at Sam's house just after dawn to ask Sam what it took to be saved. Sam answered John's questions and led John through the sinner's prayer.

Sam challenged John to show his sincerity by coming to church with Sam the next day to confess his faith publicly. The next morning, John arrived before Sam and they went in together. After some initial hesitation because he felt unworthy due to being a sinner and working as a popcorn vendor in a theater, John proclaimed Jesus as his Lord in front of the congregation, the only person to come forward that day.

John walked in the Lord's ways for the rest of his life: He became known to millions as Pastor John H. Osteen, founder of Lakewood Church in Houston, Texas. During Pastor Osteen's life, he helped lead over a million souls to Salvation. His friend, Sam Martin, served in the ministry most of his life, eventually becoming an associate pastor at Lakewood Church. You can read about the story of their friendship and walks with the Lord in *How I Led One and One Led a Million* by Sam Martin (Lakewood Church, 2001) from which their story was taken.

Today, the blessings of that Salvation continue as Lakewood Church is led by Pastor Osteen's son, Joel, where more than forty thousand people attend services. The church's reach is extended by active television and electronic ministries: We learned that in 2007 Pastor Joel Osteen's weekly telecasts were seen in over one hundred countries by more than seven million people, and his sermons were downloaded from the Internet forty-seven million times. In addition, all Pastor John Osteen's other children are either pastors, preachers, or in full-time ministry. Who knows how many more millions will receive Salvation during this generation because Pastor John Osteen did?

It all began with Sam Martin's conviction that he must help his friend find Salvation. We should do no less for our friends, family, neighbors, and lost sinners everywhere. Who knows what grace and goodness the Lord will invest in a single Salvation?

Glorious Gifts Are Received by Those Who Witness

The fruit of the righteous is a tree of life,
And he who wins souls is wise.

— Proverbs 11:30 (NKJV)

Praise God! God wants us to have a good relationship with Him and to enjoy all the blessings He has planned for us: Only God knows what all those blessings are because He wants to reveal them in His own time.

Because we don't know what God's plan and intended blessings are, we are vulnerable. If the enemy tries to stir up fear and misunderstandings about our God-given roles and opportunities, our faith can falter and we may be idle and unhappy when we were intended to be active and joyful. We see evidence of this problem whenever Christians say they are afraid to or refuse to share their faith.

Since we are ignorant of the intended consequences of God's plan for us, how can we learn what the remarkable blessings are that we haven't yet experienced? Two pathways are available: We can learn about what we are missing from the experiences described by those who have been obedient to God's commands; and when we obey God, all the intended blessings will be received, which we can, in turn, report to others.

From the ways we, your authors, have shared our faith in Jesus Christ, we have received blessings far beyond what we have read about or expected. Like the faithful scouts, Joshua and Caleb, whom Moses sent into the Promised Land to report on what God had placed there, we have explored a holy place relatively few have seen and written about, where witnessing and preparing others to witness are central parts of daily life. We want you to know that the experience has dazzled our eyes, caused our hearts to race, filled our ears with heavenly harmonies, and expanded our joy beyond the limits of our imaginations.

Here's an example: We have seen thousands of souls saved in just a few days at a cost of a few pennies per person, and those who have shared the Good News with these new Christians tell us that they could help save hundreds of thousands more in just a few more days if the funds were available to purchase more of the inexpensive witnessing tools they use. When we hear that, we experience the gift of imagining a world in which every Christian can be surrounded by fellow Christians living Godly lives, where there are only Christian communities and sin is on the continual decline. We see a vision of God's peace and goodness spreading over the Earth through His people after such a change in a way that has never occurred before. We wake up filled with the gifts of excitement and boundless energy to help create the reality of that vision.

As faithful witnessing scouts for God, we want you to know and experience the same gifts we have received. We have organized what we learned from our witnessing into simple steps that will make your own witnessing journey to the same holy places shorter, easier, more joyful, and more effective than ours have been. We feel honored to be able to share these wonderful blessings with you.

To better understand the blessings from witnessing that you haven't yet experienced, let's consider how God delivers His blessings. The love, hope, faith, and charity that light our daily lives are among the many fine gifts that we receive directly from God. We also receive delightful presents indirectly from God through what others do for us through God's plan. And when we give to God or to others in a Godly way, we gain from the good feelings we enjoy and additional benefits that God sends us through doors of opportunity newly opened by our actions. Once we are in heaven, our faith and faithful acts during life will deliver multiplied blessings throughout eternity.

Those wonderful gifts and blessings pale, however, beside the gifts of forgiveness and Salvation that we can receive through repenting of our sins and accepting Jesus Christ as our Lord and Savior. Those extraordinary gifts allow us to be filled with joy, to be free from the weight of sins and harmful events in our pasts, and to enter heaven. It's a marvelous road that God has marked out for our lives.

You will probably be surprised by one lesson we learned about God's plan: Spending more time learning how to become witness for God, sharing your faith all the time, and taking on new roles for Him in witnessing and helping others to witness are primary ways that God wants you to learn how to be more like Christ. Through your witnessing, He wants you to grow wonderfully in love, understanding, peace, confidence, kindness, and happiness. You are disconnected from many of God's finest blessings on Earth until you become a complete, continual witness, always listening to the Holy Spirit about what you can do at each moment to share the Good News of Jesus Christ with others in ways that delight hearers as well as bring you joy.

We pray that this book will help open your eyes and heart to more ways that God's love, the source of all these wonderful gifts, can fill you even more completely and inspire you to take actions that will cause you to gain still more goodness from God's plan for your life. We hope that your life will be transformed, as our lives have been, by this new appreciation for God's goodness.

Witnessing Is Much More than Attending Crusades

"Go therefore and make disciples
of all the nations,
baptizing them in the name of
the Father and of the Son and of the Holy Spirit, ..."

— Matthew 28:19 (NKJV)

Mention evangelism and many people only think of crusades led by famous preachers held in sports arenas. Go to a service during such a crusade, and you usually find most of the seats filled by busloads of Christians just arrived from their churches. Before the service is over, there will be an altar call for those who haven't yet given their lives to Jesus to repent their sins, to ask forgiveness, to come to Him, and to promise to follow Him. To loud applause, some of the unsaved will come forward, often held in the loving arms of Christian family members and friends. This kind of event is the impression held by many as to how most souls are saved today.

Let's identify some of the assumptions that might be drawn from such an impression:

- The hearts of the unsaved will respond only to testimonies by and invitations from highly skilled evangelists and pastors.
- You need to be surrounded by more than a single congregation of Christians for the Holy Spirit to move someone to come to the Lord.
- The role of family and friends in achieving Salvation is to persuade the lost person to attend a crusade.
- The unsaved can learn in a single meeting all they need to know about what it means to dedicate their lives to Jesus Christ and make a meaningful decision.
- That a single connection like this will lead the newly saved to begin attending church, studying the Bible daily, learning how to live a Godly life, and following Jesus' example.

Compare those possible assumptions to what Jesus and His disciples did. They shared the Gospel primarily with the lost, finding them wherever they might be on daily basis … whether among the multitude in the streets, within the Temple in Jerusalem, by a well in Samaria, near a synagogue outside of Israel, or inside a prison cell in Greece. Yes, Jesus did teach multitudes numbering into the thousands on some occasions. We believe that most of these listeners were seeking to learn about Salvation rather than being those who had already committed their lives to Jesus.

Could it be that some of your ideas about reaching the unsaved need revising? We will leave the answer to that question for you to decide after asking the Holy Spirit for guidance. In the meantime, here are questions for you to consider as you read the book to help you explore that larger question about how people will receive Salvation in the future:

- How did you learn about and decide to receive Salvation?
- How likely were you to have committed your life to Jesus through attending a crusade meeting after receiving an invitation to attend with a family member or friend?
- How would you feel if a family member, loved one, or friend died without being saved?
- Should people have to suffer with their sins and despair waiting for crusades to be staged before receiving forgiveness and the full radiance of God's love?
- How can more sinners be saved so that they might avoid eternal torment?

Unexpected Joys Come from Sharing Your Faith

You will show me the path of life;
In Your presence is fullness of joy;
At Your right hand are pleasures forevermore.

— Psalm 16:11 (NKJV)

Most children find it hard to share. Why? That special doll, toy, or video game probably makes the child feel special. If others have the same item or could use the child's, the child doesn't feel as special. Some carry that desire for feeling special into adulthood and exercise that desire through acquiring more and more items that few others have. That desire can distract them from developing their faith in God.

When you were growing up, your parents and caregivers performed many of the family and household responsibilities. They provided for you, took care of you when you were sick, called relatives on Christmas and Easter, visited the sick, put meals on the table, and kept the house clean. They nagged you (if necessary) to do your few responsibilities to others, such as sending thank you notes. Many people grow content with this comfortable dependence.

When not enjoying benefits you didn't earn, but gained anyway, you also learned that some things are better when you share them. You may have enjoyed speaking with friends about what was on their minds more than sitting alone. You may have liked playing games with others more than playing by yourself.

From sharing good times with others, some children learn that being thoughtful and giving to others can be more enjoyable than merely receiving. Some go so far as to later seek out life roles and jobs that permit the opportunity to give to others, including being parents, nurses, and teachers, and volunteering for work on worthy causes.

Based on our experiences as witnesses for Jesus Christ, we believe that most Christians are enormously underestimating and missing out on the blessings that God intends for them because they either don't know Christ's command to share their faith to make, to baptize, and to teach disciples in all nations (Matthew 28:18-20) or haven't yet begun fulfilling that command. The good news for these Christians is that being a witness can quickly dispel fears, build self-confidence, add joy, deliver unexpected blessings, and reveal more of God's good plan.

When you accepted Salvation from God through His Son, you received an amazing gift that has all of these desirable qualities: You were confirmed as being special in God's sight, you learned that God will look out for you and tend you, and God began sending opportunities for you to do His will through serving others in ways that are pleasing to God and to you. Unless you explore all those dimensions, however, you are missing part of the joy of life and the gift you received from God. Some of those ways of serving others include sharing your faith with them.

Here's an example of how blessings multiply from helping others gain Salvation: Don Mitchell's uncle died while this introduction was being written. Don was touched by his aunt's recounting of how she was affected by her husband's final days.

She had been vigilant to be sure that her spouse accepted Salvation and walked in the ways of Jesus. Just before he died, Don's aunt told his uncle that he would soon be in a better place, a place where his parents and five brothers and sisters already were. He visibly relaxed when she spoke of this.

She recounted his passing with quiet happiness because she had no doubt that her husband was saved and going to heaven. That's the kind of special satisfaction that Salvation can bring for all, even after the end of life on Earth when many are instead overwhelmed by grief.

We want you to learn how acting on opportunities to witness about your faith, sharing your testimony, and helping others find answers to their questions about Salvation can bring you enormous peace, joy, and fulfillment. We also want you to experience how doing more of these activities will help feelings of love, faith, hope, and charity to grow in your heart.

You Can Walk Comfortably and Confidently Along the Gentle Path of Learning to Witness

Learn to do good; ....

— Isaiah 1:17 (NKJV)

Perhaps you've seen or heard powerful evangelists share their faith. It can be quite impressive. Although God commands us not to covet what others have (Exodus 20:17), some are jealous of those abilities and are tempted to wish for such remarkable talents. Others are overwhelmed by such powerful messages and feel diminished as

Christians because their knowledge and skills are modest in comparison.

In either case, it's easy to focus on the large distance between our own experience and talents and those of the powerful evangelist rather than on what we need to do next to share our faith. When we feel diminished, many will decide not to start down the path of learning to witness. If that occurs, it's as if a young child who saw Tour de France champion Lance Armstrong on a bicycle decided never to learn to ride.

When people never start to learn how to witness, that's a shame because this path can be a gentle one that provides many more rewards than difficulties. What do you think the first step is? No, the first step isn't to enroll in a seminary.

As the Bible tells us, we each have different callings from God (Ephesians 4:11-13). Not all are called to become powerful evangelists. Some are called merely to share tracts and recordings and to perform loving acts. Most are called and given gifts to do some things between those opposite ends of the evangelical spectrum.

In chapters 5-7, you will read about a sequence of learning and teaching others how to be a witness that will make the tasks simple, easy, and pleasant. As you experience each step in that sequence, you will have positive encounters that will help you grow in confidence until you are ready for and looking to do more.

These steps begin with writing your personal testimony. (If you would like to see what a personal testimony looks like, we have included some in Appendix C.) If you aren't sure what to write about or need assistance with the writing after you've decided what you want to say, we explain how you can get help with this first activity.

Some people finish writing their testimonies in a day. Others take years. Regardless of how long it takes, the important thing is to write your testimony. Why? Your words will help many people through reading about your experiences with how God helped you with something that has happened in their lives ... even if they never meet you. They won't feel so alone, and they will know that there are answers through faith in and acceptance of Jesus Christ as their Lord and Savior.

How does this sharing happen? You can begin by making copies of your testimony and handing it to people. People who know your written testimony can also hand out copies to those who have had or are having similar experiences. Your testimony can be combined into books or placed on Web sites where people who are looking for answers can find your experience. People who read about all the good things that God has done in your congregation will be amazed and will want to gain these blessings for themselves.

Because you have a written testimony, you will also have an oral testimony. You will remember what you've written and be able to relate it to someone you meet who needs to hear about what Jesus has done in your life. By sharing what you've been through, you will create powerful empathy with people who have had similar experiences prior to gaining Salvation.

When you are ready to do more, your church can provide weekly lessons in more advanced forms of witnessing by having your church's in-congregation evangelist (someone almost all churches should have) and more experienced witnesses share their knowledge and experiences. In addition, your church can organize events to reach more people where you will have easy opportunities to begin sharing your faith with strangers while surrounded by lots of people you know, such as by holding a free car wash or providing day care.

Another good thing will happen: Because you have shared your faith, you will find that you will want to live consistently with what you've shared about how Jesus changed your life. When that happens, you will act more like our Lord. That change will be a blessing to you and to those around you.

As your life is transformed by witnessing, more people will see you as a good example and will seek you out to find why you are so much happier than they are. Those inquiries will provide more chances to share your faith and your love.

Eventually, you may find that someone you gave a tract to or to whom you spoke will accept Christ as Lord and Savior. That happy result will bring you a special joy whenever you think about it or see that person. You may also draw closer to the new Christian through your shared faith.

After that experience, you may decide that you want to learn how to play a bigger role in helping someone learn about and consider Salvation. When that happens, you may someday find yourself leading a sinner through a heartfelt prayer accepting Salvation. You may eventually see that person in heaven. Certainly, that will be a joyous reunion.

Why can all these good things occur? We are only God's agents. The Holy Spirit does the work in peoples' hearts. But our efforts can and do make a difference.

God's Plans for Establishing a Christian World Are Explained by This Book

Let all the inhabitants of the world stand in awe of Him.

— Psalm 33:8 (NKJV)

Most people need to read, see, or hear about something they don't understand at least thirty times in different ways within a month before they understand it. When we share our faith with those who aren't yet Christians or successfully encourage a fellow Christian to do the same, we are adding one of those thirty occasions to their experience.

By multiplying the available testimonies and active witnesses, and learning about how to witness in more ways, there results a rapid expansion in how many souls can be saved. Why? The number of people who will receive thirty different messages from God through His people in a month will geometrically increase. That increase in messages will help open the door for the Holy Spirit to increase the number of saved people and reduce distractions from unsaved people.

If ten million Christians shared their faith with someone different every day, those testimonies could lead to more millions being saved every month. If the newly saved learned that they should witness as well and did so, that sharing, in turn, would help lead to there soon being one hundred million Christians doing the same thing. Then, tens of millions more would be saved every month. And on it goes. Within just a few years, every person on Earth could have had the chance to receive Salvation by hearing or reading thirty different testimonies in a month.

God has a better idea than that: The methods described in this book help some people come to Salvation much faster. That means that fewer witnesses and messages are needed to light and fan a wildfire of souls being cleansed. In fact, with optimal use of the methods you will read about, many people will become saved with fewer than five testimonies and discussions of faith.

What's more, God has easy, pleasant ways for each of us to share our faith. When we use those methods, our testimonies will reach more people and have more effect. With the help of in-congregation evangelists and taking time in each church service for learning about witnessing, Christians will become more effective in sharing their faith. That also reduces how many times people will need to hear the Good News before God acts on their hearts.

There's more: Those who use the witnessing examples you will read about report that a very high percentage of the newly saved can be led to immediate baptism, regular church attendance, and sharing their newfound faith. These communications work so well that they can only be God's plan, as it is understood by us today.

We, your authors, hope you will be as excited as we are about the prospect of every person on Earth knowing as much as they want to learn about our Lord and Savior in the next twenty years. When that happens, imagine how much more love, faith, hope, and charity will surround each of us here and in heaven.

This wonderful result requires that you take action to fulfill God's marvelous plan. Start by reading this book. Act on its lessons. Share these methods with every Christian you know.

✝

Here's an overview of the book's contents to prepare you for your reading:

Chapter 1 describes some of the more important, unanticipated benefits that pastors, pastors' spouses, pastors' families, ministry leaders, Christians, and the lost gain from daily witnessing. This information will help you develop an understanding of what your new witnessing life will be like.

Chapter 2 explains the authors' experiences and ideas about having a congregational evangelist in your church as a way to light a large spiritual fire through joyful witnessing. We also explain how you can identify who should take this role.

Chapter 3 explains the importance of devoting five minutes of every church service and activity to training in and inspiration for witnessing. You will also learn ways to decide what your congregation needs to hear. A sample lesson is included.

Chapter 4 shares the parts of the Gospel that tell what we have been commanded by God to do in sharing our faith and explores ways to help people accept these commands. All Christians need to know this information to correctly consider the role of witnessing in their lives. This sharing of God's commands is an important first theme for the newly identified congregational evangelist.

Chapter 5 tells about ways to inspire and prepare all members of a congregation to write a testimony about what God has done in their lives. Reaching the stage where you have many written testimonies provides a firm foundation for making rapid increases in improving witnessing. In the meantime, you are welcome to use testimonies we share with you from Jubilee Worship Center to inform the lost.

Chapter 6 reports on what Christians at Jubilee Worship Center have told us about what they felt about and while witnessing when they started. Many were filled with one kind of fear or another. We also relate how these witnesses overcame those fears to gain peace and joy and what you can do to help people with their reluctance, concerns, and fears.

Chapter 7 presents the roles that various witnessing tools can play in preparing Christians to be effective, confident, and helpful witnesses. We share the results that have been gained from various tools used in a variety of ways.

Chapter 8 explains how your church can be the foundation for establishing effective witnessing beyond the direct reach of your congregation. We use the experiences of Jubilee Worship Center and Step by Step Ministries as examples to describe how to direct your witnessing and tools to teach Christians in other congregations how to witness more effectively and to gain more blessings.

Chapter 9 tells the importance of and describes methods for pastors starting to apply these important lessons about preparing members of their congregations to be outstanding witnesses.

Chapter 10 outlines how you can add new skills and expertise in witnessing so that you can gain more blessings in all areas of your life.

Chapter 11 unveils the insights that members of Jubilee Worship Center shared with us about what God revealed to them about His majesty and goodness through their witnessing experiences. Your faith and desire to witness will receive big boosts from learning about these remarkable experiences.

In the Epilogue, we share a vision of what needs to be done to accomplish more through witnessing.

Appendix A contains Bible verses about witnessing that you can use in considering the importance of this activity.

Appendix B has testimonies from each coauthor so you can understand our Christian backgrounds.

Appendix C contains selected testimonies from *Real Life Stories*, the book that contains testimonies from most members of Jubilee Worship Center along with instructions for how to read the whole book for free online.

Appendix D lists and thanks those who shared information with us from Jubilee Worship Center about their witnessing experiences.

Appendix E describes the importance of the resurrection and ascension of Jesus Christ in helping nonbelievers to understand the truth of the Gospel and Salvation.

We designed the information in this book about witnessing for people who have already dedicated their lives to our Lord, Jesus Christ, and want to be obedient in doing His will so that all might be saved and enjoy a wonderful relationship with Him (1 Timothy 2:1-4). Each Christian has an important, but different, role to play, a role that you may not yet know has been selected by God for you. We present important messages for pastors, pastors' wives, pastors' families, church leaders in all ministries, evangelists, mature Christians, maturing Christians, and the newly saved.

We are convinced that there are many excellent choices for you to serve the Lord as a witness by following the Holy Spirit's promptings. In fact, there are many more desirable witnessing roles and methods than we can hope to cover in a single book. As you read the book, please pray that the Holy Spirit will give you more guidance and wisdom about what you should be doing to share your faith and to encourage others to do the same.

✝

We want to help you engage in this marvelous opportunity to help create a Godlier world. For more information, please visit http://www.jubilee worshipcenter.com and http://www.step-by-step.org, and please feel free to call the JWC offices at 219-947-0301 or Jim Barbarossa at 219-787-9933 for additional assistance. You can also contact Jim Barbarossa at jim@step-by-step.org.

Contents

Chapter 1

Humbly Accept
God's Unanticipated Gifts

Discover How Daily Evangelism Provides
Bountiful Benefits for Pastors, Pastors' Spouses,
Pastors' Families, Ministry Leaders, Christians,
and the Lost

Cast your bread upon the waters,
For you will find it after many days.

— Ecclesiastes 11:1 (NKJV)

While we wrote the book, Wilfred Andabwa, an evangelist in Kenya who learned from Jim Barbarossa the witnessing methods we describe, made a trip to Nigeria to teach pastors these methods. At that time Nigeria's 150 million souls predominately observed the Muslim religion, but there were many Christians in Nigeria as well. Because the nation was filled with violence and strife, many warned the evangelist not to go there; but he went without fear because he trusted in God's protection.

Pastor Jonah Obike, who led a small congregation in Nigeria, attended the evangelist's training. Pastor Obike had long prayed that he might head a large congregation, but that blessing had not occurred. After the training, Evangelist Andabwa donated a few hundred tracts and tapes to Pastor Obike, and Pastor Obike's church members took those materials to the unsaved in their community during the following week. These evangelism teams visited people at home, at work, in the streets, and in the market to witness and to share the tracts and tapes; and the teams followed up in three days to hear what questions the lost had after thinking about the conversations and what they had learned

1

from the tracts and tapes. As a result of those efforts, approximately two hundred souls were dedicated to the Lord that week. Praise God!

A bigger surprise followed on Sunday when Pastor Obike's church was filled to overflowing by the addition of about 150 of the new Christians who had been saved during the prior week. Pastor Obike was overwhelmed to see God's power at work.

Pastor Obike wondered how big his church would be if he had begun using these witnessing methods and tools years earlier. What might such witnessing methods do for you and your church … and the lost?

Before he left Nigeria, Evangelist Andabwa trained more than four hundred pastors in these methods and left behind thousands of tracts and tapes for the pastors there to use. The pastors who received the training asked the evangelist to return, and they promised that five thousand more pastors would attend the next training.

How might such efforts change the course of Nigeria's future to reflect God's will? How many more nations would benefit from Evangelist Andabwa's teaching? How might you help train and encourage witnesses like the evangelist?

To help you fully understand the implications of Pastor Obike's experience, we would like to share with you some of the important, but often unanticipated, benefits that such daily witnessing brings to pastors, pastors' spouses, pastors' families, ministry leaders, Christians, and the lost. In the following sections, we separately consider the benefits for each group.

Pastors Build Better Christian Communities with Less Time, Effort, and Cost

I will declare Your name to My brethren;
In the midst of the assembly I will praise You.

— Psalm 22:22 (NKJV)

There are few people in most communities who work longer hours than pastors. There is never enough time for pastors to get everything done. The wear and tear on their spirits can be substantial, causing them to pray for guidance about how to do more with little time and few resources. Precious time to recharge pastors' energies and renew their faith can be hard to find: As Bishop Dale P. Combs pointed out in the Pastor's Prologue, 80 percent of pastors spend less than fifteen minutes a day in prayer and 70 percent only study God's Word while preparing a sermon. But the Lord strengthens them to soldier on despite the heavy load.

While you might think otherwise, the smaller the congregation, the more challenging these demands are on the pastor. Why? There are few other people in the congregation who can help with serving the important needs for prayer, counseling, condolence, officiating at weddings and funerals, and pastoral visits. The necessary tasks of administration also fall heavily on the pastor's shoulders.

Many congregations are quite small and will remain so without effective ways to bring more lost souls to Christ. As a result, pastors are not only working long hours with few resources; but they have too little time for their other important roles as leaders of their secular communities, providers of charity, and founders of Christian schools.

Most pastors are married and have families. As the Bible tells us, Christians must place a priority on serving their families in their roles as spouses, parents to their children, and children to their parents. Even those who have undemanding jobs find these family responsibilities to be quite challenging.

Let's add one more element to the challenge: Many pastors have little experience in saving souls outside of a church service. Of those who have more witnessing experience, their gift from the Lord is still that of a pastor, and they are going to have a harder time teaching and encouraging the congregation to share their faith than an evangelist would. As a result, even substantial pastoral efforts to lead a strong witnessing church may bring few souls to the Lord. Why? Both the pastor and the in-congregation evangelist are called to teach or equip the saints in Ephesians Chapter 4:11-12, but their roles are totally different. Either one is going to struggle by attempting to go beyond what God has selected and prepared them to do.

3

Have you ever tried to do something important for which you did not have much experience and skill? You may have worked endless hours, but the results were meager: It can feel as if you had planted low quality seed in poor, dried-out soil without adding fertilizer and water.

If you combine an effective in-congregation evangelist with an effective pastor, the two can accomplish vastly greater results together than can either one alone. The evangelist's example, teaching, and encouragement help lead many more of the unsaved to Christ, but the work doesn't end there: Those who receive Salvation then need to be taught how to grow more mature in their faith. A church is where that discipleship can best occur. Without the pastor leading a congregation, the evangelist's efforts help encourage witnessing that will assist in saving souls but will accomplish little to develop mature Christians. Without the evangelist, the pastor will have many fewer people to lead and teach.

When pastors team with effective evangelists for their congregations, congregations can fulfill more of their potential as Christian communities. Here are some of the dimensions that the in-congregation evangelist can add: The evangelist helps the congregation members to know one another better through writing and sharing their testimonies with each other, working together on outreach programs, and establishing new ministries to serve members and community residents. The combination of shared testimonies and increased communion with one another also creates a much greater appreciation for God's power in their lives and the lives of those around them ... helping encourage greater submission and obedience to God's will.

Helping lead the lost to Salvation can be a lot quicker, easier, more fun, and less expensive than you probably imagine. We'll show you the best methods we know in chapters 2 through 8. By employing these methods, a pastor can spend less time, effort, and money on witnessing, and yet accomplish more. Clearly, that increased effectiveness will only happen by being obedient to God, and experience has demonstrated that the methods we share with you can be obediently used for such dramatically better results in helping lead the lost to Salvation.

As the congregation grows, God will place more skills and talents into the congregation that are needed for developing and improving the Christian community. Among the mature Christians some will be found who can supplement the pastor's daily work in teaching, prayer, counseling, condolence, serving at weddings and funerals, and pastoral visits. In addition, the congregation will be able to afford to hire additional pastors to tend them in specialized roles such as leading youth activities, praise and worship, and small groups. Beyond that, administrative help will be more affordable. Pastors know about these advantages that stem from larger size — it's one of the main reasons they would like to have larger congregations, so that more good works can be done through drawing on the church's enhanced resources.

Unanticipated gifts are received after the congregation grows and matures in faith and observance because God will have demonstrated greater power and influence in its members' lives through witnessing: A congregation that becomes focused on evangelism also grows more capable and effective in all the desirable roles and work that a Christian community requires. Why? The church members become more heedful of the Holy Spirit and act more often in accord with God's plan for the church. Acting under the guidance of the pastor and evangelist, almost everyone in the congregation will become more active and observant in all dimensions of being a Christian. Their interactions with one another will be more Godly, their surrender to God's plan for their lives will be more complete, they will spend more time doing good works, they will be more open to the teachings of the pastor, they will be more faithful in their tithes and offerings, and they will be better able to avoid sin. The work that pastors need to do for each person in such a congregation will be less.

With reduced demands, pastors have more time for prayer and reflection, planning how to improve the church, building their knowledge and skills, and recruiting and training others to help. Pastors will also be able to spend more time with their families and play richer and more satisfying roles as spouses and parents.

5

Like a parent who looks with pleasure on grown children following God's purposes, such a pastor can receive more satisfaction from the work of and enjoy greater opportunities from building an improved Christian community in the church, one that becomes a shining light, a good example, for the non-Christians in the local community. Surrounded by such blessings, the joy of being a congregational pastor can greatly increase while the lonely burdens shrink.

To summarize what we've shared, adding the role of in-congregation evangelist who leads an effective witnessing program is like properly planting a mustard seed into fertile but fallow soil. Until planted, the seed cannot grow into its enormous potential as a mustard plant. After the seed is planted and nourished, the resulting mustard plant provides many more mustard seeds, mustard plants, food for humans, and places for birds to roost. The potential always existed for this growth to be produced through combining good seed and rich soil with enough moisture: The seed and soil must be combined like a pastor and an effective in-congregation evangelist with the right moisture (the living water of the Holy Spirit) to gain the full spiritual harvest.

Here's another way to see the potential: Think of a congregation as being like partially planted good soil (a small, faithful community of Christians) that can yield a larger harvest by planting many more witnessing seeds (inspiring members who are gifted to be evangelists to act in that role and those who don't witness to start) through having an in-congregation evangelist regularly lead the congregation to witness. The Christian community cannot grow into its potential size, strength, and goodness without an effective in-congregation evangelist to help plant and nourish witnessing seeds that deliver the fruit of new faith among the lost through activities that will also cause faith to grow in each existing believer.

Pastors' Spouses Enjoy More Time with the Pastor, Stronger Marital Relationships with the Pastor, and More Opportunities for Family Members to Grow as Christians

Do we have no right to take along a believing wife,
as do *also the other apostles, the brothers of the Lord, and Cephas?*

— 1 Corinthians 9:5 (NKJV)

The phone rings as 3:23 a.m., and your spouse, the pastor, wearily rises to attend to a parishioner who is deeply disturbed by a spiritual crisis. The struggle with the enemy who is in the world continues for the rest of the day, and you don't see your spouse again until the next day. Was this just another day in the sacrificing life of a pastor's spouse? Well, probably, except that this was your twenty-fifth wedding anniversary, and you had special plans for the evening. After prayer, the pastor's spouse grins and bears it, hoping to celebrate later during some quieter time.

There's a special Christlike servant's role in being a pastor's spouse: Your needs almost always come in last or near last in the congregation. Pastors' spouses know that and are usually quite patient. But it would still be nice to have more time together.

How does having a congregation that's more active in evangelism increase the time pastors can spend with their spouses? Prior to there being any growth in the congregation or any more resources available to the pastor, outreach programs to witness provide plenty of new opportunities for spouses to work side-by-side with the pastor in meeting the lost. Under these circumstances, pastors' spouses can feel like they are providing more than moral support for their overworked spouses. In addition, new ministries will be established and led by existing members of the congregation: These new ministries will take on some of the pastor's responsibilities, reducing at least some of the emergency calls. Finally, with a congregation that's growing in faith and activity, the needs for individual members of the congregation to call on the pastor will probably be reduced.

When a pastor's spouse witnesses with the pastor, the bond between pastor and spouse is strengthened through this service for the Lord. When the shared witnessing helps stir more hearts for Him, the joy of having the experience together can make the many daily sacrifices of being a pastor's spouse seem even more worthwhile.

When the congregation grows, the church receives new gifts and relationships through knowing the newly saved, adds more finances, can make Christians among the original congregation happier, and is blessed by a more loving environment that can improve the pastor's morale. Each of these blessings can help provide more time for pastors to be with their spouses.

Some spouses find that they are better at witnessing and helping others witness than their pastor spouses are. When that occurs, spouses can be sources of strength and inspiration in this work for the pastors who may want to spend time talking with their spouses about and working on improving witnessing.

Pastors' spouses also do a lot of child rearing without benefit of much participation from the pastor. A church that conducts more outreaches for evangelism will find the pastor's family working together at a car wash, a block party, or a parade. On those occasions, the pastor has a new kind of opportunity to be a spiritual and a parental leader of the family: As a result, the pastor's children can learn more about the importance of the pastor's and the church's work. These Godly experiences can fill a spouse's heart with joy from experiencing more ways that having a pastor for a spouse can be a blessing for the spouse and family.

There is perhaps no greater gift to a pastor's spouse than hope for a better life on Earth and more rewards in heaven. As each new Christian enters the pastor's church, that hope for achieving more in serving the Lord grows. On a purely personal level, hope also grows for more time with the pastor.

Pastors' Families Enjoy More Time with the Pastor, Stronger and Healthier Relationships with the Pastor, and More Opportunities to Grow as Christians

... the women and the children also rejoiced,
so that the joy of Jerusalem was heard afar off.

— Nehemiah 12:43 (NKJV)

Family time with the pastor is too limited and therefore precious to a pastor's family. To begin with, the hours when children are awake, not in school, or otherwise occupied are all too few. When no emergencies intervene, school days present opportunities for just a little time together in the morning and a longer time in the late afternoon and early evening. Saturdays are often busy days dedicated to the pastor preparing a sermon, and Sundays are usually even busier.

Because of the confidential nature of the pastor's work, much of what the pastor does cannot be discussed in detail at home. Also, pastors need to be Godly examples, denying many potential sources of dinner-table conversation to pastors and their families.

Evangelism adds an important new dimension to the family's ability to see and understand the pastor's work through witnessing together, loving those who are lost and hurting, and forming new friendships as a family. Let's take a look at what that experience might be like during a Saturday car wash held in the church parking lot. Dad and son may be washing cars, spending good bonding time, while mom and daughter are preparing and serving food for those who have brought their cars to be washed. Mom and daughter may begin sharing their faith with a family that doesn't have any food at home. If the hungry family is also eager for prayer, dad and son may be called over so that the pastor's whole family can join hands with the hungry family for prayer and later enjoy friendly conversation. If the hungry family starts attending the church, the two families may soon be sharing potluck suppers there. Should any of these new acquaintances dedicate their lives to the Lord, the celebration of that commitment can be enjoyed by the pastor's family in a very personal way.

9

Can you imagine the joy that the pastor and the pastor's spouse must feel as parents to help their children have such Godly experiences through showing Christ's love? Such a gift can come more frequently from serving God through witnessing as a family.

One of the great opportunities that God provides for parents is helping children learn how to take on more responsibility. By learning to witness, the pastor's children can gain more confidence and ability to successfully invite friends, neighbors, and schoolmates to attend Sunday school and youth services. In the process of being obedient to God in these ways, the children will grow in faith and maturity. Some children may also find that they enjoy these experiences so much that they will feel called to become pastors and evangelists as Bishop Dale P. Combs was called to teach as a child.

Successful witnessing by church members frees some of the pastor's time to be with the whole family as well as with his or her spouse. As congregation members share more and more pastoral responsibilities in addition to helping save more souls, the pastor can assign a schedule so that important responsibilities (including emergencies, for example) can be shared equally among several people during those hours when families can be together.

Everyone remembers being a child playing on a sports team, performing in a musical group, or competing in an academic event and hoping that mom and dad (or a guardian) will be there to provide moral support and to enjoy whatever is accomplished. Those occasions are special to parents as well. Pastors who have appointed effective in-house evangelists are more likely to have attracted enough new Christians and resources to be able to ask others to cover pastoral responsibilities so the pastor can attend such wonderful events. That's important because it's a much greater trial for a child to miss having enough attention from a parent than it is for a spouse to miss an important occasion with the pastor.

Ministry Leaders Grow in Faith, Skills, Accomplishment, and Self-Confidence

I lead in the way of righteousness, ...

— Proverbs 8:20 (KJ21V)

Every congregation has many leaders who work to fulfill the church's purposes including heads of various ministries, choir directors, Sunday school teachers, greeters, ushers, and church board members. Without these many leaders, the work of the church wouldn't be accomplished through the pastor's efforts alone. An in-congregation evangelist is a great gift to these leaders by stirring up the congregation's members to be more active in exercising their faith through all types of volunteering for the Lord.

When volunteering increases, there's another benefit for leaders: Some of those who have been leading without any assistance suddenly have the opportunity to learn how to train and lead others in performing the same tasks. Someone who is at the bottom of the totem pole at work may now be directing others to accomplish important tasks with the congregation. Beyond that, a church that encourages witnessing will develop leaders who can move outside of their comfort zones, enabling them to become better leaders and Christians by taking on challenging new tasks and being more open with others.

Some church leaders may not have witnessed except by being a good example, one of the acts Christians are called to do. Other ministry leaders may have been Christians for a long time and become complacent and less active in sharing their faith with the unsaved. That's especially likely for those who grew up in church and have lived a life filled with God's blessings for the faithful. Wouldn't it be wonderful if these leaders could grow more active and capable as witnesses?

An unexpected benefit of having in-congregation evangelists at Jubilee Worship Center was that each lay-led ministry initiated witnessing outreaches. These efforts not only added to witnessing, these

11

new outreaches also built leadership skills among some of those in these ministries who hadn't been leaders of the congregation before.

Why was this growth in experience and skills for leading witnessing activities important? One of the most significant sources of spiritual gains within a congregation comes from God's hand being seen more often in the lives of the church's leaders and those they help: There's nothing like seeing God's power and will in action to encourage more faith. Witnessing leads to requests for prayer, prayer leads to God's intercession, and those who receive comfort, aid, and guidance often dedicate or rededicate their lives to the Lord. Those consequences of witnessing stir new depths of faith among all believers who observe and hear about the occurrences.

Witnessing also helps turn some Christians into leaders of the congregation who had not played that role before. For some, the experience of writing and sharing their testimonies with others helps them gain a voice for and self-confidence in serving the Lord. For others, understanding the need to witness through the teachings of the in-congregation evangelist convinces them to listen more carefully to the Holy Spirit who directs them to exercise leadership in areas where none exists in the congregation. Some Christians with low self-esteem will find that God has planned great things for them: With the Lord's help, some will find value in themselves that they never knew existed through taking on leadership roles for the first time. Through Christ, insecure followers can become mighty spiritual warriors for Him.

Perhaps the most unanticipated effect of witnessing is that some of the newest Christians will be on fire for the Lord and will immediately set a good example as witnesses. Here's an example: Jim Barbarossa wrote his testimony shortly after he was saved and immediately began leaving copies wherever he went, including on the windshields of cars in parking lots he used. That kind of personal witnessing example from a new believer has to help fill a congregation with energy and excitement.

Christians Gain the Full Favor of the Lord
by Overcoming Shyness and Eliminating Fears

"Let your light so shine before men,
that they may see your good works
and glorify your Father in heaven."

— Matthew 5:16 (NKJV)

Many Christians might as well be invisible to the lost. Why? These Christians are shy and stay in the background. Even their good works aren't necessarily viewed as Godly acts by the unsaved, but may instead be seen as merely the conflict-avoiding steps of a timid person unless Christians mention their faith to friends, neighbors, colleagues, and strangers.

There's good news: Researchers tell us that shyness is a trait that can be overcome by becoming more socially active. What incentive does a shy person have to become more active? Witnessing for the Lord is a command that many shy Christians don't realize applies to them. What better way to gain helpful social experiences than by serving the Lord?

Made aware of the command to testify and provided with powerful tools, even the shyest person will soon feel comfortable handing out tracts and tapes in the company of others who are more outgoing. With enough experience doing that, the shy Christian will eventually say "hello" to someone while passing out such tools. If the tract or tape contains the Christian's own testimony, it's a small step from "hello" to talking about that Christian's trials and becoming a source of compassion for someone who is going through a similar trial.

Step by step, the shy Christian can become a more outgoing Christian. When that happens, the angels in heaven are probably rejoicing because they know that more souls will be saved.

An in-house evangelist can play a special role for shy Christians, by helping these people decide to write and learn how to prepare their testimonies. Revealing so much about themselves in a written testi-mony, especially concerning their past sins and difficulties, can be especially challenging for shy people. Writing about sins and diffi-

13

cultics helps lower barriers to being open with others about their faith. Lower those self-imposed barriers to sharing, and listeners will lower their barriers, too, and as a result shy people can build connections to people they would like to help.

Answers to our witnessing questionnaire from members of Jubilee Worship Center told us that shy people gained boldness for witnessing because most listeners were understanding and supportive of their faith sharing. As a result of experiencing these reactions, these shy people felt more affirmed as worthy individuals and in their faith.

Shyness doesn't only affect a Christian's ability to testify. It also inhibits all other human connections. When shy Christians become outgoing, all parts of life are enhanced. Shy Christians will also gain by having more Christian friends and acquaintances ... and being closer to them, connections that benefit everyone.

Shyness isn't the only barrier to effective witnessing. Christians who aren't shy may instead be tied up in emotional knots by fears placed in their minds by the enemy who is in the world. God doesn't send us fear of speaking about our faith, but many Christians don't realize that and don't combat this kind of fear as they should.

We also asked the congregation at Jubilee Worship Center to tell us why they were reluctant (if they ever were) to witness before joining the church. Many reported a long list of fears that had previously hobbled their willingness to share their faith. Here are the specific fears about witnessing they described in order of the frequency the fears were mentioned:

- Rejection by hearers
- Wouldn't know what to say
- Would get into a debate
- Would say something wrong
- Would make a mistake
- Listeners would bring up the witness's past bad behavior
- Would receive a hostile reaction from listeners
- Would look stupid or crazy

Looking at this list will remind some readers of the reasons why many people avoid door-to-door sales jobs. Unfortunately, these fears about witnessing are tied to something far more important than providing cosmetics or brushes, both for the lost and the saved: Some people may never hear about the Gospel unless we tell them, and many will need to hear about Jesus from a variety of people before the message will sink in and be appreciated.

Not being willing to speak up about the Lord can be a soul-threatening decision as well, but many nonwitnessing Christians may not realize that. As Jesus told us in Mark 8:38 (NKJV):

> For whoever is ashamed of Me and My words in this adulterous and sinful generation, of him the Son of Man also will be ashamed when He comes in the glory of His Father with the holy angels.

An in-congregation evangelist can be helpful in deflating fears about witnessing through addressing such concerns, explaining that God doesn't want anyone to feel fear while witnessing, and teaching how witnessing can be an easy, effective, and joyful experience. After conquering their fears about witnessing, these Christians can learn to overcome their fears brought on by the enemy who is in the world that also affect other areas of their lives. When that happens, it will be a more joyful experience for them to live as Christians.

Many people first learn to witness by sharing their faith with unsaved family members. Imagine the joy they experience when their families are united in service to the Lord! When we asked members of the Jubilee Worship Center what had been their most memorable witnessing experiences, the eloquence and depth of feeling were most vivid when telling about helping parents, spouses, children, and grand-children receive Salvation. (If you would like to read about some of these experiences, you will find many of them quoted in Chapter 11.)

Almost as eloquent and moving were descriptions we received of helping people deal with serious illnesses, harmful addictions such as to drugs and alcohol, depression, broken families, and self-destructive thinking through repentance, accepting the Lord, and gaining His help with those problems. Witnesses report tears of joy when Salvation also led to healing of the body and spirit for the newly saved through the Lord's mercy. Until having had such experiences, some witnesses hadn't realized that Christ can act through them to do miracles today. What a wonderful gift it is to see His power and goodness in action in such supernatural ways!

For those who have been shy or lived in fear, an in-house evangelist brings another unexpected blessing: After being trained in joyful witnessing, their children learn to share their faith without being self-conscious or afraid. Scientists tell us that children are often more shy or fearful after observing a parent behave in either way. With ministry leaders and parents modeling friendly, confident witnessing, children will gain a better start in life, both as witnessing Christians and in their other activities.

Even in a small congregation, members may only have nodding acquaintances with most other people in the church. That's a missed opportunity to fully appreciate God's goodness. After the first edition of *Real Life Stories* was completed, members of Jubilee Worship Center were startled to find out that most people in the congregation had been helped by the Lord in miraculous ways.

That one volume contained more examples of miracles than most members had read about in their entire lives. Yet most of those miracles were not known until revealed by those who had received them. Imagine the wonderful benefits that will be gained when most Christians share written testimonies and we can all regard God's attention to and gifts for us with awe!

Knowing more about one another also brings benefits to church members by helping them find others with similar interests and backgrounds. When that happens, new ministries may be established by warm hearts to serve others who are suffering from the problems that once troubled these Christians. From those ministries, new blessings will arise for their Christian leaders.

The Lost Gain Compassion, Meaning, Companionship, Hope, and Salvation

... just as I also please all men *in all* things, *not seeking my own profit, but the* profit *of many, that they may be saved.*

— 1 Corinthians 10:33 (NKJV)

Reading the testimonies from Jubilee Worship Center reveals many powerful messages about how God works in our lives. He stays patiently with us while we are on the low road to terrible troubles brought upon us by our sins, and He waits to rescue us when we ask for His help. When we use illegal drugs, He wants to free us from the chains of that attraction; when we become dependent on alcohol, He wants to help us appreciate joyful sobriety; when our bodies are wracked with pain and deadly disease, He wants to heal us and let us rejoice in good health; and when we are disgusted with our behavior, He wants us to be cleansed of our sinful past and to walk in happy faith. Even our sins help bring us to Him. When we are broken in spirit and body by our mistakes, we search for answers beyond our strength and capacity and listen better to His answers.

Where does witnessing fit into this picture? Christ puts the lost in the path of witnesses who can explain about God's power and love by describing what God has done in the witnesses' lives. When we share in loving ways how terrible problems, like those the lost are experiencing, have been overcome through faith in Jesus, troubled souls are soothed by hearing about the Lord's compassion. The lost also gain by receiving compassion from a witness, feeling God's caring through the witness's attention and supportive words and actions.

Whether downcast by pain resulting from sin or through living a life without Christ, many Jubilee Worship Center members told us they felt empty in ways that made them continually sad until they received Salvation. Many saw no purpose to their lives and felt a profound pain that alerted them that something important was missing.

What a great gift it is for such purposeless, hurting people to hear from a witness that God had developed good plans for everyone before they were born. Anyone would naturally want to know what those plans are and how to fulfill them. Questions about God's purpose for their lives then become planks in a strong bridge the lost can cross to learn from a faithful witness about all the gifts that Salvation brings.

What purpose does life have without God's love and direction? Immediately upon receiving Salvation, we gain Divine meaning for our lives through the services He directs us to do. In performing services for the Lord, we find satisfying meaning beyond what we ever imagined, and our steps lightly skip along our Divinely appointed path. What joy that provides!

To help prepare this book, almost all members of Jubilee Worship Center completed questionnaires about their lives before Salvation, faith, and witnessing experiences (see Appendix D for a list of contributors). From these answers, we learned that the lost often feel alone as well, even in the midst of a crowd. They may party with revelers but still feel as if no one cares whether they live or die, or about what might happen to them.

Until they receive Jesus as their Lord and Savior, they do not know His constant and caring companionship. No matter what happens (good or bad), Jesus wants to speak with them through the Holy Spirit, receive and answer their prayers, and be a warm presence in their lives. Witnesses can explain the loving companionship they enjoy with the Lord and help the lost to understand what they are missing by ignoring or rejecting Him.

Being kind to a hurting person is always appreciated, but that kindness is received as a moving, life-changing compassion when the witness has walked in the shoes of the hurting. When we share our painful experiences, we become living proof to the lost that it's possible to go from feeling hopeless to being hopeful and able to give aid to others. It's one of God's most wonderful gifts to the lost to discover this compassion.

If you saw someone who needed to be pulled from a burning wreck, you would probably find the courage to help. Many of the lost are living with a conviction that their lives are worse than a burning wreck, and that there is no way they can be saved from their problems.

They live in a dark dungeon of hopelessness that leaves them feeling helpless.

It's easy to forget how desperate people can become when they are weighed down by their sins and the consequences of their mistakes. They often believe that they are unworthy of love and cannot be forgiven, they cannot forgive themselves, and they see no possibility for improvement. It's a dreary, horrible way to live. To go from feeling totally hopeless to grasping a confident hope through faith in Jesus is one of the greatest gifts anyone can receive ... and all it takes for this gift to be received is for a willing witness or written testimony to be given so that the Holy Spirit can open and soften the hopeless person's aching heart.

During such witnessing, the lost person can begin to feel loved and gain hope that there might be a better future. When you share with the lost about how to gain Salvation, you will often describe a pathway to an improved life on Earth and later in heaven that has not been understood by the lost. How can those who haven't heard about Salvation hope to grasp what they don't know about?

How did your life change after you accepted the Lord's Salvation? If you are like us, it was the greatest gift of all. Everything changed for the better after that.

You can help to provide those wonderful improvements by simply speaking to the lost so they can understand what they are missing and decide to accept Salvation. If you had a billion dollars to give away, you couldn't do as much for others as by sharing with the lost the Good News of Salvation: God will make crooked places straight for those who repent of their sins, believe in and accept the Lord Jesus as their Savior, and dedicate their lives to serving Christ. God bless all those who witness!

✝

In Chapter 2, you will read about the importance of having an in-congregation evangelist to teach the importance of witnessing and how to be an effective witness. We also discuss how to identify who this evangelist should be from among members of your congregation.

Chapter 2

Employ All the Talents and Energy in the Body of Believers

Light a Spiritual Fire
with a Full-Time Evangelist in Every Church

*But you be watchful in all things, endure afflictions,
do the work of an evangelist, fulfill your ministry.*

— 2 Timothy 4:5 (NKJV)

When the Apostle Paul wrote these words to Timothy, Paul believed that his days on Earth were coming to an end. Paul wanted to help prepare Timothy to carry on the important work of taking the Good News about Jesus Christ to those who had not yet heard. As long as one person has not heard and understood about Salvation, our work as witnessing Christians isn't done, despite the challenges we may face to do so. That's what Paul wanted us to remember.

In practice, Paul was simply reaffirming to another generation what all followers of Jesus had been commanded to do by Him: After being saved through His grace, we must help others receive the same gift. Why was that message important in the early church? Few had heard of Jesus, and many who had heard disputed His Divine nature. Jesus knew how important this task was because it was his last direction to his eleven disciples in the book of Matthew. (See Matthew 28:19-20.) Last messages are remembered best, and our Lord was again perfect in His wisdom in choosing this message.

When Paul was still called Saul, he had a hard heart toward Jesus and the early Christians, being a leader in rebuking, punishing, and stoning them. Paul only accepted Jesus as Lord and Savior after He appeared in His blinding glory on the road to Damascus and asked

20

Paul why he was persecuting Him. God's plan wasn't to repeat that method of conversion, as was evidenced by Christ sending Paul a vision of Ananias restoring Paul's sight and then directing Ananias to perform the miracle and to baptize Paul in the Holy Spirit. (See Acts 9:1-19.)

Despite this clear direction and the hard work of many great pastors, missionaries, evangelists, and witnessing Christians for nearly two thousand years, a global survey today would probably show that the majority of people on Earth either don't know about God's promises to us or don't believe those promises. That's a sad commentary on how well we are following the Lord's direction to bring His Good News to everyone.

How many lost people are there compared to those who are saved? Only God knows, but the ratio is surely no more than ten to one and may well be as low as six to one. Some would argue that the 30 percent of the world's population that identify themselves as Christians are a larger number, but many of those self-proclaimed Christians have not repented of their sins and accepted Jesus as their Lord and Savior.

If we equally divided names of the lost into individual lists for each Christian, there would only be six to ten names on each list. If each Christian immediately began making contacts, each lost person would hear the Good News very quickly. Some Christians would be done making first contact in a single day to their share of the lost. If these Christians repeated the contacts daily, most would have succeeded in getting the message across in a convincing way to their share of the lost within a month. As the number of Christians grew and more people joined in witnessing, the number of people for each Christian to contact would become smaller and each lost person would receive more testimonies. The combined effect of such a concentrated effort would be marvelous.

Some people undoubtedly have such hard hearts that they wouldn't receive the blessings of this heavenly information no matter how many testimonies they heard. But the task of fulfilling God's call to help all be saved would be as complete as Christian efforts and prayers can

21

accomplish. Christians could then keep knocking on the hard hearts and eventually many more souls would be saved.

What's our point? If everyone does some witnessing, it's not a big job. Why then is there so much work to be done? It's because most Christians don't share their faith with lost people. Many people estimate that over 90 percent of Christians have never witnessed to anyone, and most of the rest have done little witnessing. Our survey at Jubilee Worship Center (JWC) showed that the majority of church members were either doing nothing or very little before being exposed to the church's emphasis on witnessing.

Here is what one Christian woman told us about her attitudes toward witnessing before meeting in-congregation evangelists at JWC:

> I have attended church for most of my adult life and have been involved in many of the ministries of the church. I have taught Sunday school to preschoolers through adults, served as an elder, served as church secretary, served as janitor, etc., just as many other church members have done. To me, this was what church was all about, and I found great satisfaction in what I was doing. The internal workings of the church were my delight. That was all I knew.

> The churches I had attended placed little or no emphasis on evangelism …. We were under the impression that anything to do with evangelism was under the job description of the pastors and the missionaries. This was their duty and that's why we hired them. We all knew that passing out tracts or tapes or whatever was for the overboard fanatics … all this was out of our scope.

Change satisfied witnessing inaction into inspired witnessing, and Christians will quickly and easily help transform humanity in the ways that God intended. How do you get everyone busy witnessing? You need an in-congregation evangelist to light the fire of desire for witnessing and to fan its flames with teaching how to witness. Why do we say that? Because our survey answers showed that JWC members who responded (almost the whole congregation) became active witnesses after in-congregation evangelists were appointed.

In-Congregation Evangelists Teach the Call to Witness and How to Do So in Loving, Effective Ways

"But the Helper, the Holy Spirit,
whom the Father will send in My name,
He will teach you all things,
and bring to your remembrance all things that I said to you."

— John 14:26 (NKJV)

If deciding to witness and learning how to do it well were as easy as breathing, everyone would already know God's promises. If the decision to witness and learning how were as difficult as brain surgery, there would be many fewer believers than there are.

Deciding and learning how to ride a ten-speed bicycle are good parallels to the difficulty of deciding and learning how to witness effectively. Most people don't have too much trouble deciding they want to learn how to ride a bike. When the desire to learn is strong, the learning period is usually just a few weeks long as new skills in balance, coordination, and shifting are learned. There are intermediate steps where you need help such as knowing to use and gradually remove training wheels and later having someone run along with you to provide support while you master how to balance. After you can balance, you can work on using the gears properly, a subject for which a lesson will help. If you then like riding, you can learn from others how to train and race. For lifelong enjoyment, you will need to learn to tune your bike by using simple tools. Once these skills are learned, you will rarely forget how to ride a bicycle and keep it rolling smoothly. Accomplished riders will then be able to teach others to learn the same skills.

Some will make more halting progress, stopping whenever they hit a difficulty. These people may need many years to be able to master riding and tuning a ten-speed bike. Some will never get that far. These people can still gain benefits from their learning efforts. Without being able to tune their own bikes, they can pay the local bike shop for routine maintenance. Those who never get the knack of using gears can enjoy riding a bike that doesn't require changing gears. Even youngsters who cannot learn to balance a bicycle can still learn to ride a tricycle and enjoy lots of fun and good exercise that way.

Let's consider what's actually required to decide and learn to witness. Helping people decide to witness is pretty easily accomplished. Jim and Carla Barbarossa can explain the command to witness and the consequences of not witnessing effectively enough during a weekend series of meetings so that 70 percent of the people attending church services will repent of not witnessing and agree to write and share their testimonies. If you would like to learn more about how this is done, you can contact Jim and Carla at jim@step-by-step.org, and they can provide examples.

Experience at JWC demonstrates that teaching people who are willing to witness how to do so takes a lot longer than persuading them to do so. The first step the JWC evangelists use is to ask each person to prepare a written testimony.

Now, that sounds simple … but it's not easy for many people. What's the record? Although Jim and Carla have been working as in-congregation evangelists at JWC for several years and continually emphasize written testimonies, only a little more than half the congregation has provided a written testimony.

Of those who have provided their written testimonies at JWC and answered our survey, about 40 percent completed the task within three months and two-thirds within a year. Another 8 percent finished in the second year, and 2 percent finished in the third year. Many people are still working on their testimonies several years later.

Why is there such a long delay? Some didn't decide right away to prepare a testimony. In addition, 12 percent of those who prepared written testimonies said they needed help from someone else. A number of those who haven't finished are working with others or say they still need help. Over 20 percent of those who needed more than three months to write their testimonies couldn't initially decide what to include.

There may be an unspoken reason, too. When we look at the subjects described in the *Real Life Stories* testimonies, it's clear that they often deal with emotionally painful and embarrassing subjects such as abuse, addictions, criminal activity, depression, divorce, and growing up in broken homes. Surely it's not pleasant to think about those difficulties again. From this track record for writing testimonies and these replies, it's clear that turning most Christians into testimony writers isn't fast or easy.

As with learning to ride a bicycle, there are benefits for witnessing efforts while most testimony writing takes place. An important witnessing door opens as soon as a church has some written testimonies (a level of preparation that may occur within just a few days): Those testimonies can be immediately shared with the lost by those who are fired with zeal to share the Good News whether or not they have written their own testimonies.

Usually the person who writes a testimony will find having such a tract makes it easier to approach other people and to know what to say: The written testimony is a dress rehearsal for sharing a verbal testimony. In addition, people who have experienced similar trials and paths to Salvation can use someone else's testimony by sharing a tract and discussing the testimony; those who haven't written a testimony can simply mention that "I went through something like that." For those with no testimony and no similar experience, a tract can still be helpful in overcoming shyness and fear. These people can simply hand out the written testimonies and practice smiling as they do.

When enough people have written their testimonies, the church will also have the opportunity to publish a book of testimonies as JWC did in *Real Life Stories*. Such books provide several advantages:

- It's easier to attract someone's attention with a free book than it is with a tract or tape.
- Those who read the book are more likely to find a testimony that fits their circumstances.
- Witnesses find it easier to speak to strangers when they can offer a free book.

- Witnesses who wrote a testimony in the book usually enjoy pointing to their pictures on the cover, autographing the book, and giving it as a gift.
- When passed along to others by those who were moved by reading the testimonies, the book has the potential to help open many hearts to the Lord.
- Examining the book can help pastors in other churches decide to add in-congregation evangelists and follow the path we are describing for becoming a fully witnessing congregation.

Many people have observed Christians sharing their faith in ways that make those observers feel uncomfortable. Such a discomforting memory is often recalled while listening to someone who is bold in espousing witnessing. That's too bad. It's a sad commentary about the quality of witnessing that few Christians have had a chance to observe loving, kind, and effective methods of witnessing.

Overcoming such negative images is one of the reasons why the in-congregation evangelist's task is aided by speaking for five minutes during every church service, Bible study, religious occasion, and congregational activity to discuss the reasons for being witnesses and how to do it well. While messages about general subjects are usually remembered and understood well only after thirty communications, experience at JWC suggests that some people needed to hear messages about the importance of witnessing hundreds of times before they could overcome hard hearts and ignorance about witnessing.

Why are messages about witnessing so much more difficult to appreciate than many secular subjects? We should all remember that witnessing is one of those activities where the enemy who is in the world has a large stake in stifling progress. Imagine how much harder it would be to learn how to ride a bicycle if someone were shouting in your ear that it's not worth doing, that you will never succeed, that you will be badly injured, and that you look foolish.

In addition to what we've described, the in-congregation evangelist should help church members grow as witnesses in as many ways as possible. Here are some of the important tasks:

- Messages about witnessing are written and delivered during five-minute segments in each service, Bible study, and church event.
- The evangelist meets individually with those who haven't yet decided to write a testimony to address whatever concerns they have about this activity.
- The evangelist assists those who are writing testimonies and recruits others to assist witnesses with the writing.
- Once a testimony has been prepared, the evangelist teaches the author how to use it effectively as a witnessing tract.
- The evangelist also plans, organizes, and directs outreach activities so that people who live and work near the church will be drawn to meet witnesses and receive testimonies. JWC has used block parties, car shows, free car washes featuring free food and prizes, participating in parades, and picnics in the park to help attract the lost to their church.
- The evangelist builds on the church's outreach activities by visiting those who came to the outreaches and visit the church.

As you can see, there's a lot of work to be done. It's not surprising that even pastors who are good at teaching how to witness don't get around to doing all these things. As a result, most churches are full of nonwitnessing Christians until they hire a full-time in-congregation evangelist. As the church grows beyond a small size, full-time in-congregation evangelists will need help, as well.

At JWC, "fire starters" were recruited by the in-congregation evangelists to help with all these tasks. Adding fire starters is a great blessing for the church because each person brings special gifts that permit their contributions to bear different fruit than what the in-congregation evangelist brings. After beginning with a full-time evangelist performing these tasks for the congregation, you can use fire starters to further multiply the attention and energies of the congregation on witnessing so that the congregation's efforts to save the lost grow by several hundred times. What a great blessing!

Gifted In-Congregation Evangelists Should Be Identified from within the Church Membership

*If we receive the witness of men,
the witness of God is greater; ....*

— 1 John 5:9 (NKJV)

By knowing the personalities and habits of those in the congregation, an in-congregation evangelist can be more effective in addressing the witnessing needs. For that reason we advise every congregation to employ an in-congregation evangelist from among those who already attend the church.

With fewer than sixty people in the congregation, this can be a part-time, paid position. With sixty or more members, each congregation should have its own paid, full-time evangelist.

We recommend that an in-congregation evangelist be employed before any choir leaders, youth pastors, or assistant pastors are hired. In this way, a small church can be more faithful in following Christ's commands, grow faster, and become more effective in serving the needs of those in the congregation to grow as Christians.

For those congregations with financial problems, this approach also makes the most sense: The evangelist will accelerate growth in attendance, which will lead to receiving more tithes and offerings.

If a small congregation finds it hard to afford paying an evangelist, the part-time role can be temporarily shared among a number of people who work eight to ten hours a week as volunteers. There's a potential blessing in starting this way: The volunteers can find out how much they like being evangelists and which are best at teaching and encouraging witnessing. Those who don't become full-time, in-congregation evangelists can continue as fire starters in assisting the in-congregation evangelist.

Who should become in-congregation evangelists? You want the most gifted teachers and encouragers of witnessing. God has already decided and prepared some Christians to be talented and eager to perform this role. You simply need to identify who those people are.

Here's an example of how the right person can be revealed. Jim and Carla Barbarossa had been looking for a church where they could serve as in-congregation evangelists for two years. The churches they visited had room for pastors and teachers but no interest in having in-congregation evangelists. During this time, they often shared the concept of having in-congregation evangelists with other churches around the United States.

At JWC, they sat in a back pew for a year believing that no local church wanted their involvement as evangelists. Discouraged by that conclusion, they didn't join a local church. To their surprise one Sunday night, Bishop Dale P. Combs shared a message he had received from the Holy Spirit: Jim was to be the church's evangelist. Bishop Combs revealed at that time that he had been praying for a long time that the Lord would send him an evangelist to work with him in training the congregation to reach their community.

Today, Jim and Carla travel to many churches and hold conferences at JWC where they describe what an in-congregation evangelist should do and help Christians to understand if God has given them evangelistic gifts and called them to work in that role. If you would like to find if you have these gifts and this calling, contact Jim and Carla at Jim@step-by-step.org and ask about the DVDs on this subject.

Let's look at some seemingly appropriate, but wrong, ways to choose an in-congregation evangelist. Here are the three most common mistakes: A pastor might conclude that the right person to choose is (1) the congregation's most active witness, (2) someone who has been ordained, or (3) a person who has at least been to a Bible college.

While it's possible that the congregation's most active witness would make a great in-congregation evangelist, it's more likely to be a coincidence than a certainty. While someone who does a lot of witnessing clearly has a passion for witnessing, that same passion may not apply to teaching and encouraging others to witness. In addition, the gifts of teaching and encouraging witnessing may not have been given to a wonderful witness. A further problem can occur because people who have been witnessing for a long time usually favor a few methods, haven't learned any others, and don't want to learn any new ones. As a result, great witnesses may not be able to help everyone in the congregation to find and learn witnessing methods that fit them well.

An ordained person probably has teaching gifts. That's one important part of being an in-congregation evangelist. The process most people go through to become ordained, however, rarely emphasizes developing skills in teaching and encouraging witnessing. As a result, the ordained person may not have a background in the various ways to witness.

Most ordained people feel called to teach people from the Word about how to live as Christians. Being an in-congregation evangelist could feel like an artificially narrow role for most ordained people. You also have to check if the ordained person has a passion for teaching and encouraging witnessing.

Similar concerns apply to those who have been to a Bible college. The amount of Scripture that you need to know to be an in-congregation evangelist isn't very great. Anyone could learn what's needed in a brief amount of time (Appendix A contains most of the verses that are helpful), so this degree of qualification isn't necessary to be an effective in-congregation evangelist.

What's the lesson? Pastors should be led by the Holy Spirit in identifying the in-congregation evangelists the Lord has provided rather than relying on what they know about peoples' pasts. A good way to begin is to check for which people feel called to this work.

Many congregations will be surprised when they ask if any of their members feel called to be in-congregation evangelists. It may well be that people have been called for years to evangelize but didn't see how they could regularly leave their homes for itinerant travel due to family responsibilities: Few of those people will have ever thought about being an in-congregation evangelist right where they are.

Let us share with you the experience one woman had with learning that she was called to be an in-congregation evangelist after hearing Jim and Carla teach about the gift of the evangelist and witnessing. Prior to recognizing the calling, she had grown up in church and worked in a dance ministry for over fourteen years to minister to people and serve the Lord:

Friday night and Saturday morning I learned so much about … evangelism and understood how easy it was for me to share my faith with others. I began to think and ask within me, "God, what's my purpose here on Earth?"

I always wanted to lead more people to the Lord, but I always thought it took too much time and that I didn't know enough of the Bible to do this. As you taught, my heart felt an even deeper passion for lost souls. I was getting excited and wanted to start right away.

When you said that God would speak to our hearts and indicate who the evangelists were … I couldn't sit any longer … I couldn't contain my tears.

The same week I shared with my pastors what I had learned and the calling God gave me during your conferences the past weekend. I stirred them up also. They gave me an opportunity to share for a few minutes with the leaders of the different departments in our local church … I motivated them with testimony tracts I made and some made theirs within the days that followed.

I've been giving out the two testimony tracts of my own at gas stations, stores, restaurants, and even to people on the street selling water, the newspaper, or those asking for money. I just tell them that Jesus loves them and I invite them to church.

As you can see from this experience, the passion and inspirational impact of a gifted in-congregation evangelist are hard to miss. If a mistake occurs in choosing an in-congregation evangelist, however, pastors need to be quick to replace the wrong choice with an appropriate one.

✝

Now that you have an inspired and gifted in-congregation evangelist, what's next? Your evangelist needs to begin teaching and encouraging witnessing in five-minute segments during each church service, Bible study, and church activity. That's our subject for Chapter 3.

Chapter 3

Pay Attention to
Jesus' Great Commission

Dedicate Five Minutes in Every Church Service and
Activity to Build Enthusiasm and Capability
for Witnessing

Finally, brethren, whatever things are true,
whatever things are noble,
whatever things are just,
whatever things are pure,
whatever things are lovely,
whatever things are of good report,
if there is any virtue
and if there is anything praiseworthy —
meditate on these things.

— Philippians 4:8 (NKJV)

Most Christians don't appreciate that they are supposed to be active witnesses. Many will have attended church for years without hearing much about this important commission from God. Hardly any have heard about witnessing from an evangelist who is equipped to teach and inspire them.

When evangelists Jim and Carla Barbarossa visit churches for the first time, they generally find that 97 percent of the people in the congregation have never helped lead someone to the Lord. This sad fact demonstrates in part that it's not obvious to people who may be willing to witness what they should do: They need lots of help to learn. Consider this comparison: How many people learn to ride and maintain racing bikes by listening to speeches on the subject a few times a year?

So what's to be done? An in-congregation evangelist could hold classes for teaching and encouraging witnessing. But a class in witnessing will probably draw a small percentage of a congregation, and mostly people who already witness. In contrast, five minutes dedicated to having in-congregation evangelists and fire starters teach and inspire witnessing during each service, Bible study, and any other activity will reach everyone in the congregation. As Romans 10:17 (NKJV) reminds us about reaching unsaved people, "So then faith *comes* by hearing, and hearing by the word of God."

The continuity of these five-minute communications creates a much greater frequency of information than could be accomplished in any other way, allowing the messages to sink deeper into peoples' hearts, minds, memories, and souls. These sessions show a commit-ment by the pastor and congregation to becoming a fully witnessing church that helps convince those who don't witness to begin. This commitment is especially important for reaching people who have hardened their hearts against witnessing, and these five minutes can also provide members new to a witnessing church with continual instruction about witnessing from the beginning of their connection with the church.

The most important reason for employing this practice is because spending time this way works very well for increasing witnessing activity. Let's look at the evidence based on what happened at Jubilee Worship Center (JWC) according to our survey. For one thing, few had written testimonies before worshipping at JWC. Now, more than half the adults and many of the children have. For another thing, fewer than a quarter ever shared their testimonies before coming to JWC. Now, all survey respondents report either sharing their testimony or passing out copies of other peoples' testimonies. Almost everyone reported an increase in their own witnessing; the exceptions were those who had always been active witnesses.

When asked about the effect on the church of spending five minutes on witnessing in every service, Bible study, and church activity, over three-quarters of survey respondents in the congregation described something positive. The most frequent positive answers mentioned encouragement, good teaching, and stimulating more witnessing.

When asked about the personal effect on them received from these teachings, over three-quarters of JWC survey respondents also described benefits. Almost all of those who gained personal benefits described feeling more encouraged to witness. Hearing these teachings by the evangelists and fire starters was cited by survey respondents as being the most useful thing that the church had done to make people feel more comfortable and enthusiastic about sharing their faith.

Here is one woman's description of how these five-minute teachings affected her:

I am blessed to be a member of Jubilee Worship Center for many reasons, but one is because God sent Jim and Carla here to lead us with many new ideas of telling people about Jesus. We were first taught by listening to Jim's and Carla's "Take 5's" and then encouraged to write our own testimonies and pass them out, which I did. Then came the *Real Life Stories* book that we had the opportunity to take to businesses and neighborhoods. I thought, "I can do this!" It gave me somewhere to start and someone to go with. Lisa Z. was very supportive the first time I went with her. Fear had held me back [from witnessing] for many years but I was ready to take those baby steps and keep going.

Then I was asked to do a "Take 5" and the same fear was there again. I prayed for several days and God gave me a "Take 5" that I was in awe of … I truly learned that God will give the inspiration and equip us for whatever the task ….

I have seen our children grow because they were asked to write their testimonies for the *Real Life Stories* book. Lisa Z. is training by doing "Take 5's" weekly in Sunday school, and the children themselves are also doing "Take 5's" in children's church. How natural it will be for them to witness since starting at such a young age.

Because of what Jim and Carla have taught, I now feel confident and equipped to go out and witness.

What a great blessing these brief teachings brought her and her children in serving the Lord! In teaching, pay particular attention to the youth in your church. Most Christians receive Salvation before age eighteen. Because of their strong connections to friends, young people are much more likely to be interested in learning about God from a friend than from an adult they don't know. These five-minute teachings within your youth ministry will probably help lead more souls to the Lord and to participation in your church than the combined efforts of the adults. If such a young new believer is the first soul to be saved in that family, the new Christian may be able to help bring his or her family to the Lord as well.

Having shown the importance of these five-minute teaching sessions, who should be the teacher? Consider that not everyone is called to do this kind of teaching. If the pastor has been led by the Lord to have an in-congregation evangelist, an in-congregation evangelist will be called by the Lord to serve. The evangelist, in turn, needs to ask Jesus for direction as to who else should teach witnessing. Some of these people will and others will not realize that they have the calling. Some others may want to teach but are not called to do so by the Lord: The evangelist needs to pray about whether to accept those people's teachings. If in doubt, a rehearsal can be held with some other witnessing teachers to see what everyone thinks.

If you have been given the gift of evangelism, the next two sections will help you realize the full potential of your gift.

How to Teach Witnessing Five Minutes at a Time

*"Now go; I will help you speak
and will teach you what to say."*

— Exodus 4:12 (NIV)

36

It's one thing to have five minutes to teach witnessing; it's a far more important thing to teach well. Let's begin with preparation. Pray for the Lord to guide you to Scriptures, songs, stories, and events that you should teach (and see the next section). Ask Him what He wants you to do with those subjects. If you are a fire starter (a volunteer who is in training to become an evangelist), discuss the topic you are called to share with your in-congregation evangelist and you will probably receive some valuable suggestions.

Once you've established what He wants you to teach, write out the lesson. If you are the only speaker, you can prepare a speaking outline. If it is to be a drama, you'll need to write a script and provide directions.

Check what you've written to be sure it's about witnessing. You must not address other subjects during these five-minute segments. A good test is to imagine that you are talking to a lost person. Would that person know that you are speaking about Christians sharing their faith with unsaved people? That's a relevant test because your witnessing church should have lots of lost people attending. When these people accept the Lord, they will be prepared to become witnesses right away.

Practice your planned teaching until it goes smoothly. Time your practice. You should never go over five minutes unless you have asked the pastor at least two days in advance for an additional minute or two. Please keep in mind that this is not the norm; the norm is five minutes. When you speak, take a timer with you and stop speaking before three hundred seconds pass, even if you are not done. Otherwise, you will create disputes in the church by exceeding your authority from the pastor. As a result of wanting to complete what you've prepared, plan to speak for at least thirty seconds less than five minutes so that you won't run out of time.

If you have a subject that cannot be covered in five minutes, see if you can carve out the heart of it and do that part in five minutes. If not, break up the subject matter into five-minute subsegments. Then you can teach the subsegments sequentially during Sunday services so that the pieces can be tied together into one message that is presented over several weeks.

Pick the right time to teach so that you'll have the largest audience and good attention. During Sunday services, it works well to speak just after the offering is received. If you open the service with the teaching, late arrivers will miss what you have to say. If you teach at the very end of the service, some of those who resist witnessing will walk out early. During small group Bible studies, you can teach at the end because most people would be embarrassed to leave a small group. You can also speak at the end for men's groups and women's ministries.

At JWC, witnessing teachings are held after the second worship song in youth meetings. In kid's church, the teaching follows the offering. Timing is flexible during Sunday school. Teach at every grade level, but vary the content to reflect the age of the hearers.

Whether you are an evangelist or a fire starter, you need to be properly prepared for your teaching:

- Pray for strength to resist the enemy's battle against your teaching.
- Be ready to speak without reading your text.
- Dress appropriately.
- Arrive early.
- Make eye contact with the listeners throughout the teaching.
- Hold the microphone so it is very close to your chin (if people cannot hear you, the teaching does no good).
- Speak clearly, distinctly, and loudly enough (have someone at the back of the church or hall give you a hand signal if your voice needs to be easier to hear).
- Speak in a loving way and feel love for your listeners as you talk.
- Stay on your subject.
- End with a challenge, or explain the lesson if you are sharing a testimony or describing a failure.

If you cannot do all these things, you should wait to start teaching until you can. Here's a special problem to watch out for: Resistance to the messages can cause the evangelist or a fire starter to become angry with the congregation. That anger will do much harm. If you find that anger within yourself, turn the teaching responsibilities over to those who are still filled with love about sharing these messages until your heart is again filled to overflowing with love towards the congregation.

It sounds like a lot to do, doesn't it? Is it worth it? Here's what one JWC congregant had to say about the experience of sharing a five-minute teaching about witnessing:

> When Jim [Barbarossa] says, "Are you ready to let God stretch you?" I know the Lord is getting ready to do something in me. Do I like to be stretched? Not all the time, but when I look back I am glad I was. It helps me grow. I myself don't like to do "Take 5's" all that much, but I want to be a vessel that can be used. If it pleases God, then I want to do it. I see what it has done for our local body and in me. So I am thankful to have taken part in such a great thing.

What to Teach about Witnessing

"Behold, I stand at the door and knock.
If anyone hears My voice and opens the door,
I will come in to him and dine with him, and he with Me."

— Revelation 3:20 (NKJV)

Not everyone wants to hear that Christians should be witnessing for the Lord. Be prepared for strong negative reactions. Jim Barbarossa notes that "when people are not sharing their faith and you keep talking about sharing your faith, they feel threatened and go into the attack mode. They attack your character to get the eyes off their not sharing their faith. Those who already share their faith are usually very excited to hear what God is doing through other people sharing their faith."

The First Year

Because of resistance, there's a helpful order for teaching about witnessing to gain the most benefit: Start with the Scriptures that say we must share our faith. (We've included helpful Scriptures on this subject in Appendix A.) There's no point in trying to teach people how to witness who don't believe they are supposed to do so; you just annoy them. In the process of teaching that all must share their faith to people who don't accept that command, you'll also deepen the commitment of those who already feel it is the right thing to do.

Based on Jim's and Carla's experiences, reviewing those Scriptures that command witnessing should be the only subject covered during the first two months that you teach. Christians should feel deeply challenged to share their faith before you explain how they can do so. Those who are not witnessing should be encouraged to allow God to search their hearts, to repent for not witnessing, and to ask God's forgiveness and for help to change and be teachable. Naturally, you will need to return to the commands to witness from time to time for new people who haven't heard or understood the requirement to share their faith.

After the teachings have convinced many people that they need to share their faith, you should begin to prepare them to do it effectively. Over a period of ten months or so, the teachings should focus on writing a personal testimony to be used as a witnessing tool, first as a flyer or a tract. (See examples of written personal testimonies in appendixes B and C.)

During that time, you should teach the importance of giving away copies of testimonies and explain good ways to do so. Otherwise some people who write testimonies will not want to share them. Be prepared to give a lot of encouragement to reluctant testimony distributors.

Prepare witnesses to overcome the common fear of receiving negative reactions when they share their faith. This fear is a problem because most Christians are more concerned about gaining approval from other people than from God. It helps witnesses to understand that when people don't accept a flyer or a tract, those people are rejecting the Lord, not the witness. Some witnesses have other kinds of fear, including meeting with and speaking to strangers. Be sure to regularly address any fears about witnessing that your church's members express.

After about thirty people have prepared written testimonies, you should purchase plastic displays large enough to hold quantities of four selected testimonies and add a message to the display saying "Free: Take One." Witnesses should then be taught to take displays filled with testimonies to businesses and to ask for permission to leave the display and testimonies in a prominent place. Witnesses will be surprised by how many businesses will be happy to accept these displays. Explain that those who place the displays should go back regularly to restock the displays with different testimonies. JWC members have been able to place and maintain fifty-three such displays in area businesses.

At the end of teaching for a year, you should have enough testimonies to print a book containing all the testimonies written by your congregation. Put a color photograph of each testimony writer's face on the cover to help those who receive the books to realize that the donor is an author. Within the books, you should also add all the essential information about how to achieve Salvation.

These books can provide amazingly effective ways to attract someone's attention: Everybody likes to receive something for free, and the joy is increased when an author whose picture is on the cover autographs the gift book. Even very timid people can learn how to effectively share their testimonies by using the book as a tool.

The Second Year, and Thereafter

Your teachings in the second year should begin to demonstrate the many different ways to use the book of testimonies as a witnessing tool after you have one available. For example, when you are out in public, expect the Lord to prompt you to give a book to various people. When you receive that prompting, go up to the person and ask if you can give her or him an autographed copy of the book. If he or she agrees, ask for her or his name and inscribe the book with that name ("To 'name:'") followed by a personal note of appreciation.

Write that your story is on page such-and-such and that you hope they will enjoy the book. Include a written offer to answer any questions they have about the book by calling you, add your telephone number, and sign your name. Here's a sample you can use that describes giving the book to a service station attendant:

To Sam:

Thanks for checking my oil today. I appreciate your good, friendly service.

My story is on page 37. I hope you enjoy the book.

If you have any questions about what you read, please call me. My telephone number is 404-329-1234.

(Signed) Bill Witness

Check back with the person three days later to ask their opinion of the book. Then you can ask whether they have accepted Jesus as their Lord and Savior. Invite them to join you in church whether or not they are reborn.

The first Sunday after the books are ready, put seven books into individual bags and challenge each person to take a bag of books, to give away one book a day during the following week, and to follow up with each recipient after three days. Repeat this challenge each week for two months. By repeating this challenge weekly, people can build a habit of witnessing once a day over the next sixty days. After that, it will be second nature to look for witnessing opportunities and to follow up appropriately. At JWC, about 80 percent of the members participated in such a book distribution, an exceptional percentage for any outreach activity.

At the same time, develop a book display that will contain at least fifteen books and is appropriate to place in businesses. Challenge the congregation to ask business owners and managers to accept these displays and to put them in prominent places. Once again, the people who place these displays should restock and replace the displays when they become broken or unattractive. JWC was able to place more than a hundred book displays. A third of survey respondents report being successful in getting the displays in locations where many books were taken including restaurants, an armed services induction center, a donut shop, county offices, a pizza shop, a police station, a print shop, a furniture store, a carpet store, a bank, a resale shop, a bar, a liquor store, and a health club.

If your church has a heart for helping prisoners, these books are very helpful for prison ministries. Prisoners have lots of time to read and they can be heartened by learning about how God has helped others with serious problems to turn their lives around.

As you can imagine, printing so many books is not cheap, but it's also not prohibitively expensive compared to other outreaches: JWC reports that the cost of printing 50,000 books (a one-year supply at the current rate of distribution) was about the same as what the church spent to send fifteen congregants on a brief foreign mission to South America. Unless your church has a lot of discretionary funds that can be shifted to this purpose, you should also teach the congregation to make additional offerings to pay for such witnessing tools. At JWC a box is kept at the base of the altar where contributions specifically for witnessing materials can be made.

Encouraging such donations delivers an added benefit to the members who do not tithe (providing the first 10 percent of income to the local church) by bringing them closer to tithing. Many do not realize that they have been robbing God. Those who tithe will be honored by God for their additional offerings; as Malachi 3:10 describes, God will open the windows of heaven for those who make tithes and pour out blessings that cannot be contained. In addition, those who contribute for witnessing materials will often place more value on sharing the books with the lost and following up in three days to help the lost receive Salvation.

After book distribution is going well, you can introduce those who are using the books exclusively to also distribute tracts, audio tapes, and CDs that do not contain their testimonies but are appropriate for a specific unsaved person. After sharing books, these tools are helpful during follow-up visits to expand the lost person's understanding of what Salvation is about. Many unsaved people who have little time to read will find it easier to listen to a CD as they commute to and from work or travel to do errands. Some testimony tracts will have been written after the book edition is prepared, and you can provide newer, more relevant testimonies in this way. By sharing all of these materials in appropriate ways, the lost see that witnesses are generous, caring, and willing to help, and are thus much more willing to engage with the giver.

After individual witnessing is going well, the teaching agenda can be expanded to explain the benefits of and methods required for various group outreach activities such as auto shows, free car washes, block parties, and gift wrapping in malls. These group outreaches are a blessing to those who are still shy while witnessing. Each time such an event is planned, it is also important to use the five-minute segments to encourage people to participate.

After the first year, it also helps to vary the ways that the teaching is done. People at JWC especially like the dramas that are performed by the church's youth. The more creative the way the message is presented, the longer people will remember it. Be inspired!

The messages should also vary with the season and event: Christmas and Easter services and plays bring many of the lost to church, and the messages then should speak directly by witnessing to the lost rather than just encouraging the saved to witness. A good message at these times is to have someone share his or her testimony and also describe how she or he felt about receiving Salvation.

A Teaching Example

I urge, then, first of all, that
requests, prayers, intercession and thanksgiving
be made for everyone — ....

1 Timothy 2:1 (NIV)

The teaching example that follows is five-minute lesson prepared and presented by Jim Barbarossa that many people at JWC cited as having made a lasting impression on them that encourages witnessing.

†

Do You Have Blood on Your Hands?

Several years ago, I was in a public building, waiting for the elevator to come down. When it came down, I saw a man on a stretcher with several paramedics around him. As they wheeled him past me, several more paramedics came in. As this was happening, the Spirit of God told me to go and lay my hands on him and pray.

Immediately I heard a second voice:
That voice talked me out of doing what God said.

The next morning as I looked at the newspaper, I was shocked to see the man God had told me to pray for on the front page.

Dead!

Yes! He died. I do not know if he knew Jesus. I do not know if the people around him knew Jesus. I don't know what would have happened if I would have obeyed God and prayed for the man.

But this I do know. When I disobeyed the Spirit of God, I was in rebellion.

And rebellion is SIN.

When God leads us by His Spirit to pray for or witness to someone and we disobey, we are in sin. We, all Christians, are responsible to share the truth that we know.

I had to do as David would have. I had to repent for my disobedience and ask for forgiveness and purpose to do it right the next time.

Ezekiel 3:17-18 (KJV) — *Son of man, I have made thee a watchman unto the house of Israel: therefore hear the word at my mouth, and give them warning from me. When I say unto the wicked, Thou shalt surely die; and thou givest him not warning, nor speakest to warn the wicked from his wicked way, to save his life; the same wicked* man *shall die in his iniquity; but his blood will I require at thine hand.*

This man's blood was on my hands.

Imagine what the conversation would be like if it was possible for a person to come back from hell and confront the person God had assigned to witness to them.

Christian: What is this? What is on my hands?

Soul from Hell: It's Blood! It's Blood! It's my Blood!

Christian: Blood? Why? What is this about? I don't understand.

Soul from Hell: You never told me. You never told me.

Christian: Told you what?

Soul from Hell: You never told me about Hell. You never told me of the fires of Hell.

Christian: Who are you? Do I know you?

Soul from Hell: Don't you remember me? I was your friend.

Christian: Who are you?

Soul from Hell: We worked together. We went to school together. We had the same friends. We grew up together. We shared everything. But you never told me.

Christian: I wanted to tell you, but I was afraid.

Soul from Hell: Afraid, afraid of what? Nothing could be more frightening than the fires of Hell. The fear of God and the reality of the fires of Hell should have been enough for you to overcome your fear and tell me. You knew the truth and never told me. You never gave me a chance. **My blood is on your hands.**

Then out of the dark came several demons.

Soul from Hell: I don't want to go back. Help me. Help me. Help me!

Christian: I'm sorry. I'm sorry. I'm sorry. Oh Jesus.

Soul from Hell: Help me. Help me. I don't want to go back. **If only you would have told me.**

If this could happen, how many souls from Hell would have the right to confront you? How much blood is on your hands?

The truth is that nine out of ten Christians have blood on their hands and have hardened their hearts to the part of the Gospel that tells them to be a witness, that tells them to be a minister of reconciliation, that tells them to go into all the world and preach the Gospel.

†

Some readers may be surprised to see such a direct and powerful appeal to witness by talking about helping friends avoid eternity in hell. Why should that message be a surprise to any Christian?

Many churches don't say much about sin, especially sins of omission, or hell these days. As a result, many Christians haven't thought through the tremendous potential costs to others and to themselves in losing heavenly rewards by not witnessing. When Christians stop to consider what's at stake, hearts are immediately opened to the message.

The problem is even greater than that. An increasing number of Americans believe that many religions (including non-Christian ones) can lead a person to eternal life in heaven: This belief is often expressed as "All good people go to heaven." Your congregation probably contains some people who aren't firm in their belief that only repenting of their sins and accepting Jesus as Lord and Savior can lead to such a heavenly future.

These challenges of helping people who have an inaccurate understanding of God and have incompletely submitted to the Lord by not witnessing bring up another reason for the pastor and in-congregation evangelist working as a team: Each will share messages that stir reactions among the congregation that identify more teaching needs than either alone could. By sharing the calling to build faith and encourage good acts based in faith, they can mutually reinforce the importance of what all Christians must do and help people draw closer to God.

Several sample five-minute teachings about witnessing are available in a PDF file. You can obtain them for free from Jim Barbarossa by sending an e-mail to jim@step-by-step.org.

✝

In Chapter 4, we go into more detail for helping your congregation's members to understand and accept the responsibility to be complete, continual witnesses. We begin with Jesus' commands for each of us to be witnesses for Him and go on to provide practical advice about how to help people accept those commands based on our experiences.

Chapter 4

Open Christian Hearts
to Act on Jesus' Commands

Infuse Personal Responsibility
to Continually Witness

Therefore encourage one another
and build up one another,
just as you also are doing.

— 1 Thessalonians 5:11 (NAS)

Most Christians believe that witnessing is something that others are supposed to do. Starting from such a misunderstanding, few will go from inaction to being effective, continual witnesses. Making that transition is a significant journey, and the first steps will only be taken after clearly understanding that the journey is required. God's unanticipated rewards wait for those who take the necessary steps.

In this chapter, we examine what each Christian needs to know about why effective witnessing is an important *daily* priority. We provide perspectives that can be understood either by reading the Bible or this book. We also encourage you to turn this chapter into teachings to share with your congregation so that more may understand that they should be continually seeking out and acting on opportunities to share their faith.

Follow the Directions Found in the Gospel

"Whoever desires to come after Me,
let him deny himself, and take up his cross,
and follow Me."

— Mark 8:34 (NKJV)

What are the most important aspects of being a Christian? Jesus addressed that question when He was asked, "Teacher, which is the greatest commandment in the law?"

Jesus said to him,
"'You shall love the LORD your God
with all your heart,
with all your soul,
and with all your mind.'
This is the *first and great commandment.*
And the *second* is *like it*:
'You shall love your neighbor as yourself.'
On these two commandments
hang all the Law and the Prophets."

— Matthew 22:37-40 (NKJV)

Clearly, one of the ways to follow this teaching is to be filled with God's love towards everyone else, seeking to love others as much as God loves you and as much as you love yourself.

Someone filled with God's love would surely want to help others receive the greatest gift that he or she has received from God. Most Christians would agree that gift is Salvation. When you share your faith to encourage people to become saved, you are simply showing the love that Jesus told us we should express toward others.

Why are you supposed to express so much love? God knows that it is far better for you to love than to do anything else. When you love, all your thoughts and actions will be properly directed, and your thoughts will continually be on Him. From this perspective, you can think of witnessing as a way that God wants to help you to come closer to Him.

Beyond those foundation teachings, what else did Jesus have to say that bears on sharing your faith? Let's start with the fundamental question: Who is supposed to witness? Everyone! Here are some of the directions that Jesus gave on this subject, organized into a sequence that makes the command to continually witness clearer:

"Therefore whoever confesses Me before men,
him I will also confess
before My Father who is in heaven."

— Matthew 10:32 (NKJV)

"Go home to your friends,
and tell them what great things the Lord has done for you,
and how He has had compassion on you."

— Mark 5:19 (NKJV)

But when He saw the multitudes,
He was moved with compassion for them,
because they were weary and scattered,
like sheep having no shepherd.
Then He said to His disciples,
"The harvest truly is plentiful, but the laborers are few.
Therefore pray the Lord of the harvest
to send out laborers into His harvest."

— Matthew 9:36-38 (NKJV)

"Go therefore and make disciples
of all the nations,
baptizing them in the name of
the Father and of the Son and of the Holy Spirit, ..."

— Matthew 28:19 (NKJV)

> *"And he who does not take his cross*
> *and follow after Me is not worthy of Me."*

> — Matthew 10:38 (NKJV)

> *"More than that, blessed* are *those*
> *who hear the word of God and keep it!"*

> — Luke 11:28 (NKVJ)

Some might argue that Jesus was only speaking about what His apostles should do. Paul's words make it clear that the command to witness moves forward to present-day Christians:

> *And the things that you have heard*
> *from me among many witnesses,*
> *commit these to faithful men*
> *who will be able to teach others also.*

> — 2 Timothy 2:2 (NKJV)

The command to witness is ignored by most Christians in the United States. Why? There are several reasons:

- Few Christians have read the entire Bible.
- Many of those who have read the Bible have ignored the words that Jesus spoke that concern witnessing.
- For those who rely on church services to learn what to do as Christians, witnessing may only be mentioned in an occasional sermon or a special evangelism teaching for those who are interested. With infrequent attention, it's easy to forget to witness every day.

In helping your congregation's members to become effective, continual witnesses, you'll need to be sure that the Bible verses quoted here are regularly read, studied, understood, remembered, and continually followed.

52

Beyond Jesus' command to witness, there's another Bible verse that explains the practical importance of witnessing:

> *So then faith* comes *by hearing,*
> *and hearing by the word of God.*

> — Romans 10:17 (NKJV)

A teacher might express this idea by saying "Learning follows repeated exposure."

When you understand that the lost need to hear from the Word frequently from lots of people in many different ways, you can start your journey to becoming an effective, continual witness. Only when every Christian is actively witnessing can it be expected that all the lost will have heard the Lord's offer of Salvation powerfully and often enough to make a lasting impression.

People remember and appreciate the lessons of stories that carry emotional impact much better than teachings without stories. Hearing a personal testimony about the joyful experience of becoming free from the consequences of sin through gaining Salvation helps the lost more than simply learning about God's promises about Salvation.

What does the Bible have to say about following God's will? Here are two verses that relate to the importance of doing His will diligently through continual witnessing:

> *You have commanded* us
> *To keep Your precepts diligently.*

> — Psalm 119:4 (NKJV)

> *He that diligently seeketh good*
> *procureth favor; ....*

> — Proverbs 11:27 (KJ21V)

From the perspective of being a responsible Christian, witnessing also makes sense. If someone hadn't explained to you about how to gain Salvation, how would you have learned? Since the favor you received cannot be returned in kind to the saved person who helped you, it's only common decency to share the Good News with lost people.

There's a personal benefit to continual witnessing as well. Do you remember how great you felt when you gave your life to Jesus? Wouldn't it feel wonderful to regularly participate in and observe a similar good work?

Fulfill All Dimensions of Being a Complete Witness

"I know your works, that you are neither cold nor hot.
I could wish you were cold or hot.
So then, because you are lukewarm,
and neither cold nor hot,
I will vomit you out of My mouth."

— Revelation 3:15-16 (NKJV)

When you pay lip service to witnessing by doing the least in sharing your faith, you become lukewarm toward God; and the preceding verses explain God's attitude toward the lukewarm. Instead, He wants you to be on fire with desire to help people gain Salvation through all effective activities.

What is the primary purpose of your witnessing when it comes to helping others achieve Salvation? Let's remember that Jesus isn't limited to needing your help to save souls. He could instead take away free will and simply make all people believers, or He could just send such powerful signs and wonders that all would repent and accept Him, or He could surround each lost person with a band of angels who never stop talking about Salvation. But those alternatives aren't His plans.

Jesus wants you to demonstrate your commitment to Him by being a continually active, energetic, eager, and effective witness who regularly experiences the miracle of Salvation by often being present when it is received by others. When you witness Salvation being accepted, your faith is refreshed and strengthened … causing you to feel almost like a newly saved person each time.

After you become an enthusiastic, complete witness, the Holy Spirit will open the hearts of unsaved people you witness to so that their souls will be saved. Everything is present that's needed for peoples' souls to be saved before you witness, except that gaining Salvation requires your free-will act of witnessing to start the process. It's like the way that striking a match is the first step into turning dry tinder into fire.

Your reward from providing that witnessing spark will be to bask in the glow of the holy spiritual fire that results from your witnessing. You will feel joy every time you either see or think of the people who received Salvation after you witnessed to them. The saved people will probably pray to God thanking Him for the gift of your caring acts of witnessing, and you will be blessed again. What a wonderful plan this is for the lost and for you!

Having described the beauty of that plan, it's a shame that most Christians don't realize what God's intentions are for blessing others and them through witnessing. We asked the Jubilee Worship Center (JWC) congregation to describe their beliefs about witnessing and what witnessing they did before attending the church. Their reports on those practices and beliefs showed that there had been many misconceptions about what it means to be a witness. Presumably, those same misconceptions exist within the body of believers who haven't yet been taught about witnessing by an in-congregation evangelist. In the rest of this chapter, we respond to some of the more common false beliefs about witnessing.

God Requires You to Do More Than Be a Good Example to the Lost

> *What* does it *profit, my brethren,*
> *if someone says he has faith*
> *but does not have works?*
> *Can faith save him?*
>
> — James 2:14 (NKJV)

Some Christians believe that witnessing only requires leading lives that honor God, obeying His ten commandments, and being a light (a good example) in the world. They assume that the lost will be intrigued by the good life that well-behaved Christians lead and all the unsaved will ask Christians for advice in living like observant Christians.

While being a good example and obeying God's ten commandments are part of His plan for you, these behaviors aren't enough to be a complete witness. Why? Many lost people will never be curious about why you behave differently, ask you about why you do so, and learn that you are a Christian and what being a Christian involves and provides.

The unsaved are often so stuck in their sins that they don't notice anything but their lusts, folly, and misery. If they know nothing about Christ, how are they supposed to learn what the benefits of Salvation are?

Here's another problem of solely witnessing by living a Godly life: Other forms of witnessing are essential for the Good News about the rewards of Salvation to be understood by unsaved people. For instance, most of the benefits of being a Christian come after you reach heaven. Who can know about what will be received in heaven without God's plan for that wonderful place first being explained by someone who proclaims to the unsaved about having received forgiveness and Salvation? How would only seeing someone who isn't known to be a Christian lead a good life on Earth cause a lost person who doesn't know about God's promises to think about unknown heavenly rewards that follow Salvation? Instead, the well-behaving person is likely to be seen by lost people as someone who comes from a good family.

Think about when Jesus walked on the Earth. How might His actions have been different if He had only set a good example? He would have behaved well and kept quiet about Salvation unless someone asked him about why He led a good life. But that's not what He did: After His time came to fulfill the Scriptures, He attracted the attention of curious sinners everywhere through healing people and performing miracles to express love and to show the power of faith. After He created interest through displaying supernatural works, He talked about Salvation. You can follow His example when you attract attention by sharing the supernatural works that the Lord has done in your life. Then the lost will be curious.

Part of God's plan is actually the reverse of this misconception about just living a Godly life to attract the unsaved: *Witnessing is a way of encouraging you to lead a life that honors Him.* Only the biggest hypocrites would be comfortable sharing their faith daily with lost people while not leading a life that honors Him. Each witnessing activity spurs the witness to live a more Christ-like life.

Think about the difference between merely living a good life and living a good life that includes asking lost people who are hurting if you can pray for them, helping them, and explaining to them how Jesus can build them up. That is what it means to be a light in the world: Shine the light of the Lord by being a faithful Christian *and* a credible, nonstop witness for God's promises to all. In that way, you also become a good role model for the new Christian to become a witness and fulfill all of God's plan for the saved.

God Requires You to Do More Than Tell Unsaved People You Are a Christian

> *"But I have prayed for you,*
> *that your faith should not fail;*
> *and when you have returned to* Me,
> *strengthen your brethren."*

> — Luke 22:32 (NKJV)

When asked how they shared their faith before attending JWC, a number of people commented that they let friends, neighbors, and co-workers know that they were Christians. That's certainly a good thing to do, but is it enough to help lead someone to Salvation?

We didn't ask these people to describe what these conversations were like, but merely identifying yourself as a Christian may not tell others much more about what you believe and have experienced than does checking a box on a form to indicate that you are a Christian. Without more information, the lost person may not be able to distinguish you from the person who claims an affiliation with Jesus, but who isn't saved.

What's more, the lost may perceive your assertion as a discussion ender rather than a conversation starter. Why? A statement of your allegiance to Jesus without a testimony about what Salvation has done for you may leave unsaved people unsure how to respond.

Here's an example from a different context of how assertions about beliefs can leave someone else speechless. Imagine if someone you have a good relationship with unexpectedly told you that he or she regularly speaks with aliens from outer space. You probably wouldn't want to inquire too closely about those assertions because you don't know what to say that wouldn't hurt your relationship. In fact, you might respond by just smiling a little and saying something like, "How special for you." Without describing what and why you believe by explaining what Christ has done in your life, your Christian faith can seem just that strange to those whose hearts have not yet been touched by the Lord.

How did Jesus speak about Salvation to those who didn't yet follow Him? He didn't lead off by saying that He was the Messiah and that He was founding a new faith called Christianity. Instead, He would talk to people about God the Father, proper behavior, and how to gain Salvation. At a first meeting, He would often speak in parables about the kingdom of God to make the message easier to understand for those who sought His truth. What's the lesson? Jesus made Himself approachable. You should, too, by engaging in conversations that invite the hearers to join in.

God Requires You to Do More Than Silently Pass Out Tracts and Other Tools

"And you also will bear witness, ..."

— John 15:27 (NKJV)

Everyone has experienced going to a crowded event and seeing a few Christians handing out tracts and other tools to anyone who will take one. Typically, these Christians don't say anything to those who are passing by ... not even, "God bless you." In fact, some don't even reply when you say, "Thank you. God bless you."

It's easy to imagine that these people might be frozen with fear while standing up for Christ in public and are doing their best to overcome shyness. But what kind of an impression are they making? Their methods and demeanors aren't usually much different from those who are passing out lunch menus for local restaurants and flyers for closeout sales at bankrupt stores. It might appear to an unsaved person that someone has paid the people passing out the tracts and other tools to do a task that they aren't particularly interested in and enthusiastic about. If that's what it's like to be a Christian, who needs it?

Think about television programs you've seen that show courtroom trials. Witnesses are sworn to tell the truth, and lawyers for both sides have lots of chances to ask tough questions. When the witnesses are telling the truth, you can tell a lot about why you should believe them from their expressions, how their bodies move, and the confidence in their voices. When a witness is telling a lie, it's often quite clear from seeing and hearing the person, independent of the credibility of the words that are said. There are some liars who can speak deceitfully and be credible, but conversation usually does a lot to sort out the truth from falsehoods.

If the court system operated like those who simply pass out tracts without speaking, judges would only require that witnesses write out their testimonies for jurors to read. Witnesses would not need to appear or answer any questions. How well would that work for unearthing falsehoods and ascertaining truth?

Similarly, lost people need to hear about the experiences of the saved, not just receive literature from them. The tract may be thrown away in the next trash barrel (and that receptacle will often be overflowing with unread tracts). A conversation, however, can make an impression that will never be forgotten.

How important is this point? While most members of JWC described that they did not talk to anyone about their faith before attending the church, all the people who participated in the survey reported that they have included some conversation as part of their current witnessing activities. You should do no less, and even more is required.

God Requires That You Speak to the Lost about What He Has Done in Your Life

A true witness delivers souls, ...

— Proverbs 14:25 (NKJV)

Are your efforts leading unsaved people to Salvation? If you can answer yes, you are a true witness; if no, you probably need to change what you are doing.

Either merely describing yourself as a Christian or not speaking to people about your faith can make you seem proud, aloof, uncaring, and unapproachable. But you are a sinner, a sinner who has been forgiven and is now trying to live a good life through God's grace. When the unsaved find that you are like them except for what Jesus has done for you, it's much easier for them to be interested in your experience and what you have to say.

Here's an analogy. Imagine that you have a severe skin rash that's driving you crazy. You've tried everything and been to dozens of doctors yet gained no relief. All you can think about is that rash. People walk up to you all the time and make suggestions for getting rid of the rash. You ignore them because you quickly realize that you know more about your affliction than they do. But one day someone comes up and says: "I had a rash like that for eight years and no one could help me." You immediately notice that the person doesn't have a skin rash now. You would eagerly ask: "What did you do to get rid of it?" You would then pay full attention to the answer.

What are the elements that created such open-minded interest? You start off by explaining how you are like the person who has the affliction. Then you demonstrate that you don't have the affliction any more. The afflicted person will then be curious about what you did that helped.

Let's put these elements for creating interest into a witnessing context. Someone who is depressed after being divorced will be

60

interested in talking to another person who has been divorced and depressed and now has a happy marriage and leads a joyful life. If Salvation is part of that message, the depressed, divorced person will listen. In the process of sharing relevant experiences, a heart will be softened and opened. Salvation can follow.

Here is where a tract based on your testimony may make sense to enrich the conversation. Your written testimony prepares you to describe the circumstances and benefits of your Salvation with others. In addition, your written testimony can be shared by someone who hasn't had your life experience in gaining and benefiting from Salvation. Someone who wants to think about what you said can also take the tract for further study. If you include information on the tract about how to contact you, a dialogue can continue.

God Requires That You Follow Up on Your Conversations with the Unsaved

But if we walk in the light
as He is in the light,
we have fellowship with one another,
and the blood of Jesus Christ His Son
cleanses us from all sin.

— 1 John 1:7 (NKJV)

When you go to the doctor about a serious illness, your doctor will ask you to come back to check on how your recovery is going. If one treatment doesn't work, another one will be substituted. If you don't return on a regular basis, recovery may not occur.

Leading a Godless life is much like having a serious illness that requires constant attention until recovery occurs. The witness is in the role of the doctor and must realize that this lost person is going to need regular support and encouragement to gain Salvation and to learn how to live as a Christian.

Having a single conversation about Salvation isn't much different from what a receptionist does in scheduling an initial appointment for a patient to see the doctor. You need to follow up by being sure the unsaved person learns more about Salvation and living as a Christian and to provide explanations and support as needed from there.

You cannot rely on the lost person to take the initiative. Here's why: Doctors find that most patients don't take the tests that are recommended and often stop taking medicine before they should. Wise doctors make calls to see how patients are doing who don't make follow-up appointments. In addition, the enemy who is in the world will try to fill the unsaved person's mind with discouragement, making your help all the more important.

You should certainly make yourself available if the unsaved person wants to contact you. More importantly, you should also schedule regular times to check on this person. In this way, you can diagnose how the lost person is doing in repentance and wanting to learn more about Salvation. If you haven't heard from the person after an initial discussion about Salvation in three days, you should reach out to him or her. Otherwise, the memory of your first conversation will fade towards nothingness.

Letting the lost person know you are interested in staying involved to help solve his or her problems will encourage the unsaved to contact you and to be more receptive when you follow up on your previous conversation.

God Requires That You Pray with and for the Lost

And on the Sabbath day we went
out of the city to the riverside,
where prayer was customarily made; and
we sat down and
spoke to the women who met there.

— Acts 16:13 (NKJV)

Prayer will both strengthen you in witnessing and call forth God's re-sources to help you be more effective. Prayer will also help you con-nect your heart with an unsaved person. The lost people will also learn how to pray when you pray aloud for them.

Prayer is helpful before, during, and after witnessing. Before witnessing, you should pray that the Lord send you lost people and fill you with resolve and resources to witness for Him. During witnessing, you should ask unsaved people if they would like you to pray for them. If they agree, pray aloud and make the kind of prayer that the lost person would make if he or she knew the Lord and understood how to pray. After you have witnessed, pray that God will touch the unsaved person's heart and help with any sins, afflictions, and problems the person is struggling with. In addition, you should continually pray that you will be able to play the role that God wants you to play in this person's life.

Without such prayers, your effectiveness will be limited. You will also be expressing pride and arrogance by believing that your resources are enough to help the lost. Without prayer, you will seem to the unsaved like a concerned social worker or physician, rather than someone who is trying to help them make a connection to the Lord. Prayer will indicate that you are drawing on supernatural resources from Him, and your behavior will be more Godly during and after prayer.

This need for prayer to be an effective, continual witness is part of God's wonderful plan for you. He wants a closer relationship with you, and these prayers help that occur. He loves you that much!

God Requires That You Help Provide Material Help for the Unsaved

Am *I my brother's keeper?*

— Genesis 4:9 (NKJV)

The unsaved include everyone from billionaires to poor beggars. While the lost billionaires will mainly need spiritual resources, many of the unsaved poor people will also need physical resources. You may be witnessing to someone who has no home, is seriously ill, and hasn't eaten. Your testimony, warm conversation, and prayers won't be enough for this person: You need to show the Lord's love by helping to provide those physical resources as part of expressing your love.

If taking on this responsibility concerns you, the Lord is probably helping you to understand that your heart needs further cleansing. Remember that witnessing is one of the ways that God tests and perfects us. If you are unsure about this requirement, consider what Jesus said:

> " ... *whatever you did for one*
> *of the least of these brothers of mine,*
> *you did for me."*

> — Matthew 25:40 (NIV)

Be prepared to help. Keep your schedule flexible enough that you can take more time to help someone the Lord sends into your path. Carry some extra money to be able to purchase food for people. Learn about resources that can help people who need physical help as well as spiritual healing.

God's plan is a blessing for you by providing more ways for you to express love. With such plain opportunities to help that would move even the hardest heart, it's easier to love other people as much as we love ourselves.

God Requires That You Attract Resources to Witness to and Provide for the Lost

> *"Sell what you have and give alms;*
> *provide yourselves money bags*
> *which do not grow old,*
> *a treasure in the heavens*
> *that does not fail,*
> *where no thief approaches*
> *nor moth destroys."*

> — Luke 12:33 (NKJV)

As Jesus reminded us, the poor will always be with us. He wants you to help them as well as the lost. Therefore, it is even more blessed when you help the poor who are lost.

Many people feel torn at this point: How can they hope to provide for the material needs of unsaved poor people when they feel they have little extra for themselves? The answer lies in being willing to make sacrifices to help unsaved poor people and to tell about the needs of these poor people so that other Christians will help with offerings to assist them.

Directly helping the unsaved poor is not the only reason to seek offerings. You will also need resources to provide tracts, books, CDs, DVDs, and other tools. By asking for offerings, you are also providing an opportunity for other Christians to be more faithful to God so that they will be more blessed by Him as Jesus described in Luke 12:33.

Chances are that many people will be willing to help who wouldn't otherwise think to make an offering. In addition, some of these people will then feel called to serve unsaved poor people. If you don't ask for such help, you aren't fulfilling God's charge to you. You are being like a person who has the answer but refuses to speak to anyone.

Some people don't like to ask for money. That's being arrogant. At the Last Supper, Jesus washed the feet of His disciples to make the point that we should all humble ourselves and serve others. It's good for us!

Some people don't believe they can gain enough money to make their efforts worthwhile. That belief is denying God's infinite power to work His way.

God Requires You to Find and Act on More and Better Opportunities to Witness

> *"For to everyone who has, more will be given,*
> *and he will have abundance; ...."*

— Matthew 25:29 (NKJV)

In the parable of the talents, Jesus taught that the kingdom of heaven requires that the Lord's servants create gains by making good use of what He provides them on His behalf. What greater gains can you provide than using whatever talents and resources you have to help inspire more hearts and souls to be dedicated to and guided by Him?

The Holy Spirit speaks frequently to each Christian in a small voice that many ignore to their soul's peril. A good place to find more and better opportunities to witness is by listening to the Holy Spirit's voice more carefully and acting faithfully.

In doing this, realize that God knows a great many things you don't. While it may be appealing to speak to a large group in hopes of bringing larger numbers to Christ, God may know of a single soul needing Salvation who can open doors that will lead millions to Him (as occurred when Pastor John Osteen was saved). You see this idea of winning key souls exemplified by Jesus personally visiting Saul of Tarsus after He had risen because He knew what a powerful spiritual warrior the Apostle Paul would become after he was saved.

Your work isn't just to help save souls, but to help save the souls God leads you to. Remember that God has planned out your life long before you were born. He placed you where you are for a reason. If you stay in prayer and act in faith, you will find the parts of that plan that relate to witnessing. And in letting God guide your witnessing, you will learn to become more obedient.

God Requires You to Recruit More Witnesses

> *Therefore we also, since we are surrounded*
> *by so great a cloud of witnesses,*
> *let us lay aside every weight,*
> *and the sin which so easily ensnares us,*
> *and let us run with endurance*
> *the race that is set before us, ...*
>
> — Hebrews 12:1 (NKJV)

What's a good way to be sure that you are a complete, continual witness? Recruit and train lots of other complete, continual witnesses who will surround you at all times. Their presence will provide a tangible reminder to perform all aspects of being a complete, continual witness.

Many improvement programs rely on fellow participants to help people discipline themselves. An alcoholic who goes to Alcoholics

Anonymous meetings admits publicly that she or he is an alcoholic and talks about his or her struggles. Each alcoholic also has another alcoholic as a mentor to keep tabs on her or him. Certainly God wants us to do the same in mentoring others for witnessing.

Some will point to the role of the in-congregation evangelist and say that only those people should encourage and teach others to witness. That assertion denies the value of what you have learned as a witness: You know lessons that God wants you to share with others that your in-congregation evangelist doesn't know. You should at least teach those you help lead to Christ to do what you have done both by your good example and by regular discussions of what to do as a complete, continual witness.

Perhaps it's easiest to think about this requirement in terms of your own family. If you were the first one to be saved and become a complete, continual witness, why would you not want to share those blessings with your loved ones? If that's true for your family, why wouldn't it be true for your friends? And so on.

There's also a responsibility here: You shouldn't help people receive Salvation and then leave them to backslide into their old ways. There's no better way for a new Christian to become confirmed in the faith than by becoming a complete, continual witness as soon as he or she is able.

†

Are you convinced that you should become a complete, continual witness? Check this new learning in prayer to see what God has to say to you. And in the meantime, there's another pathway that will help you become convinced when you try it. In Chapter 5, we explain how to prepare your testimony and assist others to do the same as a helpful step toward experiencing God's wonderful plan for you as a complete, continual witness.

Chapter 5

Prepare to Touch Lost Souls

Inspire and Teach Every Christian to Write a Testimony

And he departed and began to proclaim in Decapolis
all that Jesus had done for him;
and all marveled.

— Mark 5:20 (NKJV)

As we authors mentioned previously and cover again later in this chapter, the first step in becoming a complete, continual witness is to write your personal testimony. Both the authors and the readers of written testimonies gain many benefits.

How do Christians benefit from writing testimonies about what Jesus has done in their lives? It's simple: Writing your testimony is a discipline to help you overcome pride and hypocrisy through revealing your hidden failures and how God saved you from your mistakes. Otherwise, it's easy to fall into pride — believing your thoughts and actions are more important than the Lord's and not honoring and praising Him for what He has done for you. Unless you are publicly humbled by your testimony, you may hypocritically judge other Christians and the lost as though you had never sinned rather than loving them as fellow sinners.

Your written testimony will also remind you of what the Lord has done for you. If your soul is troubled, you can reread your testimony to strengthen your faith and increase hope that God will help you again.

By writing your testimony, your pastor, in-congregation evangelist, and congregation will find it easier to know you. You'll gain many more Godly connections.

There are also indirect benefits from writing a testimony: After more Christians read about and learn from your experiences of being helped by the Lord, you will live in a wiser and more loving Christian community. Everyone who reads your testimony will gain compassion for the pain of others. When you or others use the testimony to share your experiences with the unsaved, more lost people will be saved. When that happens, you and the community gain from the fellowship with, prayers by, and love of more Christians.

How do Christians benefit from inspiring and teaching other Christians to write a testimony? In this way, you will learn about more miracles that God has done, and thinking about those miracles will help you to hold Him in greater awe and reverence. As a result, your faith will grow and be more firmly based.

In this chapter, we explain how to write your testimony, to inspire others to write theirs, and to teach testimony writing. Before you do those things, however, you need to know what makes a good written testimony.

Become Familiar with the Qualities of a Good Written Testimony

And there are also many other things that Jesus did,
which if they were written one by one,
I suppose that even the world itself
could not contain the books that would be written. Amen.

— John 21:25 (NKJV)

One of God's purposes for your testimony is to open hearts, both saved and lost. This purpose is important for another reason: Wanting to open hearts to hope encourages many people to write testimonies. In our survey of Jubilee Worship Center (JWC) members, the most common reason for deciding to write a testimony was to help other people. Many other JWC members said that they recognized the value of a written testimony for witnessing, another way of helping others.

You can best touch hearts by describing your experiences that demonstrate essential knowledge about God and what it's like to have a relationship with His Son, Jesus Christ. You don't know what the unsaved know and don't know: It's best to assume that they have no knowledge about how to be a Christian, why that's a great way to live, and what the eternal rewards are. Let's break down the kind of information that's needed into categories and look at what testimony qualities are most effective for achieving God's purposes.

A Good Written Testimony Shows That God Exists

Then fear came upon all, and they glorified God, saying, ...
"God has visited His people."

— Luke 7:16 (NKJV)

How can you be saved if you don't believe in God? Showing that God exists is a fundamental proof that needs to be provided for doubters and atheists. A good way to demonstrate that He exists is by showing how He has affected your life in undeniable, supernatural ways.

God does supernatural things that are so amazing that anyone reading an account of such an event will be struck with awe and wonder. For example, powerful examples can be found in testimonies by people who have suffered from terminal cancers, repented of their sins, asked Jesus into their lives, prayed for help, and were so well healed by God that the cancer totally left their bodies and never returned.

Healing isn't the only way that God provides awe-inspiring super-natural interventions. Some people describe how God saved them from fatal accidents through His hand. Other people tell about extraordinary favors that God has shown them under difficult circumstances in re-sponse to their giving thanks for past blessings and praying for help.

Most Christians have responded to promptings from the Holy Spirit (the small, still voice within) that kept them from harm, directed them to opportunities, or gave them great peace. Those experiences also show God's presence in our lives.

Some people have never suffered from great difficulties or spiritual trials, grew up in church, and have easily resisted most temptations. Many of these people are members of families and communities that have been greatly blessed by God. These Christians can describe the remarkable peace that God has placed in their hearts and minds. Feeling deep and abiding peace based in spiritual comfort is so rare these days that most unsaved people will be astonished to hear that someone has felt that way for most of a lifetime.

Chances are that God has displayed Himself to you in many different ways over your life. How many of those encounters can you build into a single testimony? You just need to select the most powerful ones for making an impression on those who doubt that God exists.

Christ's resurrection from the dead and His ascension after being raised are also powerful evidences that God exists and that Salvation is real. You can learn more about this evidence by reading and becoming familiar with the information in Appendix E.

A Good Written Testimony Shows That God Can Do What People Cannot

"Lazarus, come forth!"
And he who had died came out bound hand and foot with graveclothes,
and his face wrapped with a cloth.
Jesus said to them, "Loose him, and let him go."

— John 11:43-44 (NKJV)

Many people believe that God exists, but that He is distant and uninvolved in individual lives. Many of those people assume that they must rely on the laws of nature, help from other people, and their own efforts to accomplish good things. Learning about God's extraordinary interventions can change those mistaken beliefs.

As we observed before, God does many miracles in secret. Those miracles display His existence and what He can do that people cannot. If you have experienced miracles, then you have the evidence for this characteristic of God's power and love as well.

But most people don't experience the kind of dramatic miracle that Jesus did in bringing Lazarus back to life after he had been dead for four days. However, all Christians have had problems that they could

71

not solve by their own efforts or through the help of others where God made a difference.

Think about abuse. Those who have experienced abuse are often blameless victims, yet they carry painful and deep physical and emotional scars. Who can take that pain away from them? Many people who have been abused report gaining permanent happiness and peace through receiving Salvation. Such examples certainly suggest that God can do what people cannot to anyone who is still suffering from the aftermaths of abuse.

Consider addictions. Media reports regularly describe how difficult it is for addicted people to give up smoking, various illegal drugs, alcohol, pornography, and gambling. If the Lord helped you to eliminate one of those addictions, those who are still stuck with addictions will recognize that you must have had powerful help to stop those harmful activities.

Let's reflect about forgiveness. Many people feel guilty and condemned by all the bad things they have done. Christians find that Salvation eliminates those feelings. Someone weighed down by guilt about past actions will be encouraged to want Salvation after learning that the Lord can help in this area.

When choosing which parts of your life with God to share in your testimony, focus on those aspects of Divine help where the lost people you usually meet have the most trouble. If you know any unsaved people, you've heard their complaints and sadness. Think about what you would have liked to know about God's ability to help before you knew the Lord as your Savior and include that essential information in your testimony.

A Good Written Testimony Shows That Life with the Lord Is Better Than Life without the Lord

"And they overcame him by the blood of the Lamb
and by the word of their testimony, ..."

— Revelation 12:11 (NKJV)

Many people feel that life is a continuing sequence of bad experiences. They have given up the bright hopes of youth and don't believe that their lives could ever again be joyful. Some of these people may claim to be Christians, but many of those have not committed their lives to the Lord or have fallen away from their faith. As a result of living without God's grace, they don't realize that their voluntary separation from God is what makes their lives feel empty and sad and their prospects seem unpromising.

Christ has changed you. Those who didn't know you before you were saved don't realize what those changes have been. Your testimony should spell out those differences so that others can appreciate God's blessings for your life through Salvation. The most impressive examples are large increases in your joy and improvements in your behavior under circumstances where many people struggle.

Let's say that you went through a divorce, formerly used foul language, yelled at people, and were grumpy. If you now feel great, use good language, and say only nice things to people while flashing a radiant smile, your testimony and presence will present a stark contrast for those who want to change in the same ways.

Some changes are observable by others, but other improvements can only be appreciated by living them or hearing about them from witnesses. Be sure to share those internal improvements with others. Here's an example: Many people report feeling hopeless all the time. If, despite continuing challenges, Salvation has enabled you to feel continual joy instead, that's an area that only a testimony can reveal.

After your behavior and interior life improved, you also experienced better feelings about your circumstances. Be sure to relate those good experiences.

Those who don't have a relationship with Jesus don't realize how great it is to never be alone, to always have someone present to listen to you, and to know that you are loved. Be generous in explaining about how your relationship with Him has improved the quality of your life.

A Good Written Testimony Shows That Witnessing for the Lord Is a Great Blessing

... the testimony of our conscience
that we conducted ourselves in the world
in simplicity and godly sincerity,
not with fleshly wisdom
but by the grace of God,
and more abundantly toward you.

— 2 Corinthians 1:12 (NKJV)

Your written testimony can help the unsaved understand your motives so that your message will be better accepted. The lost spend most of their time thinking about themselves and what will please them. As a result, they have a stunted ability to love and grow through fellowship with others. Because of that self-absorption, many unsaved people will see your testimony as a bizarre act and be skeptical of your motives. Some will think that you want their money. Others will be concerned that you would like to order them around. Some skeptics will ascribe other selfish motives to what you are doing, such as a desire to get attention. After they understand that you are merely following Christ's commands to love and serve others, and gaining joy on Earth from your service, they will react differently to your witnessing.

Jesus has transformed you through the experience of becoming or being a continual, complete witness. Lost people also need to know about that part of your transformation. The unsaved will gain by realizing that to benefit the most by accepting Jesus Christ as Lord and Savior, they will need to learn to witness as you do. Since the process of going from not witnessing to being a continual, complete witness is an extensive change, give the lost a sense of that process. If they appreciate that it wasn't easy for you to share the bad things you used to do or experienced, they will be more affected by your testimony.

If you haven't had any important experiences yet in sharing your faith, be sure to tell about deciding to prepare your testimony and what that decision and act of obedience did for you. As you gain experience in sharing your written testimony, you can add those perspectives to

74

this section. A personal testimony is a living document and should be updated as the Lord moves you onto new paths and shares more light with you.

A Good Written Testimony Specifically Shows What a Person Gains by Receiving Salvation

> *But, beloved, we are confident of better things concerning you,*
> *yes, things that accompany salvation, ...*

> — Hebrews 6:9 (NKJV)

Many people who read your testimony will have an inaccurate idea of what benefits Salvation provides to the redeemed. One of the best ways you can help lost people hear the Holy Spirit more clearly is to specifically describe what great gains Salvation brings to those who are saved.

Here are the key elements received from Salvation that you should mention:

- Your sins are forgiven, washed away, and forgotten by God as though they never occurred.
- You are changed so that you will no longer want to live just for yourself and to sin.
- You will never be alone again.
- You will have the Holy Spirit within you to guide you to make good choices.
- You can call on God for help at any time, and He will listen to you.
- Jesus will lead you to fulfill the plans that God made for you before you were conceived.
- You will spend eternity with God and Jesus in heaven after you die.
- Through your obedience in following His ways on Earth, you will gain treasures in heaven that you will enjoy forever.
- You will spend eternity with family and friends who have received Salvation.

Naturally, your testimony will be more affecting if you share what these wonderful benefits have meant to you.

A Good Written Testimony Shows the Lost How to Receive Salvation

> *... behold, now* is *the day of salvation.*
>
> — 2 Corinthians 6:2 (NKJV)

When the unsaved first learn about Salvation, it seems too good to be true. Parents teach us to beware of offers that seem to be so wonderful: There always seems to be a catch to such offers that isn't obvious. But the offers that we should be skeptical about come from people, not from God. Here is the message you should share:

All have sinned and suffer from having done so. That suffering will increase if you are not redeemed before you die. Eternal punishment is the price of unredeemed sins.

But there is an alternative: God loves you so much that He sent His only Son, Jesus Christ, to die in a cruel and painful way so that all might be saved from punishment for their sins. God is love. Someone who loves you will do anything for you: God is the same way.

How do you gain Salvation? You need only to open your heart and speak sincerely to Jesus, admit you have sinned, accept the consequences of your sins, sincerely be sorry that you have sinned, believe that Jesus was sent to die for your sins and to redeem you and rose from the dead and ascended to heaven, ask Jesus to lead your life from now on, and agree to serve Him with your whole heart.

It's a wonderful thing to serve Jesus because He has only good plans for you, plans that are better than you would devise for yourself.

Here is a sample prayer that you can use in your written testimony that contains the elements for gaining Salvation:

"Dear God,
I have sinned.
I am very sorry that I have sinned.
I know that I deserve Your punishment for my sins.
I ask You to forgive me for these sins.
From my whole heart I accept that Jesus Christ is,
and will forever be, my Lord and Savior,
that He died and rose again to be with You in heaven.
Take my life, Jesus.
I surrender my life to you.
From this moment on, I will live my life according to the Bible
and to serve You.
Thank You for taking away my sins and
giving me everlasting life in heaven.
In Jesus' name I pray.
Amen."

A Good Written Testimony Shows the Newly Saved What to Do after Receiving Salvation

For if when we were enemies we were reconciled to God
through the death of His Son,
much more, having been reconciled,
we shall be saved by His life.

— Romans 5:10 (NKJV)

A new Christian needs help to develop into a loyal servant of the Lord. Your written testimony can provide important directions to lead the new believer onto the right path. Otherwise, the enemy who is in the world will try to convince the new Christian that nothing has happened and to pull the believer away from faith in and commitment to the Lord.

To help you with this section of your written testimony, here are instructions to the newly saved based on what JWC included its latest edition of *Real Life Stories*:

✝

1. Find a Bible-believing, doctrinally sound church and attend every time the doors are open.
2. Attend Bible studies and Sunday school.
3. Get a Bible, and read it every day.
4. Pray every day, morning, noon, and night.
5. Tell people what Jesus has done for you.
6. Write out your real life story, your testimony, and give it to people.
7. Make a public profession of your faith by being baptized in water.
8. Be joyful that you've been set free. Death cannot hold you, and hell can't have you.

You belong to God no matter what happens in this life. As long as you continue to walk with Him, you will be with Him in Heaven.

✝

You have our permission to quote these instructions in your written testimony.

A Good Written Testimony Shows How to Contact You and Others to Get More Information about Salvation

Immediately the father of the child cried out and said with tears, "Lord, I believe; help my unbelief!"

— Mark 9:24 (NKJV)

Few people will read your testimony and decide to receive Salvation before talking to you or someone else. When the Lord is tugging hard on the hearts of unsaved people, you want to be sure that human encouragement is readily available as well.

We recommend that you add the following information to your testimony: your name, the name of a faithful witness at your church (in case you cannot be reached for some reason), the name and address of your church, and the telephone numbers that are most likely to reach someone without having to leave a message. It's also helpful to give instructions about the best times to make contact with you, the witness, and the church. You should mention what time your church holds services and encourage people who read the testimony to introduce themselves to a greeter or usher as someone who is learning about the Lord and Salvation. If you are not going to be present at a church service, alert someone who will be there to be on the look out for people who have read your testimony.

A Good Written Testimony Is Headed by a Powerful Title That Attracts the Lost

> *Now Pilate wrote a title and put* it *on the cross.*
> *And the writing was:*
> *JESUS OF NAZARETH,*
> *THE KING OF THE JEWS.*
>
> — John 19:19 (NKJV)

Titles attract the attention of the lost by creating a bridge between the secular concerns of the unsaved and Christ's forgiveness. If you would like to see examples, we encourage you to look at the testimony titles in Appendix C and the rest of *Real Life Stories*.

Let's take a few of those titles and review their attention-getting potential. "The Marijuana Test" is a powerful title that will attract notice from people who have jobs and regularly smoke marijuana. Many workplaces now require random drug tests, and some heavy marijuana smokers live in dread of those tests. This testimony isn't about marijuana tests, but about resisting peer pressure to smoke marijuana, by describing the opportunity to respond to such peer pressure as a test of character. Marijuana users will gain a new perspective on their smoking after the title grabs their attention.

Another powerful title is "Arrested for Attempted Murder!" Anyone who has a temper and gets into violent confrontations may want to read more about that testimony. Sadly, there's no double meaning here: This is a testimony of someone who was arrested for the attempted murder of his wife before he repented and changed his ways.

A title with more general appeal is "Don't Give Up. Look Up!" Almost everyone becomes discouraged some of the time. This title will appeal to anyone who is feeling discouraged. The secular meaning of the title is to be more optimistic and hopeful. The spiritual meaning of the testimony is to rely on God. This title shows the best kind of double meaning because the title makes a positive connection between secular thinking and spiritual belief.

"I Couldn't Feel a Thing" has a similar power to reach many people. Some will see this testimony title as referring to surviving an accident, a stroke, or other severe illness. Others will see this title as a description of the kind of grief people feel after losing a loved one or following a divorce. Some others will identify this title with being abused by another person and the dissociation that helps an abused person reduce the emotional pain. The testimony is actually about developing such a hard heart that you don't care about anyone else and take advantage of others.

We are sure you'll find a very inspiring and interesting title that will draw in those who need to read your testimony. We believe you will have a joyful time with this part of writing a testimony: It's a lot of fun to do, and the Holy Spirit will help you develop Godly ideas for a title.

Write Your Testimony as the First Step in Becoming a Complete, Continual Witness

I will remember the works of the LORD;
Surely I will remember Your wonders of old.
I will also meditate on all Your work,
And talk of Your deeds.

— Psalm 77:11-12 (NKJV)

The first step toward becoming a complete, continual witness is to write your testimony. When you do this, you honor God. You also gain great benefits.

If what you've read so far hasn't convinced you to write your testimony, we encourage you to consider some of the thirty-six reasons to write your testimony that were formerly displayed on the Web site www.olsonhouse.org. Here are a few of our favorite reasons from that list: Your testimony

- can influence hearts to seek and gain Salvation.
- will bring you closer to God.
- strengthens Christians and helps renew their faith.
- gives hope of life free from current problems.
- demonstrates gaining the life that others seek, alive in a real person.

Many people wonder why bad things happen to good people. While none of us can know why God chooses bad things to happen to anyone, a possible intent could be to provide experiences of overcoming bad things through His help in order to deepen faith and help believers become more powerful witnesses for Him. Whatever His purposes are surely it's good to demonstrate His goodness through your testimony about how He strengthened and rescued you from sin.

Certain fears may tempt you to not write your testimony. Common fears include:

- being embarrassed by others learning about your past failings
- hurting the feelings of those you write about
- upsetting family members who aren't saved

Similarly, you may delay working on a written testimony by telling yourself that you are:

- too busy.
- not ready to begin.
- unsure how to start.
- being picked on by the people who are encouraging you to share your experiences.
- waiting for a sign from God to begin.
- looking for detailed guidance from the Holy Spirit.

We encourage prayer as a source of guidance, but you should also realize that actually working on your testimony is the fastest and easiest way to turn your good intentions into results and to gain specific guidance from God.

Relax when you start: Remember that your first draft doesn't have to look very good. In fact, if it's hard for you to write, just record your testimony in spoken form and ask someone in your church to help you write a draft from the recording. Plenty of people will be glad to read and comment on your draft testimony. From those reactions, you'll find the Holy Spirit giving you lots of good directions.

If you have no idea of what to write, have a discussion with your in-congregation evangelist or your pastor about the following list. Then turn your answers into notes to help organize your thinking.

1. What you thought about writing your testimony when you first read about or heard of the task
2. What your initial reservations were
3. What inspired you to want to write a testimony
4. How you believe you should organize your thinking and writing
5. What help you might need and how you can get it

6. How you can fit this work into your daily schedule
7. How long you think it will take
8. How you believe that you will feel differently after you've finished writing
9. What you plan to do with your testimony

Once you have examined those areas, you can use the following outline, based on the first part of this chapter, to draft the sections of your written testimony:

1. God exists.
2. God can do what people cannot do.
3. God changed my life by saving my soul.
4. God gave me joy through sharing my faith.
5. God wants to give you blessings when you receive Salvation.
6. God presents Salvation as a gift when you follow these directions.
7. God will improve your life as a new Christian when you follow these directions.
8. You can get more information about Salvation from me, another witness, and my church.

After you have finished with a draft, add a title that will attract those who will be helped most by your testimony.

The Lord has done an enormous number of good things in your life. You could probably write many volumes describing those good things. You may wonder, then, how you can reduce all of that goodness into a single written testimony.

How long should a written testimony be? The answer depends on what you have to share. Most people find that items one through four on the preceding outline can be addressed in between 750 and 2,500 words. There's no problem if you need more words or require fewer. You can use the information we wrote in this chapter to help you with items five through eight on the outline.

How long does it take to write a draft testimony after you have developed your notes? Some people feel so inspired that they can complete that part of the task in just a few hours. Others will need as many as twenty hours. In either case, if you devote half an hour a day to working on your draft, you should be done with drafting within six weeks. With writing and editing help, you can probably turn your draft into a final version in another five to ten hours over the following two to three weeks.

Here's one last piece of advice: Be heartfelt in what you write. No one is going to be looking for outstanding literary skill in your writing, but all will be looking for honest, caring information designed to help them. When you write from the heart, other hearts will respond.

Writing a draft of your testimony is such an important step that we encourage you to stop reading this book until you finish a first draft of your testimony. If you find that you are stuck in any way while creating a draft and haven't received the support you need for your pastor or in-congregation evangelist, Bishop Dale P. Combs will be glad to help you. You can call him at 219-947-0301 or you can send him at an e-mail at jwcpastor@jubileeworshipcenter.com. Jim Barbarossa will also be glad to help you. You can call him at 219-787-9933 or you can send him an e-mail at jim@step-by-step.org.

Inspire Other Christians to Write Their Testimonies so They Can Start to Become Complete, Continual Witnesses

Blessed are those who have learned to acclaim you,
who walk in the light of your presence, O LORD.

— Psalm 89:15 (NIV)

Congratulations on drafting your written testimony. Good job! The Lord is proud of you, and the angels are smiling. You should feel terrific. Now keep working on your testimony every day until it's just right. Get all the help you want.

If you didn't follow our directions and write a draft testimony yet, go back to the last section and get started! We don't want you to miss the joy of complete, continual witnessing any longer than necessary.

Think of the things you love to do now that you initially procrastinated about before trying. We promise you will love sharing your written testimony once you know the right ways to do it!

Going from just being a testimony drafter to becoming a complete, continual witness will take you some more time and effort. You'll learn more about what to do in Chapters 6 through 11. For now, a good second step in becoming a complete, continual witness is encouraging other Christians to write their testimonies by explaining how you feel about the experience, describing what you did, and sharing your written testimony with them.

You will gain a deeper appreciation of God's grace through this service. You will work with people who have been rescued from terrible situations. In addition, you will work with people who have been spared from serious trials by their faith in the Lord.

By simply starting to write your testimony, you are now qualified through experience and faith and well equipped with the Lord's help to inspire those who haven't written their testimonies. Hearing about what you gained from writing your testimony or draft and asking about your experiences will be much more interesting and relevant to Christians than reading the words we, your authors, have provided. Feel free, however, to use what we've written in this book to explain to others why writing a testimony is a great thing to do.

When we asked members of JWC why they decided to write a testimony, a number reported that they responded just because they were asked: No one had ever asked them before. For some Christians, it will be that simple to get the ball rolling. Here are some other common reasons from our survey of why people decided to write a testimony listed in the order of how often they were mentioned:

- Other people could be helped.
- A written testimony provides a good witnessing tool.
- The Lord or Bible reading directed this be done.
- I want to help save more souls.
- I want to be obedient to God.

When you refer to these reasons as you speak with other Christians, chances are you will touch hearts among those who haven't yet written their testimonies.

Even if you know someone well, you probably don't know how he or she feels about writing a testimony. You can make faster progress in being helpful to them if you start off by witnessing about what it was like to write your testimony. Here's a list you can use to share your experiences:

1. What you thought about writing your testimony when you first read about or heard of the task
2. What your initial reservations were
3. What inspired you to start writing
4. How you organized your thinking and writing
5. What help you needed and how you got it
6. How you fit developing a written testimony into your daily schedule
7. How long it took you
8. How you feel differently now that you've finished
9. What you plan to do with your testimony

Having shared what you did, it's then appropriate to ask the person about his or her own thoughts and experiences on the subject. Here is a list of questions that might be helpful:

1. Have you ever read a testimony written by someone you know?
2. If "yes" to question 1, what did you think of what you read?
3. Would you like me to read my testimony to you?
4. Would you like to hear why I share my faith by using a written testimony?
5. Have you ever thought about writing your testimony?
6. If "yes" to question 5, have you written one?
7. If "no" to question 5 or 6, does the idea of writing your testimony appeal to you?
8. If "no" to question 7, why not?

9. Do you know what Jesus had to say about sharing our testimonies?
10. How can I help you learn more about the benefits of writing your testimony?
11. Would you like to read some more testimonies?
12. When would you like to talk again about writing your testimony?

Be persistent in following up until you've addressed all of the person's concerns. Get other people involved who also share your joy in witnessing through written testimonies: This is particularly helpful for those who are afraid of being embarrassed or are concerned about how family members will react. Bring new materials to read or to talk about every time you speak with the person. If necessary, ask your in-congregation evangelist or your pastor for help.

Help Other Christians to Write Their Testimonies so They Can Start to Become Complete, Continual Witnesses

"But if You can do anything,
have compassion on us and help us."

— Mark 9:22 (NKJV)

Once you have helped inspire someone to want to write a testimony, you can shift to helping her or him perform the task. We suggest that you take note of the concerns you heard during the process of helping them decide to write a testimony. Your help should focus around dealing with those concerns.

In addition, you should ask people how they like to learn how to do a new task. Do they like to read something? Do they prefer to have a conversation? Do they do better by working with someone? Whatever the answers are, shape your help to reflect that learning style. If that way of working is different from what you feel comfortable with, we suggest you enlist someone who is more comfortable to assist in that way.

Once a person understands what the testimony writing task is, explain that setting deadlines for the various steps can help avoid procrastination and the onset of new fears. Deadlines also give you a way to check on how the person is doing. Here is what such a schedule could look like over approximately two months:

I. Answer Preparation Questions (2 weeks)
    A. What experiences have you had that would help others understand that God exists?
    B. What experiences have you had that show God doing what people cannot do?
    C. How is your life different now from before you accepted Salvation?
    D. What are your most moving experiences of sharing your faith?
    E. What are the blessings of receiving Salvation?
    F. How does a lost person gain Salvation?
    G. What should a newly saved person do?
    H. How should someone get more information from you and your church about Salvation?

II. Review Preparation Question Answers with You or Another Helper (1 day)

III. Select Experiences to Include (1 day)

IV. Draft the Experience-Based Individual Parts of the Testimony (2 weeks)
    A. God exists.
    B. God can do what people cannot do.
    C. God changed my life by saving my soul.
    D. God gave me joy through sharing my faith.

V. Get Comments on the Drafted Parts of the Testimony and Draft the Rest of the Testimony (2 weeks)
   A. God wants to give you blessings when you receive Salvation.
   B. God presents Salvation as a gift when you follow these directions.
   C. God will improve your life as a new Christian when you follow these directions.
   D. You can get more information about Salvation from me, another witness, and my church.

VI. Revise the First Part of the Testimony and Get Comments on Second Part (2 weeks)

VII. Make Final Revisions and Select a Title. (1 week)

During the revisions, it will be a good idea to get reactions from an editor. Ask your pastor or in-congregation evangelist if someone in the congregation has volunteered for this role. If an editor hasn't yet volunteered, perhaps you can help find one within the congregation. If that doesn't work, freelance editors can be found by using a search engine on the Internet to look for "freelance editors." After such a search, you will find many sites listing people who have experience in preparing materials for books.

In the future, these written testimonies will be combined into a book. (You can see an example at http://www.step-by-step.org by downloading a copy of *Real Life Stories*, the book of testimonies published by Jubilee Worship Center.) You'll want to have some consistency of style and format to make the book more appealing. In addition, an editor can focus on clarity and grammar so that the other reviewers of testimony drafts can pay most attention to how moving the stories and language are. Editors and reviewers are also good sources for suggesting titles.

Keep in mind that the person who writes the testimony is responsible for its content. Don't dictate what should or shouldn't be said or how to say it. If the person is in doubt, encourage prayer as the way to clarify her or his mind.

You may, however, want to supply some standard materials (with a few choices) for the last four sections of the testimony. In this way, the writer can individualize the messages without having to reinvent all of the information by studying the Bible.

To receive a free copy of a testimony in tract form, send an e-mail request to jim@step-by-step.org that includes your postal address and telephone number.

Feel free to draw on this chapter and any other sources that provide what you find to be helpful information about writing a testimony. You have our permission to make copies of this chapter to share.

†

Be sure to have fun writing your testimony and helping other to do so; otherwise, it's not a God-directed activity. But there may well be some more fear, anger, frustration, tears, and sadness for the Christian to experience who is writing his or her testimony. Be prepared to supply loving comfort and support. Ask others to pray for those who are working on their written testimonies. We talk more about overcoming fear in Chapter 6, and you may find helpful suggestions there both for you and those you wish to help with writing their testimonies.

Chapter 6

Put on God's Spiritual
Armor Every Day

Encourage Christians
to Lose Their Fears of Witnessing

Put on the whole armor of God,
that you may be able to stand against the wiles of the devil.
For we do not wrestle against flesh and blood,
but against principalities, against powers,
against the rulers of the darkness of this age,
against spiritual hosts of wickedness in the heavenly places.

— Ephesians 6:11-12 (NKJV)

How can it be that so many people do not know about the benefits of Salvation and how to gain it? How can so many people have heard of Salvation yet rejected this most valuable gift? Paul reminds us in the Bible verses from Ephesians 6:11-12 that receiving Salvation is opposed by the enemy who is in the world. As a result, you can expect opposition to helping others learn about, appreciate, and accept Salvation. Despite such opposition, you know that God can do anything. When you put on His holy armor to do His will as Ephesians 6 encourages Christians to do, you can resist all opposition!

Surveys show that a tiny percentage of Christians have ever helped lead anyone other than a family member into receiving Salvation. That observation suggests that the ways in which most Christians share or practice their faith outside their families isn't what God intended if everyone is to be saved. Obviously, then, you need to change what you are doing in sharing your faith and to teach others to do the same. If you don't, unsaved people will suffer without hope on Earth and their souls will be lost for all eternity. It's as simple as that.

Naturally, you have a direct responsibility to help nurture the lives and souls of your grandparents, parents, aunts, uncles, children, cousins, grandchildren, and other family relations. Keep praying for and encouraging these people to come to the Lord.

However, don't limit your efforts to just those people, even if there is more work to be done with them. Billions of people are mired in unbelief or belief in false gods; they need your help, as well. Some are friends, neighbors, and acquaintances. Some work next to you as colleagues. Some serve you at the grocery store; others take away your trash. Some will be new acquaintances and play tennis with you today. One reason that God placed you where you are is to help those people around you to come to Him.

Many lost people live thousands of miles away and are strangers to you. In the past, just a small percentage of Christians were called to be missionaries in faraway places. With today's inexpensive mass communications, you can easily reach beyond your family, community, work, shopping, and interests to touch lives on all continents by sending your written testimony through the mail and over the Internet. Your written testimony can help save more souls in other nations than a mid-twentieth-century foreign missionary could ever hope to reach. What a great opportunity God has given you!

God has truly blessed us with this amazing opportunity to share His goodness by helping lost souls wherever they can be found. As a result, your responsibility to share your faith is much greater than in previous generations. Mass communications also make it easy to teach other Christians to do the same.

What's missing for this great opportunity to be fulfilled? All Christians need to gather more courage and overcome any fears and indecision that stand in the way of helping souls to join with the Lord. In this chapter, we address common fears about witnessing and how to overcome those fears so that you and others you share this book with can know how to become complete, continual witnesses.

How many Christians are hobbled by such fears and indecision? Few Christians write their testimonies. Some of that can be due to ignorance, but you can get a sense of the role that fear may play by observing that many people who agree to write their testimonies never do. Opposition from the enemy who is in the world has either paralyzed or neutralized the wills of these believers. After writing a testimony, an even smaller percentage of Christians then continually hand out what they have written. A tinier percentage of Christians who pass out their testimonies also have conversations with lost people about what's in those testimonies. For each type of witnessing activity, the enemy constructs new doubts and fears to snag, delay, and distract potential witnesses from doing what unsaved people need.

Fear is a powerful weapon for the enemy who is in the world to use against Christians to discourage witnessing. Fear can turn an intelligent, caring person into a paralyzed statue so overcome with confusion as to become inactive. Authorities on fear report that most people while afraid:

- cannot think clearly.
- don't appreciate when substantial risks are present.
- put off making decisions.
- look for someone else to save them.
- find it difficult to take action after choosing what to do.
- take actions slowly.
- are extra courteous and shy while acting, sometimes to the point of ineffectiveness.

Those who are slightly afraid become less decisive. When fear leads to indecision, concerns about possible negative consequences make it hard for fearful people to pick a direction and act on it.

Let's look more closely at common fears about witnessing and how to overcome them so that you and others you share these lessons with can become complete, continual witnesses.

Act on Your Fear of God
and Become Braver in Doing His Work

Surely His salvation is *near to those who fear Him, ...*

— Psalm 85:9 (NKJV)

... and most of the brethren in the Lord,
having become confident by my chains,
are much more bold to speak the word without fear.

— Philippians 1:14 (NKJV)

After Jesus ascended to heaven, His disciples and apostles proclaimed the way to Salvation in the face of grave dangers that included violent crowds, floggings, long imprisonment, assassination attempts, stonings with intent to kill, and crucifixion. Despite those physical risks, the disciples and apostles understood that they should fear God more than what mere men could do to their bodies. Those obedient Christians accepted all the physical risks and kept speaking.

You should follow their example regardless of what your fears are. God will protect you when you do. As you draw closer to Him, He will draw closer to you.

To better understand God's will, let's consider what it means to "fear" the Lord. When the Bible talks about "fear" of God as in Psalm 85:9, the meaning of that kind of "fear" is closer to "hold in awe" and "hold in reverence" than it is to the kind of fear you might feel when facing an angry lion or an armed robber. You need to understand and remember that whenever you don't draw close enough to God by following His commands, you aren't fearing (holding in awe and reverence) Him enough.

A good test of your relationship with Him is whether you feel closer to Him when not witnessing than while witnessing. God wants you to feel terrible when you don't witness and great while you do. He wants you to find His will more important than your fears.

Let's look at how to build moral courage to witness by first understanding fear and then learning how to overcome it. Fear is felt in many forms. Some fears are appropriate, triggering helpful actions to avoid dangers that have frequently caused you substantial harm. A good example is being careful not to touch hot metal with your bare fingers. You've touched hot metal before and know from experience and observation that a severe burn can result, continuing pain will follow, and ugly scars may remain.

If you've experienced more reasons to be afraid than most people, paralyzing fears will probably arise more often. A person can be overloaded by frequent, intense fears into being unable to respond appropriately. For example, imagine that you have been with someone who after drinking alcohol has repeatedly beaten you. Many children grow up with a fear of such an abusive parent. Many spouses live with this fear of a violent, drunken husband or wife. The power of fear to paralyze people into inaction is well demonstrated by observing how many adults who could seek safety from such abusive and violent people continue to put themselves at risk from such dangers. Even more eloquent evidence of fear's power to coerce compliance is how many adults are cowed into marrying abusive drunks after having been abused as children by a drunken parent.

As a lighter example, consider that some people would rather face any humiliation rather than ride on a roller coaster, while many other people are extremely happy while riding on these fast-moving attractions. You may find both reactions to roller coasters being experienced by different people in the same family. Many people who are afraid of roller coasters also fear heights or experience motion sickness on such rides: Merely seeing a roller coaster can be enough to trigger fear for these people.

These examples display something important about fear: It's almost always an acquired perception based on a painful experience. However, you don't only rely on your own experiences and observations to become afraid; many of your fears come from what you've been told by others. If someone says that it was terrifying to share his or her testimony in church or with a stranger, you will be much more likely to feel the same way if you haven't written or shared your testimony.

Other fears about witnessing can be triggered by earlier experiences that you indirectly connect to the current situation. For example, your teachers may have taught writing and speaking skills in such harsh ways that you were left feeling afraid of receiving painful remarks about whatever you write or say — fears made worse if judgmental family and friends have made harsh comments after reading or hearing uncorrected versions of what had been written or said. Ask someone with such painful memories to write and talk about her or his Christian testimony, and those fears based in painful learning experiences and comments of others may be revived.

A clue to the mental foundations underlying fears about writing and speaking a Christian testimony can be found in many peoples' discomforting dreams about being naked in public while everyone else is clothed. Those who aren't yet confident in writing and speaking in public often imagine that those testimony-based witnessing activities feel as if they are the same as the embarrassing exposure that occurs in such unpleasant dreams.

It is well known from surveys that most people would do virtually anything to avoid speaking in public, no matter what the cost. As an example, some intelligent, well-educated people take lower-paying jobs so that they won't have to give presentations. Some sales people choose to lose commissions rather than make speeches at public gatherings of potential customers. Part of this fear is experience-based: Many people have had bad experiences with public speaking, and almost everyone has seen someone make a royal fool of himself or herself while speaking publicly.

But experience isn't your fate. Many people have overcome fears and learned to enjoy activities that used to cause them to tremble. For instance, experiences in a swimming pool and with diving can terrify youngsters who can't swim, yet many of the most terrified eventually learn to successfully perform and enjoy these activities.

Let's take stock of your feelings for a minute so this discussion won't be so abstract:

- What fears have caused you to be indecisive?
- What fears have paralyzed you into inaction against your self-interest?
- How many of those fears have you put behind you?
- How many of the fears do you still feel, but you've become courageous enough to act appropriately despite them?
- What forms of witnessing activities are you afraid to do?
- What experiences have contributed to these witnessing fears?

Obviously, people can overcome even well-based fears; you've done it. What's involved? One of the best ways to reduce, to control, and to overcome fear is to prepare and rehearse. When confronted with a situation that triggers a fearful response, knowing what to expect and do can make the difference between being paralyzed by fear or indecision and taking the right actions to accomplish a successful result.

Consider those who fight forest fires. They may face flames hundreds of feet high generating temperatures high enough to melt steel. A sudden switch in the direction of wind-blown flames can incinerate these fire fighters. A little fear may be a good thing for the fire fighters, but too much fear makes the dangers greater by slowing reaction time. Despite constant exposure to extreme risks, people who fight forest fires keep their cool and systematically deal with the dangers. These people aren't all natural heroes. How do they gain the courage to deal with their highly justified fears? They learn by practicing during controlled burns designed to create firebreaks in forests.

People in other professions also rehearse what to do when in terrifying circumstances. Race drivers, for instance, attend special schools where they learn how to keep control when brakes fail and tires blow out at high speeds. Airline pilots routinely practice in simulators that allow instructors to induce extreme conditions, "mechanical failures," and "accidents" that the pilots need to respond to. The same is true of those who captain supertankers. If you live near a nuclear power plant, you'll be relieved to know that those who operate such plants receive a similar kind of simulation-based training to deal with reactor emergencies. With enough practice, dangerous situations they face feel more familiar, enabling them to make quick, correct decisions and act appropriately.

Much of this training presumes that there will be no one around to help and no time to get help: That's secular thinking. In becoming a complete, continual witness, you should get all the help you need.

As a Christian, you have an even greater resource as well; you have God, the greatest force in the universe, to help and protect you. That Divine help is better than the full-body armor that medieval knights wore to resist injury during tournaments and battles. God is there for you whenever risks arise, and He can send an army of angels to help you. When direct intervention isn't required, you can count on being filled with the Holy Spirit to direct your mind and body. To draw on those Divine resources, be sure to pray for His strength before you witness. With God's help, the proper preparation, and practice, you can overcome your fears and become the complete, continual witness that God wants you to be.

Prepare to Overcome Common Witnessing Fears

*"These things I have spoken to you, that in Me you may have peace.
In the world you will have tribulation; but be of good cheer,
I have overcome the world."*

— John 16:33 (NKJV)

In the same way that overcoming the fear of diving into a swimming pool is different from developing courage to fight a forest fire, neutralizing the effects of each fear that keeps Christians from sharing beliefs and experiences requires a different type of preparation. In the rest of the chapter, we share how to overcome the most common fears about witnessing that can cause indecision and inaction. This information will be helpful when you counsel Christians about various common fears whether or not you experience these fears. We'll start with fears that discourage people from writing their testimonies and go on from there to discuss types of fears that reduce other kinds of witnessing.

Overcome Fears That Return When You Think about Your Past

Therefore take up the whole armor of God,
that you may be able to withstand in the evil day,
and having done all, to stand.

— Ephesians 6:13 (NKJV)

This is the day the LORD has made;
We will rejoice and be glad in it.

— Psalm 118: 24 (NKJV)

Before you can write a testimony about what God has done for you, you have to think about the past. You might normally avoid reviewing your life because you don't want to reexamine old sins and problems.

Here's why such resistance occurs: If you have ever been in an automobile accident, you will probably feel nervous and be extra cautious whenever you return near the place where the accident occurred. All of the fear and pain you felt then will come back to you.

The same thing can happen when you reexamine your life, even to write a testimony about what God has done for you. The enemy is the father of lies and likes to take such moments to encourage you to believe that you could fall back into those or worse circumstances and sins.

Remember, instead, that God knows all about you, and He has forgiven you. He has lifted you up so that you can have joy and peace even when your circumstances are trying. Now that you have His forgiveness, direction, and support, why are you fearful of thinking about your life before He saved you? Is your faith sound?

When fears about the past before you were saved return to you, start praising the Lord for delivering you from those circumstances and sins. Tell Him that you know that He has a good plan for your life, and you are expecting great things from that plan as you draw closer to Him. Thank Him for putting His whole armor around you, surrounding you with holiness, so that no harm can come to your immortal soul. If you have some praise and worship music available, play encouraging hymns and songs. Keep focusing on Him until your past as a lost person seems remote, small, and unthreatening. Compared to God, your past is an insignificant mote of dust that He can flick away with a tiny part of His fingernail. Tell the enemy to flee and as you do quote John 16:33 (NKJV):

> *"These things I have spoken to you,*
> *that in Me you may have peace.*
> *In the world you will have tribulation;*
> *but be of good cheer, I have overcome the world."*

to prove that you are right.

After you overcome any initial panic about considering the most fear-ridden parts of your past, practice thinking how grateful you are to God to be free of those days, problems, circumstances, and sins. Develop a habit of thanking God for His love whenever you are reminded of your most painful memories: You'll feel as if you are being bathed in unlimited love and approval when you do. It's as if you have put an impermeable coating of love over your painful memories. When you can look forward to mentally reviewing those events because those memories open up your heart to feeling and appreciating more of God's love, you'll know that you have the upper hand over the fear and pain.

Overcome Fear of Embarrassment about Revealing Your Past

> *Stand therefore, having girded your waist with truth, ...*

— Ephesians 6:14 (NKJV)

> *"... your joy no one will take from you."*

John 16:22 (NKJV)

People usually feel differently about you after they know more about you. Fear of embarrassment is about being afraid that people will think less of you. Some fearful people imagine that other people will only think about the worst parts of their pasts. In its extreme form, people fear being taunted or becoming a victim of other kinds of adverse attention after revealing an embarrassing past.

Knowing how much people like to smirk over a "juicy" story is one reason some people fear embarrassment from sharing past mistakes and problems. Everyone has either heard or passed along gossip. Gossip's appeal is usually based on discovering that a proud person is a hypocrite (such as a moral leader of a community engaging in the sins the leader has repeatedly condemned) or learning that someone with a good reputation is trying to keep past bad behavior quiet (a "solid citizen" who formerly reveled in a sinful private life). The contrast between the public face and the hidden private reality attracts attention from gossips.

By comparison, most people applaud, appreciate, and encourage someone who reveals a troubled past, repents of any wrongs he or she has done, and now leads a better life. You've probably been in church when an itinerant speaker described having overcome past problems with alcohol, drugs, crime, or sexual misbehavior. Revealing that information made you much more interested in the person and her or his message; you were probably more impressed by the lessons revealed; and you were probably more likely to apply those lessons to your life and to share those lessons with people you know.

In preparing to write a testimony that describes regrettable past behavior or dreadful experiences, remember that God knows you made those mistakes or suffered those harms; and He wants you to be a witness about what He has done for you to build a better life.

In writing that testimony, realize that you are the author. No investigative reporters from *60 Minutes* are going to show up to try to make you look as bad as possible.

Instead, your testimony should focus on what God did for you. To glorify God, readers don't need to know every ugly detail about your past life. They benefit from simply knowing that you had problems that the Lord rescued you from. For example, suppose someone had been sexually abused by a sadist. That abused person's testimony doesn't need to go into those details (unless the abused person feels called to share them). The person could simply write: "I was sexually abused." If that disclosure feels too explicit, the person could write instead: "I was a victim of physical abuse."

As you read about this person, you are probably feeling sympathetic. If you, too, have experienced abuse, you'll want to learn about how that person dealt with and overcame the abuse. If you were still a lost person, you'd also want to know how the person gained joy and love through Salvation.

To help feel less concerned about sharing your past sins and circumstances, read some testimonies about life experiences like yours. If you can arrange to talk with some of these witnesses, ask them about how they felt about sharing their pasts before writing the testimony and how testimony readers and hearers have reacted to the disclosures. We think you'll feel encouraged by what you learn.

In fact, telling about what happened to you or how you sinned will leave you feeling better and more forgiven than ever before. It's a little like dealing with a heavy load. When one person carries it, a heavy load can seem overwhelming. When you share carrying the same heavy load with enough people, it's easy for each person to bear. The same holds true for painful memories.

In writing or speaking your testimony, you'll find that people will acknowledge and appreciate your willingness to share information. When people know more about what you've overcome with the Lord's help, most people will feel closer to you and want to know you better. Almost everyone will focus on what God did in your life and how that lesson can help many other people. The worse your past has been, the greater is God's glory for helping you. You are praising Him when you share the truth about your experiences. What can be wrong, embarrassing, or fear-causing about praising Him?

Overcome Fear of Hurting the Feelings of Those Christians You Write About

... having put on the breastplate of righteousness, ...

— Ephesians 6:14 (NKJV)

102

For the Scripture says, "Whoever believes on Him will not be put to shame."

Romans 10:11 (NKJV)

Many people don't like to be surprised. Some people warn family members and friends not to prepare surprise parties for them. Such people would be mortified if the local newspaper wrote about them, even if the words were mostly positive or neutral.

In addition, almost everyone treasures privacy ... especially about matters that would have seemed embarrassing if observed at the time they occurred. Some incidents can be seen as so humiliating that people will want them buried forever: You see a similar reaction when artists and authors leave wills that direct executors to destroy their diaries, notes, drawings, and uncompleted works so that no one will see uncensored disclosures in public.

Writing about others in your testimony has the potential to create bad reactions simply by surprising those people. After being surprised that you disclosed something about them, anger and harsh words may follow.

Negative reactions to being written about are often related to feeling that privacy has been violated. Even those who have acted in deplorable ways may feel they are owed your silence. In fact, many abusers threaten more harm if the abused person tells anyone.

Beyond that, some people you write about can feel betrayed, that you have broken faith with them, especially if what you share shows that person having done something wrong.

These aren't hypothetical fears: These may be fears based on accurately anticipating that some Christians will feel hurt by what you write. What can be done to avoid the fears and the hurt reactions so that you can comfortably write a testimony that refers to other people?

From our survey of Jubilee Worship Center (JWC) testimony writers, we learned that many bad reactions to being written about can be avoided by talking to the person about your plans before you write or speak. In the rest of this section, we assume that you will be writing about another Christian.

When your testimony refers to a Christian, you have a huge advantage: You can share the materials we've put in this book to explain why it's important for you to write a testimony that includes speaking about this person. The two of you can pray together about this task and have good talks about each other's feelings. See this as an opportunity for both of you to come closer to the Lord. Perhaps the other person will decide to write a testimony as well. When that happens, it may be that the two testimonies together can be used to save more souls than either one alone could. Some married couples at Jubilee Worship Center have combined their testimonies, and the results are very eloquent.

Talking to the person in advance offers another advantage: If the person isn't going to feel hurt by what you write, you quickly find out that your fear is groundless. In that case, discovering that there's no problem will be a great relief and release you to start writing.

We have often found that if you also let the person see your testimony in draft form, the person may be able to suggest ways of rewriting the testimony that make him or her feel more comfortable. Sometimes the subject will surprise you by suggesting stronger language and more graphic details than you used.

Overcome Fear of Upsetting Family Members Who Aren't Saved

... and having shod your feet with the preparation of the gospel of peace; ....

— Ephesians 6:15 (NKJV)

"I did not come to bring peace but a sword.
For I have come to 'set a man against his father,
a daughter against her mother, and
a daughter-in-law against her mother-in-law'; *and*
'a man's enemies will be those of his own household.'
He who loves father or mother more than Me is not worthy of Me.
And he who loves son or daughter more than Me is not worthy of Me."

— Matthew 10:34-37 (NKJV)

No one wants to lose good relations with family members. Jesus knew this and addressed that feeling in Matthew 10:34-37: If the choice is between keeping our families harmonious and serving Him, we must follow Him.

Notice that Jesus didn't tell us to antagonize family members for no reason or to stop loving them; He just said to love Him more and to stay in allegiance with Him by doing His will.

There's an opportunity here if you grasp it: Writing a testimony can be an act of faith that can help bring your family member to Christ.

How can that happen? Making your family comfortable with your written testimony is an opportunity to witness to any unsaved people in your family.

A good way to start is by meeting individually to explain to each unsaved family member that you are about to do something important — to share what God has done in your life so that others may be helped.

Most lost people will approve of your desire to help someone else. As a child, your parents probably taught you to look for opportunities to help others. Your younger siblings probably hoped you would act that way toward them, especially when you didn't. Your spouse and children will be glad to hear that you want to express more love and help to others; they will see themselves as obvious beneficiaries.

Then tell unsaved family members how such a testimony can encourage someone to receive Salvation and enjoy more peace on Earth and eternal life in heaven. Describe how this is a wonderful gift of love from God that you are being asked to share.

Describe what God has done for you. Explain how you felt before being saved and what your life has been like since then. Point out that many people are dealing with the same issues and how it hurts your heart to think about their suffering.

Tell your lost family members that you don't wish to cause them any discomfort or pain. If your testimony will speak about any of them, tell her or him you would like their help with the writing so that you'll get the story right and avoid making them feel uncomfortable with your testimony.

For instance, if you have a generally well-behaved family and you have been the black sheep in the past, you can explain that your past misbehavior will now serve a good purpose in warning others to live better. You can also indicate that after having written such a testimony you'll feel more committed to leading a better life. That observation should relax everyone a lot. What's a little family embarrassment about the past compared to having the former black sheep slip back into misbehavior in the present?

If you will be disclosing bad actions that a family member has done, you should be candid in explaining that intent. In describing this plan, give that loved one a chance to apologize if he or she hasn't. If that person has expressed regret and apologized, you can describe how much that repentance has meant to you and that you plan to include that in your testimony. In this way, you can remind them about the redeeming power of repentance, even for those who don't accept Jesus as Lord.

If you anticipate that the discussion could be a stormy one, you should first talk to and pray with your in-congregation evangelist or pastor to gain direction for what to do to avoid unnecessary anger and hurt feelings. Consider if it will be important to be joined by the evangelist or pastor when you meet with your family member.

Ultimately, you will have to rely on God's love for you and the love you feel for God to guide you. Many family members can be softened quite a bit by extra expressions of love. What can you do to create more peacefulness before you tell about your plans to write a testimony?

Always pray just before you speak until you have peace about what needs to be said. The Holy Spirit will guide you to walk and talk in love.

Overcome Fear of Witnessing at Work

> *... above all, taking the shield of faith*
> *with which you will be able to quench*
> *all the fiery darts of the wicked one.*

> — Ephesians 6:16 (NKJV)

And my God shall supply all your need
according to His riches in glory by Christ Jesus.

— Philippians 4:19 (NKJV)

Workplaces often have thick policy manuals about what you can and cannot do as an employee. Many of those manuals indicate that you cannot talk about your faith at work. Sometimes those manuals go so far as to indicate you will be fired if you discuss religion.

Because many people don't have much extra money, the potential of losing a job can stir a lot of fear. In extreme cases, some people will imagine their families living on the streets instead of in an apartment or home.

Those fears are overdone. We are told by the Bible that God and Jesus will supply all of our needs. Surely there's another job where an honest, hard-working, witnessing Christian can earn a good living.

The reality at work typically isn't much like what the manuals say. Supervisors may give those who work for them memos describing personal philosophies and how to work together better. Co-workers often take coffee breaks and lunch together away from their assignments and develop personal relationships that outlast the job. While working late, it's not unusual to have personal conversations. If you like someone, chances are that you'll see also them outside of work.

Through all these contacts, more and more personal aspects of your life will be revealed. If you are an avid bowler, chances are that everyone you work with will soon know that. If you are an enthusiastic Christian, why should that interest be any different?

Those who can easily find work may have already located a workplace where outspoken Christians are welcome. If God has instead sent you to a job where you are surrounded by lost people, surely He wants you to help them find peace and love in His forgiveness.

We asked members of Jubilee Worship Center about their witnessing experiences at work, and no one reported any problems being witnesses there ... even when company policies indicated that religion was not to be discussed. Once the ice was broken by sharing a testimony, unsaved people usually initiated future conversations about the member's faith.

If you still feel nervous about being a witness at work, you can share your written testimony with co-workers while you are away from the premises. When co-workers share their troubles with you, offer to pray for them. Hearts will be opened because He wants them opened, regardless of what people say.

Naturally, you'll also want to be generous in inviting co-workers to attend church with you. In addition, you can hold Bible studies at your home and invite congregation members, friends, and co-workers.

Overcome Fear of Being Rejected

And take the helmet of salvation, ...

— Ephesians 6:17 (NKJV)

"And whoever will not receive you,
when you go out of that city,
shake off the very dust from your feet
as a testimony against them."

— Luke 9:5 (NKJV)

There's a painful playground experience that most children have suffered from at one time or another: Two captains are supposed to select teams from among a group of children. The quick, athletic kids are picked first, and the process slows down a lot after only unskilled youngsters are left. Sometimes hurtful comments are made (like "Don't take Joe. He's a loser.") that sting for years to come.

In similar fashion, some boy-girl activities may display similar preferences for some children over others. School dances may involve lots of girls congregating on one side of the room waiting to be asked to dance. Boys may size up the girls' appearances like examining so much merchandise, and the same girls are asked to dance again and again while some other girls aren't asked. The wiser unasked girls often overcome this painful ritual by dancing with one another.

At large family gatherings, parents brag about their children, and those who don't compare favorably to their siblings and cousins come to see themselves as second-class members of the family. Sometimes those who aren't so well esteemed misbehave to attract attention that makes them feel better.

In the classroom, it's easy to feel rejected. The kids who don't know the answers try to avoid being called on. If the teacher isn't very kind and encouraging, even those with the correct answers will keep quiet.

It's easy to imagine that some similar rejection will follow when you approach someone to share your testimony. You may imagine that the person will brusquely tell you to go away. If you choose to feel rejected, such a reaction could cut you to the quick.

What happens during such an encounter is a poor reflection of the underlying reality: Some people may not want to hear about your faith, but simply sharing what Jesus has done for you may plant a seed that can later sprout into faith and eventually lead to Salvation. Even the person who acts rudely today may later feel guilty for having treated you badly. Many people who refuse to speak to a person handing out a testimony later decide to read the testimony and are moved to receive Salvation. As a result, you should go into those situations with optimism in representing Jesus by doing His will.

Much more often than being rude, people respond politely. The kinder you are in treating the person well, the more likely you are to be well received.

It's helpful to think about what any rejection means in advance: The lost person is rejecting Christ Jesus, not you. As long as you are doing His will, your efforts will be fruitful according to His plan.

Perhaps it will help you to imagine that you are offering free samples of a delightful new product. Some people just won't want to try the product even if they would like it. Those who reject the offering in such circumstances are making a mistake, not making an authoritative rejection of the offering and the person presenting it. People who are making such mistakes deserve your sympathy and understanding. Shake it off and approach the next person!

Overcome Fear of Talking to Strangers

And take ... the sword of the Spirit,
which is the word of God; ....

— Ephesians 6:17 (NKJV)

Let Him take His rod away from me,
And do not let dread of Him terrify me.
Then *I would speak and not fear Him,*
But it is not so with me.

— Job 9:34-35 (NKJV)

After writing and passing out your testimony, there comes a time when the next step for becoming a complete, continual witness is to speak to a stranger. Many people find such a prospect to be daunting. Even those who do more witnessing than most members at Jubilee Worship Center told us that speaking to strangers about their faith was something they would prefer to avoid.

When you were young, your parents and teachers probably told you to be careful around strangers. Surveys show that such warnings create exaggerated concerns about dangers that strangers present: Most people don't realize they have more reason statistically to expect violence from a family member than from strangers.

Think about how context affects your reactions. If you meet a stranger who is working at an amusement park, you'll probably exchange pleasantries with hardly a second thought. Put that same person in a dark alley at midnight when you don't expect to see anyone, and fear may shake you.

One way you can reduce fear of speaking to a stranger is to improve your context. For instance, become accustomed to witnessing to strangers in company with people you know well in observably safe conditions. JWC regularly sponsors outreaches where a dozen or more people may be involved in witnessing during activities such as car washes, block parties, and car shows. In those surroundings, you can observe how others speak to strangers and how the strangers respond.

After you see that there is no physical danger or little likelihood of an unpleasant encounter, you can try your hand at doing the same things in the same company and settings. With enough experience, you'll soon feel confident enough to approach people who visit your church or church activity and appear to be hurting.

If you don't yet feel confident enough to approach strangers outside of a church outreach or at church, ask another member of your congregation to go with you when you first speak about your faith to strangers in other locations. If having a witnessing companion doesn't seem to help, visit with your in-congregation evangelist to discuss the concerns you have about speaking to strangers. The evangelist may be able to provide other nonthreatening, safe ways to gain witnessing experience and confidence.

Be gentle with others and yourself, and you'll make fine progress. Pray to God for His guidance when you are about to encounter someone who is a stranger. The Holy Spirit will help you to feel more confident about what to do and will let you know what to say.

Overcome Fear of Looking Foolish

> *... praying always with all prayer*
> *and supplication in the Spirit,*
> *being watchful to this end with all perseverance*
> *and supplication for all the saints — ....*

— Ephesians 6:18 (NKJV)

> *We* are *fools for Christ's sake,*
> *but you* are *wise in Christ!*

— 1 Corinthians 4:10 (NKJV)

Some Christians are embarrassed to be around those who are extremely bold in proclaiming their faith, such as those who spend hours in aggressive street ministry getting attention with loud bull horns. In our surveys of JWC members, some people told us that they didn't want to be seen by lost people as aggressive witnesses. We got the impression that these may be people who also don't like to be around aggressive salespeople.

Rather than fearing looking foolish, you should be glad when a foolish appearance attracts the interest of unsaved people. That can be one way that God will help lead them to Him. After all, children spend more time looking at circus clowns during a performance than at the imposing-looking security guards who surround the clowns. In 1 Corinthians 4:10, the Apostle Paul spoke positively about being a fool for Christ's sake because being a fool had helped save souls of Corinthians, making them wise in Christ. What's the harm of a little foolishness that serves a good purpose?

You need to focus on what He will think of you, not what other people may think or do. Here's a point that will help you appreciate that perspective: When you are focused on your own feelings rather than on the person you are witnessing to, you aren't being a complete witness. Think about getting dressed to go out for the day. While examining yourself in the mirror and adjusting your clothes, how much of your attention is on God?

Imagine instead that you work as an Emergency Medical Technician (EMT). Your priority should be to stabilize any person who is in danger of dying until you can take the person to a physician. If you aren't sure what to do, you will call a physician at the hospital and ask for directions. In any case, you need to move quickly, unconcerned about how others perceive you or your appearance.

When it comes to being a witness for Jesus, you are acting as an EMT for endangered souls. If the unsaved people around you don't get your help before they die, there will be no hope for them unless someone else becomes a witness to them. Remember that while you aren't God, you aren't Jesus, and you aren't the Holy Spirit, you can call on all of Them to help you witness by praying and listening to the still, small voice within. Then, do whatever it takes to deliver spiritual first aid to those souls.

How do you think that someone will feel about you after receiving Salvation? Undoubtedly, the person will feel grateful that you cared and were obedient in helping regardless of what initial reaction to you he or she may have had.

Overcome Fear of Making a Mistake

... and for me, that utterance may be given to me,
that I may open my mouth boldly to make known the mystery of the gospel, ...
that in it I may speak boldly, as I ought to speak.

— Ephesians 6:19-20 (NKJV)

Who can understand his errors?

— Psalm 19:12 (NKJV)

If you are a conscientious person, you may be concerned about doing more harm than good in witnessing to a lost person. Some people avoid medical and nursing careers because they don't want the responsibility of life-and-death decisions. When it comes to witnessing, these are praiseworthy but mistaken concerns.

When someone has an accident that will lead to death without immediate treatment, even unprepared, ignorant people will try to help. Why? It's clear that inaction will lead to bad results; any partially helpful action can help. Under those circumstances, a mistaken attempt to help may have no worse effect than taking no action. It's hard to feel guilty about trying under those circumstances.

All unsaved people's souls are headed for a painful end. And no one except God knows when their deaths may come. An automobile accident can take anyone's life. Surely, it's better to take some action before they die and are condemned to that painful end, even if mistakes do occur.

By applying the process for becoming a complete, continual witness that we have been describing, you also don't have much chance of making mistakes. While writing a testimony, you can solicit suggestions from those who have already written testimonies. Your testimony will be reviewed with those who are affected before you share the testimony with anyone else. Before publishing your testimony, you can review your draft with many experienced witnesses. Before speaking about your testimony, you can practice describing it to fellow Christians based on what you have written. When you are preparing to discuss your testimony with unsaved people, you can practice at first with more experienced witnesses around you for moral support and to gain ideas for improvement.

If you are worried about not remembering the Bible verses you want to share, just put the ones you need in your written testimony where you can easily refer to them. Look at the verses in Appendix A for possible inclusion in your testimony.

If you want to feel more confident about being able to describe why Salvation is truly available, we encourage you to read and become familiar with describing the information in Appendix E about the importance of Christ's resurrection and ascension.

You should also remember that Salvation occurs through the Holy Spirit. Any mistake can easily be corrected by the Holy Spirit.

In addition, a new Christian isn't yet a fully sanctified Christian (someone who lives as much as possible like Jesus). Through regular church attendance, Bible studies, and prayer, new Christians will also learn more about their faith. Any remaining mistakes you made during witnessing will be identified and corrected then.

Overcome Fear of Submitting to God

Oh, how great is *Your goodness,*
Which You have laid up for those who fear You,
Which *You have prepared for those who trust in You*
In the presence of the sons of men!

— Psalm 31:19 (NKJV)

As soon as they hear of me they obey me;
The foreigners submit to me.

— Psalm 18:44 (NKJV)

Lost people usually like the idea of being forgiven for their sins and gaining eternal life in heaven. Enthusiasm for Salvation may wane, however, when a witness first explains that being saved means turning your life over to Jesus and following Him. Having just started to get acquainted with Him, how does an unsaved person know to trust Jesus for all eternity?

You've probably had bad experiences with people who have asked you to trust them. You may be even less trusting of those who speak the most about deserving trust.

When a lost person realizes all the things he or she isn't doing that Jesus commands, it can become pretty frightening. After all, that person knows he or she is a sinner. Won't he or she just keep sinning after receiving Salvation?

Those who have been saved know that God immediately changes you so that sin isn't as appealing any more. You also have spiritual resources to help you such as prayer, the baptism of the Holy Spirit, and faithful people in your church.

You appreciate that changing bad habits takes time; you are always a work in progress in being sanctified. As you become more obedient, you feel more of His strength, love, and peace.

Witnessing is one of the ways that people who have trouble submitting to God can realize that they have more work to do in building their faith. Witnessing is the second greatest gift that God gives us after Salvation, yet most people won't submit enough to Him to find that out and gain those benefits.

When you were young, your parents may have encouraged you to try new foods and experiences. At the time, you may not have initially liked what you tried, but chances are that you later developed strong preferences from some of those trials.

If you love God, similarly give Him the benefit of the doubt and start trying ways to witness that you haven't done before. You'll find that they are much more desirable and less frightening than you now believe.

When you get past the enemy's lies about witnessing (and the enemy has a strong interest in keeping you quiet and invisible), you'll find that trying new forms of witnessing is like coming into a beautiful garden, one filled with flowering souls that respond to your thoughtful writing, comments, and love-inspired tending. Some people describe being a complete, continual witness as being the closest we can come on Earth to reentering the Garden of Eden. Now that's surely a place you would like to visit, isn't it?

How do we, your authors, know these things about doing more witnessing? We asked witnesses at Jubilee Witness Center what advice they would have for those who either don't witness or don't witness very often. They said, "Get started. You'll like it." Now that's pretty clear advice, isn't it?

†

In Chapter 7, you can learn how to take your new fearless attitude and effectively use a variety of witnessing tools to become a complete, continual witness. Feel free to return to Chapter 6 for guidance whenever you find witnessing is making you feel afraid or you want to be reminded of what to say to others who aren't witnessing because of fear.

Chapter 7

Reveal the Light of the Holy Spirit

Prepare and Provide
Powerful Witnessing Tools
for All Christians to Use

Fools, because of their transgression,
And because of their iniquities, were afflicted.
Their soul abhorred all manner of food,
And they drew near to the gates of death.
Then they cried out to the LORD in their trouble,
And He saved them out of their distresses.
He sent His word and healed them,
And delivered them *from their destructions.*
Oh, that men *would give thanks to the LORD* for *His goodness,*
And for *His wonderful works to the children of men!*
Let them sacrifice the sacrifices of thanksgiving,
And declare His works with rejoicing.

— Psalm 107:17-22 (NKJV)

Witnessing Christians who have settled into comfortable religious routines may doubt that they need to do more or different kinds of witnessing. In believing that they know exactly how to witness and are properly doing so, Christians can be just as guilty of ignoring His intentions for Christian witnessing as are the lost in rejecting Salvation.

We, your authors, were reminded of the need to try new witnessing methods in 2008 after the evangelist, Wilfred Andabwa of Kenya, visited Nigeria and explained to pastors there how to use different tools to be more effective in witnessing. Many of the hundreds of pastors who attended his trainings immediately began to apply what they had learned.

Here is a report from a pastor that made us realize how important it is to learn and apply helpful information about choosing and using tools correctly for witnessing:

> For thirty-five years in the ministry, I have not been seeing any change, and I have been asking God why my ministry was not growing. We did crusades. We did one-on-one evangelism.
>
> But our efforts were not effective until Evangelist Wilfred came to our town and taught different kinds of evangelism. From the teaching I understood that one-on-one evangelism using tracts and tapes could be very effective.
>
> I went back to my church and gave it a try.
>
> I could not believe it when I saw my church grow from 200 members to 650 in a period of four weeks. It was unbelievable!

Just think how many pastors and witnesses are eagerly praying for more souls to be saved but haven't tried any different witnessing tools or activities. This chapter is for them. You will do a good work when you share this chapter with pastors and witnesses who have a heart for the unsaved. We discuss suggested activities for preparing and sharing tools in the sequence that will be effective for most congregations.

Begin by Compiling and Sharing
a Library of Excellent Written Testimonies

Your testimonies also are *my delight*
And *my counselors.*

— Psalm 119:24 (NKJV)

In Chapter 5, we explain how each Christian should prepare a written testimony describing what the Lord has done in his or her life. Those are important instructions you need to apply: When all the elements we describe are present in a written testimony, lost people are more interested in learning about Salvation.

Many Christians will be tempted to skip writing a personal testimony, choosing instead to distribute Bible-based tracts. That "shortcut" is a mistake: A well-prepared individual testimony will help open more hearts than mass-produced Bible-focused tracts. How do we know? Thousands of witnesses have told us that personal testimonies work much better than Bible-focused tracts.

Here are some reasons why individual testimonies work better:

- Such testimonies usually come closer to addressing an unsaved person's issues on Earth than do more general tracts about Salvation.
- Sharing her or his trials and tribulations in a personal testimony provides more credible evidence that God is alive and helping people.
- Lost people are more impressed by testimonies from living people who have been helped by God than they are by Bible-based tales about long-dead people in faraway lands.
- Unsaved people usually find it easier to understand the language in a personal testimony than what they read in Bible-focused tracts.
- Written testimonies are more likely to be kept and read again than are Bible-focused tracts.
- When the person delivering the written testimony is able to say, "God helped me in this way" (whether or not he or she wrote the testimony), a lost person has to pause, question her or his beliefs, and reconsider living without Salvation.
- Written testimonies relate better to everyday experiences and thus invite more questions and remarks from an unsaved person than do general tracts.

By seeing how some pastors have expanded their churches in just a few weeks through simply passing out Gospel-based tracts and witnessing to lost people, we authors are in awe of the soul-stirring potential of instead sharing well-written personal testimonies with the unsaved. We expect that the soul-saving results of sharing testimony-based tracts will be still better after a church has created a library of member-written testimonies.

Such highly effective witnessing can occur after just a few church members have written their testimonies: One person's written experience can be a highly effective tool for thousands of witnesses with similar experiences. Praise God!

As we note in Chapter 5, churches should display libraries of written testimonies in their entrance halls, and witnesses should stock a few different testimonies in attractive containers on counters and tabletops in businesses and public buildings. By rotating which testimonies are placed in businesses and public buildings, a variety of written testimonies will be continually available to people who never come to church, and a lost person can eventually find a testimony that speaks directly to her or his heart.

Most Christians dedicate their lives to the Lord and accept Salvation when they are children, teenagers, or young adults. While young, most unsaved people prefer age-specific vocabularies applied to their interests and challenges. If you share written materials with young people that are aimed at forty-five-year-olds, you won't connect as well as you might. A well-written testimony that has been authored by a child, teenager, or young adult who faced the same life issues as a lost youth will seem like it was written just for them.

In an economically underdeveloped country, poor people who receive a testimony as a gift will feel they have been shown great generosity. Written materials of any kind are scarce. If the testimony has been translated into the local language, the impact of the thoughtfulness will be magnified. How can an unsaved recipient not pay serious attention?

Record and Share
Cassette Tapes, CDs, and MP3 Versions
of Written Testimonies

"But he who received seed on the good ground
is he who hears the word and understands it,
who indeed bears fruit and produces:
some a hundredfold, some sixty, some thirty."

— Matthew 13:23 (NKJV)

Everyone who uses tools knows that it's important to have specialized devices and gadgets designed for each task involved in a job, whether you are remodeling a bathroom or re-plumbing an old house. For instance, a screw can be better and more easily attached after you drill a screw hole. The same lesson about needing specialized tools for various tasks to complete a job well applies to witnessing.

Even in countries with advanced economies, many people don't read very well. In countries where schools are few, many poor people may be illiterate. People who can't read or read poorly can usually listen with fine understanding to a recording of a written testimony in their language. When you have a written testimony and a recording of it, you can communicate effectively with virtually everyone who knows that language.

In addition, many people who can read simply prefer to listen to new information rather than to read it. Recordings are especially useful for those who drive a lot and regularly listen to tapes or CDs while traveling. Other people like to listen to MP3 recordings while exercising. If you offer the right type of recording, you are much more likely to get the message across to these people. Recordings offer several other advantages over written testimonies:

- CDs and cassette tapes are perceived by recipients as being much more expensive than are tract-sized testimonies. As a result, people will feel like you've made more of a commitment to help them by giving such a recording.

- Witnessing recordings are listened to more often than written testimonies are read.
- With permission from the copyright holder, music can be added to a recording to deepen its emotional impact.
- Most people will remember a well-read recording better than a written testimony.
- Several people can listen to a recording at the same time.
- More testimonies can be put onto a recording than onto a tract-sized handout.
- Most people will retain a recording longer than a written testimony.
- A recording deteriorates more slowly than printed material does and can be passed along to many more people.

Recordings also provide a valuable opportunity to follow up in an impressive way with someone who has already received a written testimony. Here's how that might be done: Let's say that while providing the written testimony, you learned that the unsaved person has problems with bad feelings from having been sexually abused, is currently being treated for depression, and has a teenaged son who is an alcoholic. You can bring recorded testimonies about those subjects on your next visit to show your love and concern for the lost person.

In economically developing countries, a recorded gift of an audio cassette will be seen as very valuable by a poor person; such a gift is going to receive careful attention. In fact, the value of the gift has been viewed as so substantial that witnesses in some countries loan rather than give the recordings. This approach encourages unsaved people to listen sooner. Returning to retrieve the lent recording in three days then provides an opportunity to discuss Salvation while also reducing the costs of providing witnessing tools.

Recordings are also wonderful for reaching young people. Resonance is increased by hearing the voice of someone who is obviously of a similar age. Younger people are often more demonstrative in revealing their emotions and that can make the recording seem more genuine. When contemporary music is added, the young person's emotions can be strongly stirred.

Provide Collections of Written Testimonies in Books

Now when I looked,
there was a hand stretched out to me;
and behold, a scroll of a book was *in it.*

— Ezekiel 2:9 (NKJV)

Imagine that your favorite author walked up to you displaying a friendly smile and said, "I want to give you a copy of my brand new book." Wouldn't that be great?

Your pleasure would increase exponentially if he or she then took the time to inscribe and autograph the book. You would probably be telling about that experience for years to come. What could possibly inspire such a thoughtful and wonderful gift? It has to be a genuine liking for and interest in you. You know that you really count with that author!

How often has an author given you an autographed book that was inscribed to you? If you are like most people, you are waiting for your first one. It's a very rare occurrence to be treated with a gift that expresses such honor and generosity.

Now, imagine what it would be like to be an author who has avid readers and to provide joy to those readers. Sounds like fun, doesn't it?

When you put at least thirty written testimonies from your church's members into a book, you make it possible for testimony authors to enjoy witnessing more and to provide unsaved people with joyous experiences. With this book of testimonies in your hand, you can really make someone's day ... and eternity ... when your gift helps open the door to seeking Salvation from the Lord.

There's more good news: While few have ever seen a book filled with contemporary Christian testimonies about what God has done in peoples' lives, anyone who reads such a book will appreciate God's omnipresence, omniscience, and omnipotence in much more powerful ways. Reading a book of testimonies is an astonishing, faith-reinforcing experience for even the most committed and well-versed Christians.

Keep in mind that a book of testimonies can be either a general compilation or one aimed at a specific audience. For example, if you care about young souls, your church will produce a book of testimonies solely written by young people. That's a pretty cool witnessing tool, isn't it? Instead of reading autobiographies, biographies, or articles about young celebrities who don't follow Christ, young, unsaved people will have a chance to learn how great it is to be young, dedicated to God, and having Him fighting their battles.

Likewise, if your church has a heart for helping drug addicts, you could provide a book of testimonies by recovering addicts who have accepted Jesus Christ as their Lord, Savior, and healer. Similar compilations can be directed towards those who are alcoholics, are depressed, have troubled marriages, or are facing economic problems.

Imagine now that you are a person who has made a mess of your life. Everyone you know has preached to you about cleaning up your act, but they have usually done so in shrill and condescending ways. When someone gives you a book of relevant testimonies in a kind way, you realize that the giver cares about you just as you are, appreciates the difficulties you have been through, and wants you to know how lots of people have overcome the same kind of problems you have. The book's advice is appealing because it comes from the humble sinners who have repented: Such support may seem more loving than the way your family and friends have been talking to you. The greater the life challenge, the more you will appreciate understanding support that addressees your specific issue.

Imagine instead that you are a pastor of a small congregation whose membership has been declining for five years. You've tried everything you can think of, but you aren't helping to save many souls. You want to test out the ideas in this book. You decide to order copies of Jubilee Worship Center's (JWC) book of testimonies, *Real Life Stories*. Your congregation distributes the books to lost people and follows up every three days with those who accept the books. In two months, your congregation is substantially larger. You also realize that better results would follow if the books contained testimonies from your congregation. How long will you wait to add an in-congregation evangelist and start following the directions in this book?

Now consider being a pastor in a poor country who receives a book filled with testimonies as a gift. You realize that you have no current resources to create a book like this one. The stories amaze you, and you know they will astonish those who don't yet know about God's grace. You take the book with you to do street witnessing. After asking people what sorrows and difficulties they have in their lives, you read aloud the testimonies that address the issues. You return to the same location in three days to read other testimonies on different subjects. Your one-on-one witnessing becomes much more successful, and your ministry grows. In fact, you find that increased offerings allow you to spare a little money to print a few copies of the testimonies that seem most appealing to the lost you meet. When will you appoint your in-congregation evangelist and start preparing written testimonies from your congregation's members?

Put yourself in the shoes of someone who is committed to helping people gain Salvation. While reading a book of testimonies, you feel called to help your fellow Christians to develop and use such tools. How long will it take you to speak with your pastor about becoming an in-congregation evangelist or a fire starter (person who helps others learn about witnessing)?

If you haven't yet done this, we hope that reading this section will inspire you with an irresistible urge to write your personal testimony, create such a book with your fellow congregants, and begin sharing the book with unsaved people.

Prepare and Share
Audio and Video Recordings and Photographs
of In-Congregation Evangelists' Activities

"For I have given you an example,
that you should do as I have done to you."

— John 13:15 (NKJV)

Recorded materials can contribute to people gaining Salvation in many ways. One important application is encouraging people to serve as in-congregation evangelists. Many people who feel called to take on that role will want to test the depth of that calling. What could be better for doing that than watching an in-congregation evangelist at work?

Some pastors may also be curious to know more about what it's like to have in-congregation evangelists. Observing how this role can be conducted may be very helpful for pastors and in-congregation evangelists in starting such activities in a church.

Jim and Carla Barbarossa have recorded many of their activities on behalf of JWC and other churches' congregations. From their audio and video recordings, you can see and hear what it's like to introduce the concept of complete, continual witnessing to a congregation, to share five-minute teachings about witnessing, and to call Christians to serve as in-congregation evangelists and fire starters. They have also made photographic records of outreach activities such as block parties, car shows, car washes, and Christmas gift wrapping to demonstrate how to organize these witnessing events. If you are interested in any of the recordings or the photographs, you can contact Jim and Carla at jim@step-by-step.org.

Perhaps the most delightful witnessing records are photographs of the shining faces of new Christians just after emerging from baptismal waters. At a second glance, you notice that the pastor is facing the new Christian, an in-congregation evangelist is holding one arm of the new Christian, and the new Christian's sponsoring witness is on the other side holding the other arm. You enjoy their beaming faces as well. After seeing a photograph of such joy on Earth, anyone would feel excited to witness and look forward to being part of such a baptismal event.

Opportunities to record important evangelism and witnessing activities are virtually endless. The more Christians who see such records, the more witnessing will follow. For instance, by twice a day playing a full set of five-minute teachings about witnessing, a new witness could benefit from morning and evening reminders of what needs to be done. When that concentrated study occurs, more focus will be on witnessing than when the subject is only considered at church.

At this time, we, as authors, don't know of any recordings done by churches other than JWC to capture the practice of in-congregation evangelism. As this book gains attention through the Lord's sponsorship of its message, in-congregation evangelism will become much more common. If some of those congregations record what their evangelists do, those experiences will be available to many more pastors, in-congregation evangelists, and witnesses. As a result, evaluations of different witnessing methods can be conducted so that each person can learn from everyone else who is encouraging witnessing or witnessing.

In the future, it may be appropriate to create libraries of witnessing-related audios, videos, and photographs to be used for training programs. With as much emphasis as JWC puts on witnessing, you would think that the demand to learn more about witnessing would have been satisfied long ago. We were pleased to discover that many people at JWC want in-depth training in separate classes to further develop their witnessing skills. That reaction is a great testimony to how attractive it is to witness effectively: It's such a God-given joy that you always want to do more and become more effective.

Cover the Earth
with Electronic Versions of Witnessing Tools
That Can Be Accessed on the Internet

"So He humbled you,
allowed you to hunger,
and fed you with manna
which you did not know
nor did your fathers know,
that He might make you know
that man shall not live by bread alone;
but man lives by every word
that proceeds from the mouth of the LORD."

— Deuteronomy 8:3 (NKJV)

As mentioned earlier, now is an astonishingly good time to be an effective witness for the Lord. You can place any witnessing tool onto an Internet site, and anyone with access to an Internet-connected computer can view, listen, or read the material at little or no cost. You can also make free telephone calls over the Internet to virtually anyone with access to a connected computer. When you use these electronic distribution methods for witnessing, cost is no longer a limitation for reaching over one billion of the Earth's people. In the relatively near future, the number of people who can be reached in these inexpensive ways will increase by several more billions. To us, as authors, this opportunity is an enormous gift from God.

To show our commitment to this concept, both JWC and Step-by-Step Ministries have posted free electronic copies of this book on their Web sites. We hope that through these electronic libraries many more Christians will become complete, continual witnesses within congregations dedicated to serving the Lord in this way. In addition, pastors, in-congregation evangelists, and fire starters can lead distance learning classes about witnessing over the Internet. We hope that many gifted teachers will take advantage of these opportunities to build on what we are sharing in this book.

We also have a vision for an enormous online library of written and recorded testimonies where unsaved people can easily search out and find testimonies that address their concerns and issues about Salvation. Perhaps some witnesses will also be willing to share their e-mail addresses with lost people who want to pose questions. In this way, direct witnessing can reach a global scale for millions of people who write and record testimonies. And because online written materials can increasingly be quickly translated into many other languages through the use of software, many more people who read different languages than a testimony is written in will be able to understand about how God has helped Christians.

All of these changes will help Christians to magnify God from their perceptions of His presence with them closer to His proper size and influence as the One who watches over everyone. It is hard to imagine a more wonderful calling than to help make Him more visible to all.

Experiment with New Witnessing Tools

"You are witnesses of these things."

— Luke 24:48 (NAS)

The Bible warns against false witnesses and witnessing falsely. You can also read those verses as encouragement to seek true witnesses and to witness truthfully. The Lord's apostles didn't have electronic recordings of His voice to share, but today recordings of witnesses' testimonies can be used to gain the attention of lost people. That example should stimulate questions about what other ways of witnessing may be effective in helping unsaved people find the Lord.

With so many families having video recorders, there may come a time when it will be possible to put together video versions of testimonies that let lost people see and hear the witness before and after Jesus did His work in their lives. Should that be the case, witnesses may need help from Christians who have recently studied video communications or who are video professionals to prepare and edit the videos.

It may also be possible to take written and recorded testimonies and to turn them into dramatized readings in other languages where the local culture favors the oral traditions. A simple version of this can be done by selecting appropriate people to read translated written testimonies.

We, your authors, do not intend to lay out an agenda here. Our purpose is simply to encourage you to pray for guidance about other ways that testimonies can be made into more powerful witnessing tools for unsaved people. If you find a new way to witness or raise funds using existing or new types of tools, we hope you'll share your experiences with us so that we can learn from what you have done.

Employ Effective Fund-Raising Methods so That Enough Witnessing Tools Will Be Available

"The works that I do in My Father's name,
they bear witness of Me."

— John 10:25 (NKJV)

Would you want a soul to remain lost for lack of a tool? Of course, you wouldn't. Your reaction is all the more understandable because producing the tools covered in this chapter isn't very expensive. Printed in substantial quantities, individual testimonies cost pennies each. Recorded in similar quantities, brief audio cassettes and CDs usually cost less than sixty cents apiece. Even paperback books of testimonies can cost much less than a dollar when printed in large quantities. When these tools are reproduced in less economically developed countries, the costs can be substantially lower.

However, for complete, continual witnesses, the costs of sharing witnessing tools add up. When you distribute fifteen tracts, five audio tapes, three CDs, and twelve books of testimonies, the total cost of those tools is about $14.00. A complete, continual witness could easily distribute that many tools in a single day. Someone who is stocking gift displays in busy stores and public buildings could distribute tools costing more than $100 in a day.

There would be no need to raise funds for tools if each person simply paid the cost of what she or he shared. Unfortunately, many witnesses aren't able to afford the number of tools that God has called them to share with the lost. This limitation is particularly true of youngsters in poor families, young Christians who are in a prime position to reach many unsaved people at an age when decisions to accept Christ are often made.

We, your authors, have observed a kind of reverse correlation here: Many people with lots of money to pay for tools don't seem to distribute very many while those with little money are able to make good use of tools costing in excess of their incomes. In such a circumstance, it seems like one way the Lord can provide is by moving the hearts of those who can afford offerings above the tithes they provide to their churches to pay not only for the witnessing tools they use … but to also make offerings for tools to be used by those who cannot afford to buy enough witnessing tools.

Some witnesses may be a little careless about using witnessing tools: For example, they might share witnessing tools but never follow up to answer questions and to see what other tools are needed. All witnesses should know what witnessing tools cost as a way of encouraging good stewardship of the resources being employed.

How can any shortfall in funds for tools be made up? You should first pray for guidance about what to do. Beyond that, there is no single answer that fits all situations. One helpful next step in most circumstances will be to alert your congregation when both the supply of funds to purchase witnessing tools and stocks of tools are low. Sharing that information will help alert someone who has been blessed by the Lord with extra resources at that time that making an offering for this purpose would be a good idea.

At JWC, there is a special offering box for witnessing tools and outreaches located on the floor near the pulpit. During the time when tithes and offerings are received, members are asked to place additional offerings in this box.

After your congregation has been actively and effectively witnessing using these tools for a few months, your congregation's size and financial contributions should be rising. If new members are being well discipled, these new Christians will realize that they should be tithing and making additional goodwill offerings to help provide tools. Some of the increased funds might be earmarked to pay for witnessing tools.

There's a good parallel to a farmer who buys high quality seed in the spring in order to be able to produce a bountiful crop in the fall. With enough witnessing tools planted as spiritual seed and wise care given to those who receive the tools, it should be possible to create crops of newly saved souls attending church in due season. When that occurs, increased tithes and offerings should greatly exceed the cost of the tools that were needed to help new Christians find the Lord.

Some pastors and in-congregation evangelists may prefer to ask for a special offering to make witnessing tools available. If that is the direction you decide to go, be aware that an actively witnessing congregation of one hundred people can probably make good use of $25,000 worth of witnessing tools a year. On a per-person basis, that's about $20 a month.

Other congregations may wish to review other ways they financially support witnessing and to substitute having an in-congregation evangelist and using witnessing tools for some of those activities. This substitution should eventually result in enough of an increase in funds to reinstate financial support for some of the other witnessing-related activities.

We haven't produced a tool yet to guide you in raising funds for witnessing tools, but we hope that the suggestions in this chapter will provide some useful ideas for your prayers. In praying, always remember that God, the Maker of the universe, can easily provide whatever is needed as He did in providing manna to the Israelites after they fled Egypt. There is no reason to fear lack of support for witnessing from God. In fact, it may well be that the inspiration to become complete, continual witnesses is one of the ways that the Lord intends for a congregation to gain the financial resources needed to pay for all of its Godly activities.

†

In Chapter 8 you can learn more details about how to spread helpful information about active witnessing to people around the world. In the process, you will be able to help the Lord recruit more willing workers who will make good use of the tools for helping the lost that we have been discussing in this chapter.

Chapter 8

Share the Good News of
Active Witnessing in All Nations

Reach and Equip
as Many Willing Workers as Possible

So then neither he who plants is anything, nor he who waters,
but God who gives the increase.
Now he who plants and he who waters are one,
and each one will receive his own reward
according to his own labor.
For we are God's fellow workers;
you are God's field, you are God's building.

— 1 Corinthians 3:7-9 (NKJV)

Christians who live in the United States can easily forget how much witnessing is needed in parts of the world where there are few Christians. Despite almost two thousand years having passed since Jesus was resurrected and rose to heaven, sections of some nations are almost as untouched by knowledge of Him as they were when He walked the Earth.

A Christian can feel pretty isolated while surrounded by a crowd of people who worship idols or false gods or when living in a country where the government prohibits any kind of worship. To expect Christians under such circumstances to learn and practice complete, continual witnessing without ongoing help is overly optimistic.

Through Jim and Carla Barbarossa's efforts, Step by Step Ministries (http://www.step-by-step.org) has been blessed to learn that the Lord has generously provided a powerful way to expand His body of witnesses even where Christians are a small part of the community. In many nations, He has raised up pastors and evangelists who can quickly learn to be complete, continual witnesses. Some of these spiritual leaders can help vast numbers of other pastors learn how to be complete, continual witnesses and decide to add those who are called to be in-congregation evangelists to help their congregations learn how to witness. For God's plan that all be saved, pastors and evangelists who can help others learn to be complete, continual witnesses need to allocate a substantial amount of their time to helping other pastors and in-congregation evangelists learn.

In the following sections, you can learn how more willing witnesses can be reached and equipped so that your church can understand how to help create similar results both in your country and in all other nations.

Meetings in Cyberspace

Therefore we ought to support such men,
so that we may be fellow workers with the truth.

— 3 John 1:8 (NAS)

How do pastors and in-congregation evangelists meet their counterparts in other nations? One way is to attend Christian conferences that are held around the world. Few people will do that: It's time consuming and expensive to travel; the bed at home is a better place to sleep; there are a lot of pressing responsibilities where they are; and then there may be language barriers.

But God always has a way to be sure His will is done. In this case, He has provided the Internet, online search engines, an increasing number of people who understand English, and software translation programs that provide unprecedented opportunities for Christians to reach across oceans to grasp hands in friendship and mutual support for increasing complete, continual witnessing.

Let us explain how to take advantage of these opportunities. To get started in advancing complete, continual witnessing in other nations, put up a blog (directions for a free one can be found at https://www.blogger.

com/start) or a Web site (directions for a free one can be found at http://www.webs.com) that shares the lessons that you have learned from your experiences and this book. Software robots from search engine providers will automatically locate your pages and index your content so others can find it.

When a pastor wants to learn more about witnessing, the pastor can rely on a software-based search engine to locate your content. If the description sounds interesting enough, a click of a computer mouse sends the pastor to your information. If what you've written is in English and the pastor only speaks Arabic, the pastor can choose to employ software translation programs that will make your content available in seconds.

In most cases, the person who reads your information will be interested in witnessing. Often the seeking person will arrive at your blog or Web site with a prior agenda that's somewhat different from following the program we have been describing to you. Perhaps he or she is doing one-on-one evangelism and needs funds to travel to new areas. Or this may be a person who needs large-print Bibles for people with poor eyesight.

A relationship with the seeking person can be built by first understanding what the seeker is interested in. Then you should do whatever you can to help the person: pray for the person's efforts, suggest the person contact a resource that helps those with that particular need, or, if appropriate, send some financial help. You should pray over the requests and decide what God wants you to do.

In some cases, you will be able to help serve the request by directing the person toward information about becoming a complete, continual witness. For example, if someone decides to become an in-congregation evangelist, Jim and Carla recommend a special evangelism package they offer (available for purchase at http://www.step-by-step.org/specialpackage.html). Anyone who orders the package can also call them, and Jim and Carla will make themselves available to be mentors. You should feel free to direct people with that interest to this resource.

Jim and Carla Barbarossa do one additional thing for those who want to become complete, continual witnesses but cannot afford to purchase witnessing tools: They ask for the person's physical address and send along a box of materials about witnessing. Such a first shipment might include a copy of *Real Life Stories*, some personal testimony tracts, a DVD of a witnessing conference for pastors and in-congregation evangelists, and a few CDs of five-minute teachings about witnessing. Based on the exact nature of the person's interests, other materials may supplement this information.

Jim and Carla take the time and spend the money to send these packages by air, rather than saving a little money by using ocean freight (which may delay delivery by several months). Within a day or two after the box is received, they usually receive an astonished e-mail from the seeker who describes what a life-changing experience it has been to learn about this way of witnessing and the methods presented for helping others to learn about witnessing.

However the first contact occurred, e-mails then wing back and forth as the fortunate purchaser or recipient asks about how to apply this new learning and Jim and Carla answer. Some who make contact are not pastors and are directed to speak with their pastors about serving as in-congregation evangelists. Others are pastors looking for guidance in identifying someone with the gift to be an in-congregation evangelist. Some are pastors who are very active as evangelists, want to start implementing the program, and ask Jim and Carla to send some witnessing tools to help. Jim and Carla offer many such tools on their Web site, http://www.step-by-step.org. If the person cannot afford to purchase tools, Jim and Carla pray over the need and do what they can to help in a loving way.

A second package containing multiple copies of witnessing tools may soon be winging its way to a foreign land. Upon receipt, some pastors and in-congregation evangelists will also offer to translate the materials into local languages. In this way, the Step by Step materials have gradually become available to many more people. Many opportunities remain for such translations to be made.

Jim and Carla ask the people who receive witnessing tools to send photographs of those who are saved along with their personal testimonies. Within just a few days, wonderful baptismal photographs arrive by e-mail accompanied descriptions of repentance and heartfelt acceptances of the Lord Jesus.

In most cases, the testimonies are brief and don't follow the suggestions we laid out for you in creating an effective personal testimony. We hope that these new Christians will read and apply our instructions in the future so they can have tracts, recordings, and books to share with lost people based on their own experiences.

These heartfelt, brief testimonies can be very eloquent and moving. We have been touched to learn about people in their eighties who were saved after having never heard of Jesus before. The repentances of children from their sins often show beautifully innocent hearts. If you would like to see photographs and read testimonies of people who have gained Salvation after tract and tape outreaches outside the United States, please visit http://www.step-by-step.org/testimonies.html.

In many cases, the newly saved in foreign lands describe that they feel threatened by hostility from their friends and families who adhere to different beliefs. In fact, some new Christians experience immediate repercussions such as having financial support from parents for school be cut off. In many ways, these reports read like how the apostles expanded the early church in Acts. Our hearts, love, and prayers go out in support of those facing these trials.

If someone has been productive in using witnessing tools, Jim and Carla will do what they can to supply more witnessing tools or to pay for materials to be prepared in that country. As proof of how the funds are employed, the pastors and in-congregation evangelists often send photographs of themselves standing next to mountains of tracts and tapes. It's exciting to think about all the good that those tools will do after being presented by willing, loving witnesses. If you would like to read reports of these outreaches from different countries, please go to http://www.step-by-step.org/tapetractwhy.html.

Naturally, the route to becoming a complete, continual witness for someone who is a pastor or evangelist will be different from one instance to another. For churches in or near the United States, Jim and Carla may spend a few days on location teaching the congregation to help prepare the spiritual soil for creating a church full of complete, continual witnesses.

How have all these cybermeetings affected lost people? With God's blessings, Jim and Carla have been able to assist pastors and evangelists whose efforts have helped thousands of souls be saved. What a wonderful harvest this is for the Lord!

What are the economics of providing such witnessing tools? In some lesser developed countries one thousand tapes and CDs could be made for as little as $220 in 2008. After being shared by complete, continual witnesses, some pastors have indicated that as many as five hundred people can gain Salvation from that many tools. Of those five hundred saved people, three hundred to four hundred (depending on the country) will continue to walk with the Lord and become members of a church. Clearly, God has lovingly blessed this activity: Otherwise, such a small amount of money could not possibly create such a wonderful result.

Let's look at these economics on the scale of what a church can accomplish. Imagine that one hundred people from a church make an additional offering of $10 a month to pay for witnessing tools in foreign countries. That's $12,000 a year. You couldn't support a foreign missionary with that little money, but you could pay for enough witnessing tools to be used by complete, continual witnesses in foreign lands to potentially lead more than twenty thousand people to Salvation. Now, wouldn't that be a wonderful thing for the members of a single church to accomplish through reaching other nations with His promise of Salvation?

Let's think bigger than that to better understand God's plan: What could forty thousand churches accomplish with a similar effort? Let's assume that the success rate in helping lost people gain Salvation dropped by 50 percent to make the example more conservative. That would lead to five hundred million additional people receiving Salvation each year, more than the population of all but a few countries. Continue that effort for eight years, and an additional four billion people gain Salvation following these efforts. Fulfilling God's plan that all be saved is just that close to fruition. Are you excited? Are you ready to take action?

Let's look at some individual cases to learn how these heavenly blessings have occurred in different countries through effective leadership by evangelists and pastors who have been supported by effective witnessing tools. We start our tour in sub-Saharan Africa by visiting Kenya.

Keen in Kenya

Behold, God is my salvation,
I will trust and not be afraid; ....
Therefore with joy you will draw water
From the wells of salvation.

— Isaiah 12:2-3 (NKJV)

Evangelist Wilfred Andabwa initially contacted Jim Barbarossa by e-mail in March 2005. After much correspondence, Evangelist Andabwa started a tract-and-tape outreach on Sunday, July 8, 2005. His supply of witnessing tools for this initial outreach consisted of four tapes, three CDs, and five Gospel tracts (if you would like to see one of these tracts, go to: http://www.step-by-step.org/tracts.html) that Jim and Carla provided through Step by Step Ministries. By sharing the tapes, CDs, and tracts, Evangelist Andabwa reported that approximately one hundred fifty people gained Salvation during this first mission. Let the glory be to God!

Evangelist Andabwa recently reported that he believes that tract-and-tape outreach is the best way for believers to witness to the lost. His reasons for believing so include the following:

- The tools are easy to use: It's very easy to tell someone "I have a gift for you," and few can refuse a free gift.
- Once read or listened to, these tools work well because the messages are very clear, brief, compassionate, and relevant.
- The cost is low because the same tools can be used more than once with different people.

In the three years since starting this outreach, Evangelist Andabwa says that tens of thousands of souls have been saved after sharing tracts and tapes. He estimates that over 60 percent of these new

Christians have been baptized and joined a church. As proof, he reports that more than fifty churches have been established to serve new Christians who gained Salvation through the outreach efforts. As a result, his ministry is one of the fastest growing in Kenya.

Before using tracts and tapes, Evangelist Andabwa relied on crusades. He still conducts crusades but obtains better results from the tract-and-tape outreaches.

Since crusades are often organized by churches, most of the people who come are already Christians. From the crusades, only a small percentage of those who are newly saved become baptized (20 percent) and stay in church (5 percent). One reason is that after someone is saved through a crusade, you often don't have a way to follow up with that person. Someone who you meet through tract-and-tape outreach can be easily contacted again, as often as need be, because you know where she or he lives or works.

Evangelist Andabwa sees many other advantages for tract-and-tape outreaches compared to crusades:

- Less preparation is required.
- Scheduling is easier and more flexible.
- You reach people who would never attend a crusade.
- A minimum number of people are needed to conduct the activity.
- More contact occurs with people who aren't saved.

Evangelist Andabwa described the witnessing process that he uses as follows:

Matthew 28:19-20 (NKJV): "Go therefore and make disciples of all the nations, baptizing them in the name of the Father and of the Son and of the Holy Spirit, teaching them to observe all things that I have commanded you; and lo, I am with you always, *even* to the end of the age."

The word "Go" means to step out from our comfort zone and reach outside. That's why we use most of our time in prayers and going outside to reach the people where they are already gathered: markets, high schools, colleges, businesses, streets, slums from house to house, offices, remote areas where the Gospel has not yet reached, and unchurched areas (and planting churches there). In all these places we distribute free tapes or tracts to all the people that we meet.

We ask the lost if they can listen to the tape or read the tract over the next three days. Then we come back after three days to find out if they listened to our tape or read the tract. That's where the follow-up starts. We continue until by the grace of the Lord they are won to Christ.

As soon as they become children of God, we disciple them and train them how to go outside and witness. From my experience, new disciples are more effective and active in witnessing than those Christians who were saved long ago.

As impressive as these accomplishments are, Evangelist Andabwa feels like he is only scratching the surface. He has far more willing witnesses than he has witnessing tools to share with unsaved people. Here is his vision of what can be accomplished in Kenya:

If I had all the money that I need to buy tracts and tapes, many more people will be saved by the grace of the Lord through these tools; many more churches will be opened, the Kingdom would expand to fill Kenya in a very short period of time; and from Kenya, other parts of Africa would be reached.

If I had an unlimited supply of tracts and tapes, millions of people would be reached, and every year I would trust the Lord for one million souls to be saved in Kenya alone.

If you would like to contact Evangelist Andabwa, feel free to write to him at:

Evangelist Wilfred Andabwa
Box 9060-30100
Eldoret, Kenya
East Africa

You may also reach him by e-mail at wamps23470@yahoo.com.

Affecting All Africa

Be glad and rejoice,
For the LORD has done marvelous things!

— Joel 2:21 (NKJV)

In 2008, Evangelist Andabwa was called to share the good news about tract-and-tape ministries throughout Africa. With the assistance of Step by Step Ministries, Evangelist Andabwa began contacting pastors in other nations and offered to conduct on-site teachings about how to become complete, continual witnesses. One goal for this program was to see how many pastors and in-congregation evangelists could be affected by a single evangelist. At a minimum, it seemed likely that such trainings would help identify some pastors who would become complete, continual witnesses and lead many pastors and in-congregation evangelists in other African nations to do the same.

One of the first fruits of this calling was for Evangelist Andabwa to be invited to Nigeria, a country where Muslims outnumber Christians. Equipped with lots of witnessing tools, Evangelist Andabwa began his visit by teaching at four different churches daily for five days in Port Harcourt, leading up to a teaching in Aba Abia that was attended by a reported 435 pastors.

Like most man-made plans, this one soon proved to be inadequate to meet God's intent: Pastors and their congregations at the twenty churches were so enthusiastic for tract-and-tape outreach that Evangelist Andabwa gave away all of his witnessing tools except for a single tract and tape for each of the 435 pastors by the time he reached the final training session. Praying to the Lord for help, he was able to produce a second set of witnessing tools during the training and to distribute a few thousand of them before the 435 pastors returned to their congregations.

While the full effects of this training won't be known for some time, it's clear that it was a big success. One indication is that the pastors who sponsored the initial group training asked Evangelist Andabwa to return, promising that more pastors would attend the next training. As another indication, seventy-five days later a reported eight new churches had been established to serve new believers who received some of these tracts and tapes from willing witnesses.

At the beginnings of chapters 1 and 7 in this book are two stories describing how pastors transformed their churches by attracting newly saved people in Nigeria after applying what Evangelist Andabwa taught them. The combined results are even more impressive than the individual stories: The first twenty churches that used the witnessing tools helped lead hundreds of people to Salvation before Evangelist Andabwa returned to Kenya. Clearly, the lesson from the Lord is that it just takes a willingness to be obedient and some good witnessing tools for His will to be done in saving souls.

The scope of the opportunity revealed by Evangelist Andabwa's trip to Nigeria is truly awe-inspiring, a cause for rejoicing. Let's look at the economics required to support more of these willing workers. Jim Barbarossa estimates that Gospel-based tracts can be printed in most African countries very inexpensively. For example, a million tracts can be printed for about $6,000. As pointed out earlier, a small church could afford to support that level of annual investment in witnessing tools. It is hoped that you and your church will be moved to support some of these fertile witnessing efforts in Africa and else-where. Jim Barbarossa and Evangelist Andabwa can assist you in placing your resources into effective, willing hands.

One of the most exciting aspects of the African opportunity is that pastors there are extremely interested in supporting the development of congregations filled with complete, continual witnesses. With thousands of churches in a single nation employing these methods, God's intentions for saving souls will be followed in better ways than anyone has seen before.

By applying those lessons, the time needed to share information about Salvation to all who have not yet heard can be substantially reduced. For instance, in a nation like Nigeria where people are divided by religion among Muslims, Christians, and those who follow various kinds of witchcraft, there is a chance to develop a new community of peace after tens of millions choose to follow the Lord. Imagine how many Earthly problems would go away if most people were living in observant, loving Christian communities.

Malawi Matters

Commit to the LORD whatever you do,
and your plans will succeed.

— Proverbs 16:3 (NIV)

Before leaving Africa for now, let's take a look at another outstanding example of what complete, continual witnessing can accomplish. Pastor Lackson C. Likawa has been featuring tracts and tapes in his outreaches in Malawi since September 2, 2005. In that time, tens of thousands of people in Malawi have gained Salvation through these witnessing efforts. Pastor Likawa reports that about 95 percent of these new Christians have been baptized, joined a church, and continue to be faithful to the Lord.

Pastor Likawa began these efforts when his congregation consisted of only ten members. Today, the church has sixty members and sixteen outstation churches. But those accomplishments are just the beginning: Pastor Likawa has established a vision of changing Malawi through complete, continual witnessing by 2015.

He has divided the African nation into fifty districts, each of which has a leader and a complement of at least ten witnesses. These willing workers are busy witnessing night and day. Their goal is to help lead 2,500,000 people in Malawi to Christ by 2015. All that's lacking is to have more witnessing tools.

In January 2008, Step by Step Ministries supplied $660 to Pastor Likawa who used the money to print one hundred thousand Gospel tracts. By the end of May 2008, tens of thousands of people were saved through witnesses who shared these tracts, and each new Christian provided a testimony. Clearly, there is a thirst for the Lord's living water in Malawi.

After this success, Pastor Likawa was called to share information about complete, continual witnessing with pastors in neighboring Mozambique. We pray that his efforts will soon bear fruit there as well.

If you would like to write to Pastor Likawa, he may be reached at:

Pastor Lackson C. Likawa
Tape and Tract Ministries
P.O. Box 20575
Luwinga
Mzuzu 2, Malawi

You may also reach him by e-mail at likawachingaipe@yahoo.co.uk.

Indomitable in India

For we ourselves were also once foolish, disobedient, deceived,
serving various lusts and pleasures,
living in malice and envy,
hateful and hating one another.
But when the kindness and the love of God
our Savior toward man appeared,
not by works of righteousness which we have done,
but according to His mercy He saved us,
through the washing of regeneration
and renewing of the Holy Spirit,
whom He poured out on us abundantly
through Jesus Christ our Savior,
that having been justified by His grace
we should become heirs
according to the hope of eternal life.
This is a faithful saying,
and these things I want you to affirm constantly,
that those who have believed in God should be careful
to maintain good works.
These things are good and profitable to men.

— Titus 3:3-8 (NKJV)

While a number of other African nations have promising programs to teach and practice complete, continual witnessing, we would like to take you to India to see the opportunity to witness from a different perspective. India is a country with rich spiritual heritages, but ones that are rarely based in the Christian faith. There are parts of India where you might travel all day and never meet a Christian.

Pastor Kranthi Paul Somavarapu in India has been working with Step by Step Ministries since August 22, 2006, to teach complete, continual witnessing. In such a populous country, the opportunities to serve the Lord are clearly huge, and Pastor Somavarapu is excited about what can be accomplished.

By the end of 2007, complete, continual witnessing using tracts and tapes helped lead thousands of people to choose Salvation. Of those new Christians, almost half were baptized by someone in the ministry.

In the course of this work, Pastor Somavarapu also taught these witnessing methods to other pastors, evangelists, and Christian leaders. As a result, there are now twenty-five district leaders who are willing to teach and organize complete, continual witnessing. For 2008, Pastor Somavarapu wanted to have one hundred thousand tracts and ten thousand tapes to distribute. With those resources, he believed that the Lord would lead fifty thousand souls to Salvation.

As you can see, the geometric rate of increase in activity is startling. Many people in India are being impressed that such outreach witnessing is better than crusades and traditional missionary activities. As soon as these complete, continual witnesses experience how well this method of evangelism works, they will want to do more of it. Having reached that point, the number of witnessing tools becomes the limit to growth in numbers of souls saved.

Here's an example: Pastor Somavarapu recently visited a pastor in the Paderu Mandle in Vizag district. Pastor Somavarapu invited the local pastor to join him for a day of evangelism, and the local pastor quickly agreed. They gave out tracts from house to house, from business to business, and from person to person in the streets. That evening, they conducted a Gospel meeting in the street on the message of "Do You Ever Feel That Something Is Lost in Your Life?" At the end of the meeting, twenty-seven people accepted the altar call. Praise God! Three weeks later, the local pastor called Pastor Somavarapu to share the good news that twenty-one of the new believers were attending his church. The local pastor invited Pastor Somavarapu to return with more tapes and tracts. When the local pastor learns to follow up after three days, the harvest will be much larger. This example shows the importance of using the correct methods for being a complete, continual witness. Most of the soul harvest is not yet in the storehouse because there has been no follow-up by the local pastor and his congregation.

Because India's people speak many different languages and dialects, there is also much work to be done in translating the Step by Step materials into information that all can understand. Local Christians are happy to take on that challenge.

Pastor Somavarapu has a vision for changing all of India in the same way that Pastor Andabwa foresees for all of Africa. With enough witnessing tools, Pastor Somavarapu will organize every district in India with pastors, evangelists, and Christian leaders to provide masses of complete, continual witnesses. What a wonderful prospect that is!

You can reach Pastor Somavarapu by writing to:

Pastor Kranthi Paul Somavarapu
PRINCE PRAYER HALL
Vengalarao nagar5th lane
Arundal Pet (post), Guntur-522002
Andhra Pradesh, South India

You may also reach him by e-mail at steavforjesus@yahoo.com.

Tapping Unreached People Groups

Then Paul stood in the midst of the Areopagus and said,
"Men of Athens, I perceive that in all things you are very religious;
for as I was passing through and
considering the objects of your worship,
I even found an altar with this inscription:
TO THE UNKNOWN GOD.

> *Therefore, the One whom you worship without knowing,*
> *Him I proclaim to you: ...."*

— Acts 17:22-23 (NKJV)

Step by Step Ministries has also worked with devoted pastors who are employing similar methods of witnessing in Pakistan and Uganda. Jim and Carla Barbarossa would like you to know about these pastors. Here is a little about their experiences. If you would like to know more about them and their activities, please contact Jim and Carla at jim@step-by-step.org.

From 1999 through 2004, Pastor Naomi Sadiq led an evangelism team in Pakistan using traditional methods such as crusades. From those efforts a few hundred people gained Salvation. Beginning in 2005, Pastor Sadiq and her team switched over to tape-and-tract witnessing, and thousands of people have been saved in each year since that revision occurred.

Pastor David Tisiburu operated in a single district of Uganda until 2007 when he began working with coordinators in every part of the country. Equipped with two hundred thousand tracts in 2007, Pastor Tisiburu was able to reach hundreds of thousands of people, and tens of thousands were saved. Some of the people who received the tracts took them to other countries, and many pastors would like to learn this form of witnessing form Pastor Tisiburu.

More of the world hasn't heard about the benefits of complete, continual witnessing than has. That means that the most promising territories for sharing His promise of Salvation probably haven't been found yet. What will be the reactions of China's hard-working people when they are allowed to learn about Christianity? How well will complete, continual witnessing work on small islands where people know one another well? When there are enough complete, continual witnesses, will followers of Allah accept the Lord Jesus instead? How will those who chase the idols of the world (such as material possessions, careers, popularity, appearance, drugs, alcohol, and improper sexual relations) respond when complete, continual witnesses explain about His forgiveness and peace?

Here is where you come in: You and your church can take the Lord's promises to people who otherwise wouldn't receive the wonderful benefits from complete, continual witnessing. As you learn to become a complete, continual witness, pray for guidance about how you should reach out to the world outside your country to bring the wonderful promise of Salvation to the unsaved.

We would like to support you in this God-directed work. Please let us know your plans and questions by contacting Jim and Carla Barbarossa at jim@step-by-step.org.

†

In Chapter 9, we explain more about how important it is to set a Godly example concerning complete, continual witnessing and describe how pastors can lead their congregations to save more of the lost.

Chapter 9

Set a Godly Example

How Pastors Can Lead Church Congregations
to Help Save More of the Lost

Like the cold of snow in time of harvest
Is a faithful messenger to those who send him,
For he refreshes the soul of his masters.

— Proverbs 25:13 (NKJV)

If you are a pastor, this chapter describes activities that may assist you in leading your congregation to help save more lost people. If you are not a pastor, you can read this chapter to learn information that may help your pastor be more effective in praying for guidance about improving your church's witnessing activities.

Consider Witnessing Perspectives

Only fear the LORD,
and serve Him in truth with all your heart;
for consider what great things
He has done for You.

— 1 Samuel 12:24 (NKJV)

In offering our suggestions, we, your authors, are very aware that there is no cut-and-dry formula for pastoral leadership concerning witnessing that is perfect for all. We have prayed for guidance on this point and have been guided by the Holy Spirit to share some ideas with you as a sign of our love and caring for you.

Let's start with thinking about the end time: Jesus will return for the Last Judgment. When He does, it will be too late to save those who have not received Salvation.

Knowing that there is a cutoff point for Salvation affects how believers approach witnessing. Some pastors see His return as imminent, based on comparing the events and sins going on around us with the book of Revelation. Only God knows if that perspective is true. If it is correct, there's certainly no time to waste in improving witnessing.

In considering this perspective, it should also be noted that believing in an extremely imminent return can be harmful to encouraging people to witness: Expecting the Last Judgment to come any day can become an excuse for a Christian to do nothing about lost people and the evils in the world.

Let's consider the alternative: Jesus Christ will not be returning soon. How does that possibility affect what should be done about helping congregations to witness more?

Many pastors who expect Him to return soon refer to the possibility of the world continuing as it is by saying, "Should Christ tarry …" That word "tarry" is an interesting choice. *Webster's New World Dictionary and Thesaurus* (Simon & Schuster, 1996) provides these definitions for tarry: "1. to delay; linger 2. to stay for a time 3. to wait." When the word is applied to an ordinary person, "tarry" usually suggests someone who is distracted enough to delay attending to other responsibilities. From that human perspective of "tarry," you could imagine Jesus enjoying heaven so much that He puts off bringing the Last Judgment.

Only God can know why Jesus has not yet returned, but it seems unlikely that He is tarrying because He is distracted. Could a possible reason for Jesus not returning soon be the opposite circumstance, that God is waiting to send Jesus because Christians are tarrying in wrong pursuits rather than doing His will concerning witnessing?

Let's consider for a moment the possibility that God might be waiting for the people of the Earth to do such a good job of following Jesus that little more can be accomplished by mere mortals in bringing the heavenly kingdom to Earth. From that perspective, the Last Judgment would be a final cleanup action by Christ to deal with the remaining sinners who will not be rescued by Salvation because these unsaved people are too hardhearted. That perspective is certainly consistent with His stated desire that all be saved.

While this is not a book of theology, nor are we suggesting that we have any idea when Christ will return, it seems curious to us that many Christians assign no possible role for themselves in influencing the timing of the Last Judgment. While only by God can the existence of such a potential human role in affecting when the Last Judgment occurs be revealed, it is clear here on Earth that all Christians can affect what happens at the Last Judgment through whether they help lost people understand and consider Salvation. The number of those who are condemned at that time will be more or less, depending on what each Christian does now. Until the Last Judgment comes, souls are being condemned whenever unsaved people die. That consequence should be considerable encouragement to do more witnessing now.

Isn't it interesting that regardless of personal views about when the end times will arrive, the conclusion is almost always the same? More witnessing should be done now.

Let's now look at a smaller perspective: We would like to suggest an additional way for pastors to think about the congregations God has given them. From this new perspective, a pastor's congregation includes those who attend the church and those who would attend if someone witnessed to them. When pastors look around in a church service, they should use their eyes of faith to see the large numbers of those who should be there and aren't. From that perspective, a church filled to overflowing with Christian worshippers may be sadly empty of lost people God wants to attend that church but who need a witness to bring them.

One way to discover how a church is doing from this perspective is to sponsor a free car wash in the church parking lot. When Jubilee Worship Center (JWC) conducted such an outreach recently, almost none of the dozens of visitors reported being saved or attending a church. Yet their travels brought them by JWC on a Saturday. Presumably, they also knew how to get there on Sunday. Imagine that there were many other lost people who drove by who didn't have time for a car wash, had a clean car, or weren't hungry. It becomes clear that even with a very active witnessing program, only a small percentage of the neighbors, visitors, and passers-by are being reached by a church with many complete, continual witnesses. The size of the lost population in a church's vicinity is obviously much larger for congregations that don't do much witnessing.

What would happen if each pastor led the congregation to become acquainted with all the people who regularly work, visit, and live within a three-mile radius of the sanctuary?

- The congregation would know who was saved and who wasn't.
- Those who aren't yet complete, continual witnesses would understand how much witnessing needs to be done.
- Systematic efforts could be aimed at sharing the Good News with the nearby unsaved people.
- The needs of neighbors would be better understood so that appropriate ministries could be developed to serve those needs.
- Measurements could be used to assess how well the church is serving lost people in gaining Salvation so that more of what works for witnessing would be done to substitute for efforts that are ineffective.
- The church's light would shine brightly in that community, and everyone there would realize what a Godly example it was providing.

Some may despair of doing so much at once, especially after having paid little attention to many of these needs. Here's a suggestion: Start with a much smaller geographical radius and work outward. You could start with as little as the block where the church is located. If that is still too much as a first step, focus on teenagers and young adults in that block or an even smaller geographical area. Helping those people appreciate how to gain Salvation will open the door to gaining the resources and energy you need to accomplish everything else that you need to do.

We also suggest that a church share at least 10 percent of the resources available for witnessing tools and trainings with a church that is developing complete, continual witnesses in an economically underdeveloped area in your country or another nation. While that investment in helping to save souls may seem like a small one, many people are likely to gain Salvation through sharing your resources with an effective witnessing church that has many more witnesses than witnessing tools. At a small cost to your congregation, you can greatly increase witnessing and give more glory to God. What could be nicer?

If you have found these observations to be interesting, that's good, but please remember that we are not trying to prescribe a precise direction for you. Instead, we want to help you consider how your congregation could fulfill Christ's Great Commission in the most effective way. In the rest of this chapter, we outline some ideas for pastors to explore in deciding what will work best for their congregations.

Set Personal and Teaching Goals for Witnessing

Where there is *no vision, the people perish: ....*

— Proverbs 29:18 (KJV)

The familiar proverb could easily be rephrased to read, "Where *the pastor has* no vision for witnessing, many lost people miss the opportunity to gain Salvation." We, your authors, believe that few pastors have taken the time to describe goals for what they want to accomplish as personal witnesses and in helping others become more effective witnesses. Pastors, in-congregation evangelists, lay-ministry leaders, and members of the congregation will often be more effective after setting witnessing goals because the goals help them gain and keep focus to make consistent efforts.

Many people find it difficult to write goals for an activity. Without goals, it's easy to be inactive. If you doubt that observation, think about all the things you know you should be doing, but aren't. Do you have written goals that you review twice a day for those activities? In this section, we simplify the task of writing goals to make the process easier for you.

Start by defining what your personal and teaching goals for witnessing are. Title your statement of goals with something like "What I Intend To Do as a Witness in the Next Twelve Months." Keep in mind that brief goals are better than long ones. A goal statement that contains inspiring words will help motivate you to follow through. We encourage you to write goals that you feel God would be pleased to have you accomplish.

The elements of a good goal include what you will do, who will be affected, how they will be affected, when the effect will occur, where the actions will take place, and how much activity will be done. Let's look at an example of what a new Christian might have as a personal witnessing goal:

> I will joyfully share my written testimony
> with all of my family, friends, and co-workers
> and keep telling them about the Lord
> until they understand what Salvation is.

After one goal has been fulfilled, it's time to expand into a larger goal or additional goals. Someone who has become comfortable sharing a written testimony with people known to him or her might choose next to reach unsaved people she or he doesn't know. The expanded witnessing goal might read as follows:

> I will joyfully share my written testimony
> with three new people a week whom I don't know
> and keep telling them about the Lord
> until they understand what Salvation is.

After working on this goal for a few years, the witness may be ready to take on an expanded role, a role that includes helping others to become effective witnesses. The next expanded witnessing goals might be:

I will joyfully share my written testimony
with three new people a week whom I don't know
and keep telling about the Lord
until they understand what Salvation is, and
lovingly help one Christian a week to write a testimony.

From there, the person could later decide to do more of the same. The witness might work with four new people a week and assist six Christians a month to write their testimonies. Or new activities could be added. Here's an example of doing more of the same activities and adding a new activity:

I will joyfully share my written testimony
with four new people a week whom I don't know
and keep telling them about the Lord
until they understand what Salvation is,
lovingly help six Christians a month to write a testimony, and
provide one inspiring five-minute teaching a year
about witnessing to the congregation.

Whatever goal is selected, we recommend that it be written down and read each morning and evening. That will remind you of what you have committed to do. In addition, we recommend that you keep track of what you have accomplished at the end of each day. Take notes to remind you what follow up is needed with whom and by when.

Set a Witnessing Vision with the Congregation

And a vision appeared to Paul in the night:
there stood a man of Macedonia beseeching him, saying,
"Come over into Macedonia and help us."

— Acts 16:9 (KJ21)

A vision is a long-term view of what you are trying to accomplish. For instance, a congregation that wanted to witness to all neighbors, workers, and visitors within three miles of the church might adopt this vision: "Share the Good News about Salvation with everyone who comes within three miles of our church until all understand." As another example, a congregation that wanted to help save as many souls as possible might choose this vision: "Joyfully witness until three times as many people to whom we witness are saved each year as there are members in our congregation." A larger vision that encompasses helping other congregations to witness might be: "Joyfully witness and provide witnessing tools to other churches until thirty times as many people receive witnessing and are saved each year as there are members in our congregation."

As you can see, a congregation's vision for helping to save souls is different from summarizing what the pastor and each individual witness choose as goals. In most cases, there is a continuing interaction between individual goals and the congregational vision. A congregational vision can emerge after developing individual goals, or individual goals can be created after setting a congregational vision. Whichever starting point is used, goals can help create a greater vision, and a greater vision can help people choose more meaningful goals.

We, your authors, believe that in every case the pastor first has to have personal and teaching goals for witnessing. Why? It's a starting point for explaining to the congregation about witnessing and the importance of goals. Otherwise, Christians will have no idea what goals they should set. Many would be happy to set a goal to just help save their spouse and children, even if they are already saved.

In most cases, we also believe that a pastor should have an in-congregation evangelist selected and ready to begin before working with the congregation to set a witnessing vision. While the pastor will lead the congregation to establish the vision, the in-congregation evangelist can do much good work in preparing the way for establishing the vision.

Before setting a vision, we recommend that pastors consider using surveys to learn how much witnessing the church has been doing, to gain a sense of how many souls were saved in the last year among people the congregation witnessed to, and to identify how many lost people are located in the church's vicinity. Why is having that kind of information important? Most churches will discover and be convinced

157

by understanding that current witnessing activities aren't accomplishing enough to continually reduce the number of unsaved people around them.

While we don't know what your surveys will show, to help understand the value of the information let's imagine that a church has done these surveys and learned the following:

- Five percent of the congregation shared their faith at least once with an unsaved person in the last year.
- This witnessing helped lead eight people to being saved in the last year.
- There are 3,467 unsaved people within a three-mile radius of the church.

Most people would view those results as indicating that much more witnessing needs to be done. If the number of lost people in the area is to be reduced, the number of people being saved each year probably needs to increase to well over a hundred. Note that if information about lost people is not measured and considered, a small congregation might feel as if helping save eight souls is accomplishing enough. Such a congregation is probably growing. But we know that God cares about souls, not simply whether a congregation is growing or not.

Another useful method for developing a vision is to estimate how much activity is involved in accomplishing various tasks involved in being complete, effective witnesses. For instance, if a witness shares information about Salvation with one unsaved person a day and follows up on a regular basis, it will be very unlikely for fewer than five souls to be saved each year following such efforts. If fifty church members are willing to do this much witnessing, a large number of people are going to be saved every year.

It also helps to consider how much your in-congregation evangelism program is going to help your congregation's members become complete, continuing witnesses. For example, an inactive evangelism teaching program might require six months to obtain the first five written testimonies, while a very active program might have enough written testimonies to put together a book of testimonies within two months. As you think about that difference in witnessing accomplishments, you can see how important it is that the Lord lead pastors to encourage a person with the right gifts to be an in-congregation evangelist.

However you decide to develop your congregation's vision, remember that the commitments that people make to working toward the vision are more important than what the vision is. If as a pastor you want a larger vision than the congregation does, pray for guidance and commitment to accomplish more. As your congregation grows in witnessing awareness and competence, you'll find that the commitment to witnessing will increase enough to permit expanding the vision.

One important reason for vision expansion comes from your congregation attracting new members who are witnessing minded. Some will be long-time Christians who are looking for a witnessing congregation. Others will be new Christians who are extremely eager to share the wonderful experience of being saved.

Be Kingdom Minded

And the disciples came and said to Him,
"Why do You speak to them in parables?"
He answered and said to them,
"Because it has been given to you
to know the mysteries of the kingdom of heaven,
but to them it has not been given."

— Matthew 13:10-11 (NKJV)

In a pastor's day-to-day responsibilities, many tangible realities stand out: Is there enough money to pay the church's mortgage this month? Who will visit the sick, troubled, and mourning while you are recovering from an operation? What lesson should be taught next Sunday? How can the angry elder be calmed down? Is our attendance rising? Are the tithes and offerings growing? Will the roof last another winter? How will we find the money to heat the building?

159

By contrast, God's heavenly kingdom is mostly invisible to us except for reading what the Bible says. Progress of individual souls towards Salvation is almost totally invisible. Only by inquiring in loving and helpful ways can we even find out whether someone is saved or not. Without such careful inquiry, a pastor might have pews filled with unsaved people who don't realize it ... calling themselves Christians because their parents did, they attend church, and they exchange gifts at Christmas.

The good news is that by reaching out we can learn who is saved and who isn't, and what keeps those who are lost from accepting Salvation. If we look past the surface reality of the church to the eternal status of the souls, the process of helping develop the kingdom is simplified.

The two different perspectives may provide conflicting information. A rapidly growing church might not be helping save many souls. A congregation filled with effective witnesses might be bringing many people to Salvation while attendance temporarily shrinks because those who don't want to witness flee to less demanding pews where witnessing is rarely mentioned.

In the same way that the disciples needed for Jesus to explain His parables to them, pastors need to pray to Him for guidance in leading a congregation of witnesses. How can a pastor do better in serving the kingdom of heaven and keeping track of what's working and what isn't in witnessing to lost people? This subject is a good one for pastors who are newly determined to expand how much time they spend each day in prayer.

This focus on the kingdom doesn't mean that we, your authors, think the visible is unimportant: Pastors need to be good shepherds over their congregations' physical beings and good stewards of the resources provided to them. But we urge pastors to remember that God promised that all of our needs would be taken care of by Him. Can anyone doubt that by attending better to fulfilling God's purposes for witnessing that He will fail to provide the added physical resources needed to be good witnesses and to tend to His flock?

Beware of the Enemy's Attacks

O LORD, my strength and my fortress,
and my refuge in the day of affliction,
the Gentiles shall come unto Thee
from the ends of earth and shall say,
"Surely our fathers have inherited lies, vanity,
and things wherein there is no profit."

— Jeremiah 16:19 (KJ21)

Doubts will enter your mind about making witnessing a major focus for your congregation. Why? The enemy who is in the world will use any deception, any lie, and any trick to keep lost people from accepting Salvation. Encouraging Christians to be silent and invisible to the unsaved is a critical strategy in that spiritual battle.

In discussing the challenges of leading a congregation of complete, continual witnesses, we also don't want to paint a picture that's rosier than what you may experience. All we know for sure is that each congregation has unique opportunities and challenges.

We have had enough experiences with pastors who decided not to emphasize witnessing to know what some of the deceptions are that can lead pastors away from serving the Lord in nurturing unsaved people. In the following subsections, we refer to thoughts you may have and comments you may receive from your congregation, and describe possible ways to prepare for having the thoughts or hearing the comments.

Thought: I Want My Church to Grow

And out of the ground the LORD God made every tree grow
that is pleasant to the sight and good for food.

— Genesis 2:9 (NKJV)

It's natural to want to lead a larger congregation: Pastors can do more service for the Lord that way. A growing congregation can also be seen as a sign of the Lord's pleasure.

Problems can arise if a focus on growing a congregation becomes too important to a pastor. When that happens, harmful compromises can be tempting. One such temptation is to focus on making the church's activities more attractive to those who are already saved at the expense of encouraging witnessing. Since most Christians in the United States rarely, if ever, share their faith with lost people, the most comfortable messages for saved people say little about witnessing, do not come from an in-congregation evangelist, and avoid making anyone who is reluctant to witness feel uncomfortable.

Perhaps an analogy can help explain what we mean by not overemphasizing growth. It's natural for a human body to grow from being a baby into an adult. Provide enough nutrients and liquids, and growth follows in almost all cases. For a few children, missing hormones will fill in for genetic gaps.

Some peoples' cells receive the wrong signal from their DNA and begin uncontrolled growth that interferes with the body's healthy activities. The result of that DNA malfunction is a cancerous growth. Left unchecked, the body may be overwhelmed by the cancer, and death can result.

A church that builds a congregation of complete, willing witnesses will grow ... both by adding newly saved people and attracting those who want to be part of an actively witnessing congregation. That's healthy growth.

Before that growth occurs, pastors should be aware that there may be some losses of congregation members. Some Christians will leave for other congregations rather than participate in complete, continual witnessing. Before leaving, these Christians may be quite outspoken in their opposition to being asked to witness.

A pastor can see these challenges as part of spiritual warfare to help the congregation walk closer to the Lord, or as an unnecessary annoyance to be avoided. An analogy is that of children needing to lose their baby teeth before their adult teeth can properly come in. Opposition to witnessing is like the natural desire that some children have to avoid having their loose baby teeth pulled. As adults, we know that the baby teeth have to go, even if a dentist has to extract them.

Many pastors who want to grow their congregations report little success in doing so. Another analogy may help to explain the source of that frustration. Some people would like to look fit but have a hard time exercising enough to develop the muscles that provide that appearance. Similarly, some pastors want to grow but report that they don't do anything to increase witnessing. Think of encouraging witnessing as part of the Lord's exercises for developing a spiritually fit and growing congregation.

Thought: I Don't Want to Divide My Congregation

> *"Do you suppose that I came to give peace on earth?*
> *I tell you, not at all, but rather division.*
> *For from now on five in one house will be divided:*
> *three against two, and two against three."*

— Luke 12:51-52 (NKJV)

The Bible tells us that we should confront our fellow Christians in love to help them amend their faults. If such encouragement doesn't help, we are advised to treat unrepentant Christians like pagans and tax collectors. That example shows that when a division helps keep us from falling away from Him, divisions among people are more desirable than agreement that dilutes our relationship with God. Certainly, we should also seek to cooperate as one body of Christians with those who are doing their best to walk with the Lord.

Patience and tact can be effectively grounded first in prayer to help you develop a vision for witnessing that will avoid a harmful division. Consider your own experiences. When someone has told you that you must do something that sounded unpleasant without providing much explanation, you may recall times when you wanted to do the opposite. It's a common reaction.

Few people will resist the call to witness after understanding that Jesus has commanded it to be done by all Christians, the need is great, the consequences of not witnessing are dire for the unsaved people, and Christians gain Earthly and heavenly rewards for witnessing. In that context, asking someone to do more witnessing is a lot like asking guests if they would like their favorite dessert at the end of dinner.

After being consulted and having been given a chance to share their ideas, most people feel encouraged to support a new initiative. In fact, those who are consulted may feel like they have a stake in the outcome. You see this effect all the time in fund-raising programs: The largest potential donors are asked to lead the program and to make large pledges to encourage others to follow their lead. As a result, more than half the money may be raised before a public announcement is made that there is a fund-raising program.

The only place where a pastor has to be cautious is in avoiding identifying someone as an in-congregation evangelist who isn't well equipped to teach and encourage witnessing. People who advance their own candidacies often make the worst choices. Let the Holy Spirit point out to you the person with the greatest gift for teaching and encouraging witnesses.

Congregational Comment: Hearing about Witnessing Is a Waste of Time

> *... they found Him in the temple,*
> *sitting in the midst of the teachers,*
> *both listening to them and asking them questions.*

— Luke 2:46 (NKJV)

Five minutes from every church service and activity for teaching and encouraging witnessing doesn't seem like a lot. Even if you attend a church service or activity three times a week, that's only fifteen minutes a week. In a year, five-minute teachings add up to no more than ten hours for most people. Almost everyone spends more than ten hours a year watching reruns on television that they have seen before.

What is this congregational comment really about? In many cases, it is defensiveness on the part of someone who doesn't share his or her faith. Can you recall being a child when you had done something you knew was wrong and you were being grilled by your parents about what you had done? Each second seemed to last for several hours.

Many of the people who are listening to the five-minute teachings about witnessing feel the same way.

Contrast that reaction with our patient, omniscient Lord who would listen to anyone's teachings and then ask questions. Through His questions, people would realize their errors ... often in such profound ways that they were left with nothing to say to Him.

Hearing this comment from someone in the congregation offers an opportunity to ask why hearing about witnessing is a waste of time. From the answers, you can learn what the reason for the comment is: Does the Christian agree that our Lord told us all to witness? Does the Christian already have an encyclopedic knowledge of witnessing so this information is needless repetition? What witnessing does this Christian do? Could the teachings be improved? How would the Christian like to help improve in the witnessing teachings and activities?

Congregational Comment: I Don't Like Being Harassed into Joining Outreaches

What shall we do, that we may work the works of God?

— John 6:28 (NKJV)

A kind invitation to engage in a witnessing outreach will be interpreted by some, who don't want to witness, as being harassment. Of course, if the invitations aren't kind, they need to be.

Psychologists tell us that most people find it hard to say "no" more than eight times when asked to do something. Persistent in-congregation evangelists will often employ repeated requests to gain someone's attention. When presented with continued requests, the reluctant witness eventually says "yes" but may not mean it. That Christian may feel harassed. Perhaps there is some other way to witness that this person would like to do instead. The in-congregation evangelist should find out and encourage that alternative.

†

165

In Chapter 10, we build on this theme of finding your witnessing niche by reviewing the importance of trying lots of different witnessing activities in order to find the ones where God has gifted you with the most talent and interest.

Chapter 10

Use Your Gifts to Develop
a Full Set of Evangelism Skills

Extend Your Range of Witnessing
after Hearing about and Seeing What Others Do

Now I myself am confident concerning you, my brethren,
that you also are full of goodness,
filled with all knowledge,
able also to admonish one another.

— Romans 15:14 (NKJV)

In this book, we describe a pathway of learning to witness that goes from writing a personal testimony to becoming an in-congregation evangelist. Such a pathway can keep you productively engaged in serving the Lord for a lifetime, and we pray that you will find much satisfaction in such service.

Considering the possibilities encountered along that pathway overwhelms some people, while others pay attention to what is written and said and soon see other possibilities. In this chapter, we encourage you to think beyond what we've described so far. Why? Your calling and gifts for witnessing may be quite different from what we've described.

Prayer is always a good way to start learning whether you should be doing something different from what we've described to help spread His promises. You can also learn about other alternatives by asking others how they share their faith and by watching what they do.

Discovering alternative approaches is important because lost people are influenced to learn about and accept Salvation in a variety of ways. If you don't portray Salvation in a way that God wants His existence to be shared with certain unsaved people, souls will be permanently lost.

In the following sections, we describe some other ways of witnessing that may be of interest to you, whether or not you feel called and gifted to perform them. Keep these methods in mind so that you can share what you learn with Christians who are looking for other ways to witness.

Sing to and for Him

Let the word of Christ dwell in you richly in all wisdom,
teaching and admonishing one another
in psalms and hymns and spiritual songs,
singing with grace in your hearts to the Lord.

— Colossians 3:16 (NKJV)

Most people enjoy listening to music. Singing with others makes the experience more uplifting. Both the Old and New Testaments instruct us to praise the Lord through song. If you have a gift for music or song, surely the Lord intended you to use that gift in witnessing for Him.

If you can play an instrument, you can help attract unsaved people with public performances. If you have friends who play, the group of you can make an even more joyous sound for Him.

Here's an example: Jim Barbarossa has learned to play the shofar, the ancient instrument fashioned from a ram's horn that the Israelites used in their celebrations of God. Interest in his shofar playing often helps attract people to learn more about witnessing.

A musical program can be turned into a more witnessing-oriented event by selecting what is played and inserting some helpful messages between pieces. If you provide printed copies of the lyrics to your listeners, you can add written testimonies and Scriptures to these handouts.

Often, people who have had a good time listening to the music will crowd up afterward to speak to you. It's natural to ask listeners about themselves, to tell more about yourself, and to ask them if they know the Lord as their Savior. Some may want to listen to the music again, and you can provide them with witnessing tapes and CDs featuring music and testimonies.

Providing a regular series of performances encourages people to return regularly so that you can follow up on how they have responded to your witnessing. Future discussions will present more opportunities to understand their needs so you can be more helpful, such as by introducing them to other witnesses and sharing other written testimonies with them.

What if you can't play an instrument, but can sing? You can participate in many of the same things musicians do by cooperating with a witness who does play.

But what if your singing voice isn't so great, and you aren't very musical? Then you could organize events where those who can play and sing attract a crowd while you act as the emcee.

If you have skill as a dancer, that's another way to celebrate the Lord. Carla Barbarossa often performs dances as part of her witnessing.

What if you have skill in writing lyrics? You can take popular music that isn't protected by copyright and add witnessing words to the melody. Now, wouldn't that be fun to do?

Some people are differently talented and can write new music as well as new lyrics. When those musical gifts are dedicated to the Lord, the potential for witnessing effectively expands. Here's an example: Someone who likes the music may want to share it with unsaved friends and family, which sharing turns the unsaved person into an indirect witness.

A few people can write musicals while a few others know how to choreograph such performances. Imagine creating a whole performance that describes the Lord's Salvation. Even if you don't have that kind of skill, you could still help by assisting with the preparation and performances.

Serve and Then Witness to Lost People

For you, brethren, have been called to liberty;
only do not use liberty as an opportunity for the flesh,
but through love to serve one another.

— Galatians 5:13 (NKJV)

Loving acts can open a lost person's heart to learning about Salvation before you say a word about your faith. Each of us has special ways to show loving kindness and to encourage others to become better acquainted. In the process, you can enjoy many wonderful experiences while witnessing in your unique way.

Let's say that you enjoy baking. Most people like to eat tasty baked goods. By providing your baking as a gift, you can walk up to anyone, share a bite, and begin to develop a personal relationship. Naturally, the person who eats your baking will be polite toward you and will accept your witnessing with a more open mind and heart than would occur without the delicious treat.

Most people know how to do something well that many other people would like to learn. Many interested people haven't taken courses in your expertise because it's hard to find one, the available courses are too expensive, or their locations are inconvenient. What could be nicer than to open your home to those who want to learn? In such a friendly setting, you could certainly feel good about sharing your faith.

For those who sew, there are opportunities to help people learn the skill and make clothes that bring much enjoyment. Helping with sewing projects for important life transitions, such as making bridal gowns or palls, can provide opportunities to share your faith at times when people are thinking about life's meaning.

Poetry offers a special opportunity. Instead of just speaking to people, write them poems. Nothing pleases unsaved hearts more than someone writing a poem about them. You can do this for special occasions such as birthdays and anniversaries, or for no special reason when someone needs to see that others care.

If you can draw or paint, you can also create Christian artworks and give them to unsaved people. Opportunities abound. For instance, at a children's event most people can sketch well enough to provide face painting. While the children sit for the drawings, you can talk about the Lord.

If you know about science, you can help lost people understand about the many miracles of creation and how they show His loving hand. Some people are led to Salvation simply by appreciating how special and wonderfully created are our bodies, Earth, and universe.

If you are a good writer, you can create stories and essays that will appeal to unsaved people and help them to want the light of His glory. For instance, you can help prepare tracts and books that feature testimonies.

If you can read, you can read aloud to those who have no sight. That's a critical contribution to make for blind students who need to master materials that haven't been converted into Braille or recorded.

Those who have lost loved ones, especially those who don't know the Lord, often have a hard time recovering from their sadness. Some of these people have no one to speak to about their grief. You could volunteer at a hospice or hospital to counsel and pray with the bereaved. Such service could be a great blessing in reminding you of how important it is that all people learn about Salvation before they die.

Some people find they need a part-time job to earn a little extra money. Instead of picking the job that is most convenient or provides the most income, consider choosing work where you can serve others and have a chance to witness to them as Bishop Dale P. Combs does (you can read a description of his part-time work and the opportunities gained for witnessing in the Pastor's Prologue).

Even if you don't have a particular skill and don't need a part-time job, volunteering can put you into a position to serve and then share your faith. By picking an opportunity that interests you, your service can be a bigger blessing to lost people. If your congregation has a plan for reaching unsaved people near the church, your volunteer work can be aimed at filling a role in the congregation's expanded outreach efforts.

Disciple Large Numbers of New Christians

For I bear them witness that they have a zeal for God,
but not according to knowledge.

— Romans 10:2 (NKJV)

By addressing the sinner's prayer to God with a sincere and repentant heart, lost people are cleansed by the Lord of their sins and forgiven. When that great event occurs, it is often followed by some confusion about what this new life of submission to Jesus Christ means. New believers are vulnerable to being discouraged by unsaved people who challenge their commitment. Just at the moment when a new Christian is most vulnerable to backsliding, there is a great opportunity to help save more souls by firming up the new Christian's beliefs and helping him or her testify to lost people.

Many people miss this point and insist that helping disciple new believers has nothing to do with witnessing. On the contrary, the two activities are so intertwined that they cannot be separated.

Let's explain that point in a different way: If congregations suddenly become effective in witnessing, there will be many more new believers than mature ones. If the congregation is poorly equipped to disciple the new believers, the church will have to shift all of its resources to dealing with this influx of new Christians while curtailing witnessing by the mature Christians.

The challenge is so great that pastors need to think about how they might handle a several hundred percent increase in the congregation occurring over just a few months. You can obviously hold quite large classes, as long as you have a room that's big enough for everyone. But how will you give people a chance to meet in small groups to discuss their questions and deepen their understanding of what was just presented? It is likely that this kind of congregational growth requires churches to also offer active, small-group ministries that meet in individual homes.

Lead New Outreach Ministries

"Lord, when did we see You hungry or thirsty
or a stranger or naked or sick or in prison,
and did not minister to You?"

— Matthew 25:44 (NKJV)

At college orientations and alumni gatherings, school officials love to praise new student initiatives to serve the local community. It's easy for college officials to stimulate such activity: Simply share an encouraging word with students, and those who feel called to help others will take it from there. That's an important lesson for witnessing because many of these eager volunteer leaders don't yet know the Lord but have a heart for others.

By contrast, college-age people don't often receive the same encouragement at church to be leaders of new community outreach activities. More often, young Christians are asked to follow well-established volunteer and witnessing activities. Jubilee Worship Center (JWC) has been fortunate that its youth have been eager to be active as volunteers and witnesses, both through their own outreaches and through what JWC provides for the whole congregation.

Even in a church with an active youth ministry, it's easy for young people to miss opportunities to lead new ministries that draw unsaved people. Let's consider Habitat for Humanity, which is a good example of how a new youth-led Christian outreach can have witnessing value. This global organization is a Christian ministry, but many of the people who donate land, materials, and work to the ministry aren't the Lord's followers. Most college campuses have chapters that help build new homes for poor people by teaming with churches that have more money to contribute than volunteer time to offer.

If the youth in your church are interested in helping a poor family gain a decent home in a safe neighborhood, establishing a new youth-led Habitat ministry would be easy because Habitat provides lots of information and organizational skills. Those who volunteer can learn new lessons for building and repairing homes, organizing volunteer efforts, and sharing their faith. Those benefits are a great gift from the Lord.

Outreaches don't have to be started by young people; strong commitments to outreach ministries can develop at any age. Here's an example: Many communities lack enough good foster care. This lack is often most apparent to those who are grandparents and parents. You could start a lay-led ministry that encourages couples to serve as foster parents. Most of the people who serve as foster parents will probably be people well beyond age thirty and some won't yet be Christians. Those who enjoy this work may eventually develop an interest in encouraging adoptions of foster children. Both types of service offer good opportunities to meet and help children with pressing needs while also delivering hope to foster parents and children through Salvation.

Many churches serve the poor in a variety of ways. Community organizations are often looking to team up with churches to do more. For instance, a church can be a distribution point for surplus food gathered by other organizations from restaurants and manufacturers. Something similar can be done for distributing used clothing. A congregation with a big heart and a kitchen may provide regular meals for poor people. Some people with a heart to help the poor may not yet be Christians, and your new ministry may attract them to become involved in the charitable work and to learn more about Salvation. Obviously, poor people will also want to know about God's promises for them as He provides.

Establish and Lead New Christian Organizations

And the LORD went before them by day
in a pillar of cloud to lead the way,
and by night in a pillar of fire to give them light,
so as to go by day and night.

— Exodus 13:21 (NKJV)

Leadership counts. God gave us a great example of that lesson. Although Moses was the leader of the Israelites when they left Egypt for the Promised Land, God wanted to make sure that the people were where He wanted them to be. To make it clear, He led them with a pillar of cloud by day and a pillar of fire by night to let them know when to rest, when to move, and where to go.

In the United States and some other countries, governments provide tax-exempt status to churches and Christian organizations. In some cases, this also means that donors benefit from paying less in taxes based on how much they give. With these gifts, volunteer efforts can be supplemented so that more can be accomplished.

Most in-congregation evangelists are kept more than busy and satisfied with responsibilities for teaching and encouraging their congregations to witness and sharing witnessing tools and lessons with other congregations; however, some may wish to do more. Evangelists Jim and Carla Barbarossa are examples. In addition to operating successful businesses, serving as in-congregation evangelists, and being good grandparents and parents, they established Step by Step Ministries to gather and share resources around the world to help save more souls.

Many such opportunities exist, both to facilitate witnessing and to perform other good works. If you feel called to accomplish more as a leader, you have the potential to help many more souls.

Here's some practical advice: Start with a management team of people who have complementary gifts. When the Israelites left Egypt, Moses was concerned about being a leader because he spoke slowly and poorly. God responded by telling Moses to engage his brother, Aaron, to do the speaking. Ideally, your management team should include one person who is a very fine organizer, another person who is an excellent speaker and motivator, and a third person who is good at raising and shepherding funds. If you can add other leadership gifts as well to the management team, so much the better.

If your organization has a compelling purpose for serving others, you are emulating the appeal of Habitat for Humanity and can lead a Christian ministry that attracts many lost people to support what you do and to provide benefits. If your heart is stirred to establish and develop such an organization, you can be sure that God has ignited a similar passion in many other people who know and need to know the Lord. That stirring purpose serves the same role as the pillars of cloud and fire for attracting attention and directing people to move to the right place at the proper time.

Translate Great Tools and Testimonies

And the LORD said, "Indeed the people are one and
they all have one language, ...
now nothing that they propose to do will be withheld from them.
Come, let Us go down and there confuse their language,
that they may not understand one another's speech."

— Genesis 11:6-7 (NKJV)

The Bible tells us that mankind once spoke one language. Some people then determined that they wanted to become famous by building a city with a tower in it whose top would reach into the heavens. God didn't approve and confused them by introducing many languages and scattering the people across the Earth. The city and tower were abandoned.

The language-based division of humanity remains an issue for witnessing today. A few languages don't yet have written formats. Most witnessing tools and testimonies are available in only one language. Although we, your authors, are encouraged by the potential of translation software to provide crude meanings, good translations require understanding both languages and cultures so that proper metaphors, word choices, and subjects are employed in the other language. Top-notch translators are well paid for this work, often at rates exceeding a dollar a word. Translating a thousand-word testimony into another language can cost more than the average annual income of people living in most countries.

It will obviously require armies of talented volunteer translators to take excellent materials and render them into other languages. In the United States, few people take language study seriously and that means relatively few potential volunteer resources except to translate between Spanish and English, and French and English. In Europe, almost everyone can read and write at least two languages well.

Despite these differences in language knowledge, the same percentage of every nation's Christians probably has the ability to learn another language. Evangelists need to let it be known that translators are needed, and encourage those who want to learn languages to do so and then to use some of their skill to make tools and testimonies more available. Given the nature of what is being translated, it will also make sense for special language programs to be formed to help people translate Christian tools and testimonies.

Think of it: People who are nervous about traveling around the world can instead indulge their taste for exotic cultures by learning and using foreign languages as a labor of love for the Lord. What language would you like to use to illuminate God's glory?

Assemble Witnessing and Testimony Libraries

Love never fails.
But whether there are prophecies, they will fail;
whether there are tongues, they will cease;
whether there is knowledge, it will vanish away.

— 1 Corinthians 13:8 (NKJV)

If a book containing a hundred testimonies can make an impression on lost people, imagine what a library filled with hundreds of thousands of such books could do. Over the ages, too few attempts have been made to save witnessing materials and testimonies. As a result, the records of many of the most eloquent and effective ways to be a witness and to share a testimony have probably been lost. Only God knows what was in those materials and testimonies.

While no one can do much about what has been lost except search around for what has been misplaced, a lot can be done to be sure that current and future witnessing materials and testimonies are studied, used, and retained. We would like to encourage anyone who wants to do a big task for God to create places where witnessing materials and testimonies will be available for future generations. In addition, it would be great for witnesses to have access to such libraries to select resources especially relevant for a particular unsaved person. This goal means not only retaining material, but indexing it to make it more accessible.

As wonderful as it would be to have one great world library for witnessing, it may be more practical to have several specialized libraries that can be accessed electronically using search software. A starting point would be to create indexes of online materials whether from Web sites or blogs.

Even if you aren't drawn to such a large project, each church should have a library so that its witnessing tools and testimonies will be available for study and possible use in the future. These church-based efforts could be expanded to encourage families to obtain and retain their written testimonies. Then, a church library could be a repository of faith-based information for future generations of the family ... even if the family's own records were destroyed. For centuries, church records have been essential sources for genealogists and historians. Wouldn't it be terrific if you could find out more than just when people lived, were baptized, and died?

Seek and Encourage Witnessing Breakthroughs

He said to him the third time,
"Simon, son of Jonah, do you love Me?"
Peter was grieved because He said to him the third time,
"Do you love Me?"
And he said to Him, "Lord, You know all things;
You know that I love You."
Jesus said to him, "Feed My sheep."

— John 21:17 (NKJV)

Peter often had a hard time understanding what Jesus wanted him to do. Jesus knew that and provided extra instruction to Peter until the message sunk in. Even then, Peter would sometimes fail to follow through such as when Jesus asked him to stay awake and pray with Him in the Garden of Gethsemane, but Peter fell asleep.

If it can be so hard to understand and to do the right thing when in Jesus' physical and spiritual presence, how much more difficult must it be to obey Him when our connection is purely spiritual. As a result, mistakes and disobedience will occur in feeding the saved and lost sheep. For instance, some people need years to write a testimony … and then more years to begin sharing that testimony with anyone. Even more eloquent evidence of mistakes and disobedience comes from the thousands of brief, incomplete testimonies that Jim and Carla Barbarossa receive from the newly saved in foreign nations.

By comparison, most people can learn to drive a vehicle tolerably well within a few months. Most experts would agree that it's much more difficult and dangerous to drive than it is to witness. That comparison suggests to your authors that breakthroughs are needed for teaching and encouraging witnessing beyond anything we have seen or heard.

It may well be that some people have quietly developed highly advantaged approaches, as Jubilee Worship Center and Step by Step Ministries have done, but the practices aren't known to and understood by many other people. A systematic search for such practices should be able to locate more of them. When those practices are well described and explained, those who want to encourage witnessing can learn from the practices.

There are many opportunities to establish new organizations, activities, and research projects that will identify, describe, and teach superior practices. If you feel called to work in that area, the subject seems to be largely undeveloped.

Beyond that, there's an even richer potential opportunity to combine bits and pieces of helpful practices in new ways to accomplish more through witnessing. For example, there are many interesting pilot projects going on now to expand Christian broadcasting to unsaved people, to develop Christian tourist attractions that teach the Bible, to connect those seeking more information about the Lord with counselors, and to provide more Christian education. In most cases, it's obvious to see how such activities might be linked with each other to increase effectiveness.

What's needed is a systematic study of current witnessing practices to consider which ones might work better when combined. From there, experiments need to be designed, results studied, and lessons disseminated to pastors and evangelists. This could be a major activity for anyone with an interest in and talent for process improvement.

Looking deeper into the lessons of witnessing experiences, there are also opportunities to learn more about those who decide to accept Salvation to better understand how different kinds of witnessing have affected their interest in and understanding of the Lord's offer of forgiveness. From a deep understanding of the conditions that help people to open their hearts and understand, improved ideas might be created for witnessing. By conducting and measuring controlled experiments, the good new ideas can be separated from the not-so-good choices.

As you can see from the choices that we have outlined, there are many ways to improve witnessing to reach higher levels of effectiveness. If you feel called to work on witnessing breakthroughs, JWC and Step by Step Ministries will be glad to advise you. Feel free to call the JWC offices at 219-947-0301 or Jim Barbarossa at 219-787-9933 for assistance. You can also contact Jim Barbarossa at jim@step-by-step.org.

†

In Chapter 11, we describe the wonderful revelations that come from learning more about all of the good that God has done in the world through witnessing. After gaining that knowledge, you'll also feel your faith deepened and strengthened in wondrous ways.

Chapter 11

Rejoice in God's Goodness

Be in Awe of and Curious about
How Much Good God Has Done

*Therefore we also pray always for you
that our God would count you worthy of this calling,
and fulfill all the good pleasure of His goodness
and the work of faith with power,
that the name of our Lord Jesus Christ
may be glorified in you, and you in Him,
according to the grace of our God
and the Lord Jesus Christ.*

— 2 Thessalonians 1:11-12 (NKJV)

God's goodness is often invisible or taken for granted. For example, that person who looks so healthy may have experienced a miraculous recovery from illness ten years ago, and His healing may not be appreciated by others today unless it is described. In addition, many Christians don't stop to thank Him for the gifts that are obvious, such as being alive for another day or having enough to eat.

By lifting the veils of time, distance, and interior experience, a witnessing testimony can reveal astonishing works that will leave you awestruck. As an example of God's amazing acts, we would like to share one of Bishop Dale P. Combs's experiences with witnessing, Salvation, and faith:

A congregation member called to ask if I would mind visiting a man dying of cancer. Let me call him "Charlie." She shared that Charlie did not know the Lord and had little time left before the cancer would finally take his life.

I drove up to Charlie's home that afternoon and knocked on the door. I introduced myself: "Good afternoon, I am Pastor Dale Combs from Jubilee Worship Center, and I was asked by a member of my church to stop by and meet you folks and let you know that we are here for you should you need us."

At first the couple was hesitant to say much. They simply wanted to know who asked me to visit. When I told them, they responded, "We know her!" They then introduced themselves to me.

We stood in the front room for a moment, and there was a knock at the door. The couple said, "Excuse us, but we have been waiting for this person to come by. Could you wait a moment while we talk to her?" I agreed.

I waited in the front room until they had finished. Charlie returned and said, "I have to go into the bedroom and lay down. Would you come with me so we can talk?"

I followed the couple into the bedroom, and Charlie got into bed. He told me about his situation. "I have throat cancer. The doctors have told me there is nothing else that they can do for me and by September I will be dead."

I just looked at him, and he began to cry. He stopped crying for a moment and continued, "I have to go get a tracheotomy [a surgical opening in a blocked throat to permit air to enter and exit the lungs] in a few days to help me with breathing and a feeding tube [a way of making feeding possible when the esophagus is blocked], and that's all they can do for me."

At that moment, I knew that I could only tell Charlie one thing, The Truth! I felt the Holy Spirit move in my mind and my heart to share with him Christ's message.

I said, "The doctors have told you that you are going to die. If that is so, where do you want to spend eternity?"

Charlie replied, "I don't know! I used to believe in God and one time I served Him, but it got to be too hard. Boy, if I had known then what I would be facing today, I would not have given up so easily. Now, I don't know if God could ever forgive me."

I replied, "God loves you the same today as He did then. He can forgive you today, and you can know that you will spend eternity with Him … and not only that, He can heal you, too."

With that, Charlie asked Christ to forgive him for walking away, and through his tears he accepted Christ and was spiritually restored.

Following some instructions and exchanging of telephone numbers, I left rejoicing in what God did that day.

Time passed. I tried to reach Charlie at home, but due to his frequent doctors' visits he was never available. The summer came and went.

In the fall, I received a phone call from a young lady who had grown up in our church. She shared with me that Charlie was not the same man. "I have known him for a long time, and all he talks about is what Christ did for him that day you came to visit." She went on to tell me that all Charlie talks about is God. I was surprised to hear this because it was now November and Charlie was supposed to be gone.

Then one Sunday, I looked out into the congregation and I saw a frail man. After the service, he walked up to me and said, "Hi, Pastor Dale. Do you remember me?"

"Yes, I do! How are you, Charlie?"

"Can you believe that I'm still here? They said I would be dead back in September and here it is March!"

We rejoiced and Charlie explained what had happened since I saw him. The doctors could not explain why he was still living or how he was able to do what he was doing with so little strength.

I shared with him God's wonderful power to heal and he said, "I am believing for a complete healing."

He had brought his whole family to church for the first time. What a blessing! As time went on, he returned for other services but also missed some.

One day in late April I learned from one of his friends that Charlie had gained thirty-five pounds.

A few weeks later, Charlie showed up again at church. "The doctors say my cancer is in remission. I believe I am healed!" Charlie exclaimed excitedly. "And look at me. I have gained forty-five pounds and ate ten chicken wings for the first time in over eight months. Man, did they taste good!" Eating chicken wings was supposed to be impossible because of the tracheotomy and feeding tube. We laughed and cried together.

He looked up and said, "Pastor Combs, I never thought I would be here. I thank God for you coming to see me that day at my home and telling me that God could change me. He has and I am so thankful!" While I was still weeping over God's goodness, he continued, "The doctor said I will have this tracheotomy tube in my throat for the rest of my life and that is okay with me. I am just thankful that I am alive and serving the Lord."

I looked at him and said, "Charlie, if God can heal cancer, he can get that tracheotomy tube out too. Let's just pray and trust the Lord." We did and he went on his way.

Two weeks later, Charlie came to church. He ran to see me, "Pastor, Pastor, I'm sorry I wasn't at church last Sunday. I was at the hospital. Look, look. What do you see?" He pulled back his shirt collar and the tracheotomy tube was gone. Charlie had just seen a specialist who determined that his lungs were strong and healthy, and Charlie had no need for the tracheotomy. He showed me how he could breathe normally. God did this final change on Father's Day, June 15, 2008.

I will never forget that day in Charlie's bedroom as God came down and changed his life forever. There were no lightning bolts, no clashing thunder, just the simple prayer of a desperate man living without God who asked for forgiveness! The Bible says in James 5:15 (NKJV):

> And the prayer of faith will save the sick, and the Lord will raise him up. And if he has committed sins, he will be forgiven.

We would like to share with you other moving stories from Jubilee Worship Center (JWC) about witnessing, stories that demonstrate God's love, goodness, and power. We hope you will draw encouragement to witness from reading these stories. As inspiring as these stories are, imagine how much more exciting it would be to have played the witnessing roles that are described. If you are faithful in witnessing, God may have many such heart-warming opportunities waiting for you.

These stories appear in the remaining sections. We begin by sharing stories about witnessing that led to Salvation.

Stories from Jubilee Worship Center about Witnessing That Helped Lead to Salvation

Again the word of the LORD came to me, saying,
"Son of man, speak to the children of your people, and say to them:
'When I bring the sword upon a land,
and the people of the land take a man from their territory
and make him their watchman,
when he sees the sword coming upon the land,
if he blows the trumpet and warns the people,
then whoever hears the sound of the trumpet
and does not take warning,
if the sword comes and takes him away,
his blood shall be on his own head.
He heard the sound of the trumpet,
but did not take warning;
his blood shall be upon himself.
But he who takes warning will save his life.
But if the watchman sees the sword coming
and does not blow the trumpet,
and the people are not warned,
and the sword comes and takes any person from among them,
he is taken away in his iniquity;
but his blood I will require at the watchman's hand.'"

— Ezekiel 33:1-6 (NKJV)

Our surveys of JWC congregation members asked about their favorite witnessing experiences. In this section, we share bits and pieces from a few stories about helping lead others to Salvation. We pray that these stories will help you realize that there are many more good opportunities to share your faith than you are currently acting on.

There's a special joy in helping a family member accept Salvation. You'll read several stories about that experience in this section. If there are people in your family who aren't saved yet, we hope these stories will inspire you to share your faith with them.

God has plenty of surprises in store for those who witness to people outside their families. In those cases, resistance to accepting the Lord is often weaker than it is with family members. We hope these stories will help you feel energized to speak more frequently about your faith to people at work, people you serve, new acquaintances, and strangers.

Working in a Dementia Unit

My favorite witnessing experience was at work with James A, a resident in our dementia unit. James usually yells out loudly, "Help me. Help me." When you ask him how you can help him, he becomes very angry and combative. Because of his dementia, he does not have the cognitive ability to understand all of what he does or says.

One evening while I was arranging my medcart and charts at the nurses' station, James and several other cognitively impaired people were sitting nearby. James yelled out my name. I replied, "Yes, sir."

He asked, "Are you going to heaven?"

I replied, "Yes, sir. I am."

There was a pause. It was very still.

I asked James, "Are you going to heaven?"

He said very loudly, "NO!"

I asked him if he would like to go to heaven.

He said softly, "Yes."

I asked James if he would like to learn how, and he said, "Yes."

I prayed the sinner's prayer with James, and he accepted Jesus into his heart. Afterwards, he looked at me and said, "Thank you."

I took his hand and placed it over his heart. Then I said to him, "Let's thank Jesus. This is where He is."

James then said, "Thank you, Jesus."

I heard voices around me. Some of the residents were saying, "Praise God. Amen. Thank you, Jesus."

This was one of the best times I have ever had a work.

Visiting Mom as She Lay Dying

My favorite witnessing experience came with my mom. I discussed Salvation and confessing your sins with her. She repented and received Salvation two days prior to her passing away from lung cancer. Praise God!

Sharing with Everybody

All of my witnessing experiences are my favorites.

One time, a girl at work got saved in my car. My car is so anointed!

I love sitting around a table with tons of nations, strippers, and drug dealers sharing Jesus straight from my heart. I'll share with anybody!

It's all in the heart, baby!

Out of the abundance of the heart, your mouth is going to speak. If you just have Jesus in there, you can't help but share, to have him rolling out of your mouth every ten seconds!

Persuading a Son

My favorite witnessing experience came from watching my wife witness to my son. She asked him to go with me to the men's encounter, and he agreed. My son gave his life back to God.

Helping Little Boys Go to Church

My favorite witnessing experience came when I started taking two little boys, ages four and six, to church. On the way home on the first Sunday, I asked if they liked it.

The older one said, "Yes, I want to go back. We are gonna do a play and I get to be some guy named Jesus."

I almost cried. I took them to Sunday school and church for four years until I moved away, and then I arranged for someone else to pick them up.

They learned the books of the Bible, and I bought them *Veggie Tales* videos. They asked Jesus into their hearts one night during Christmas break while they were staying with me for a few days.

We were watching a *Veggie Tales* video and playing *Veggie Tales* cards when the older one said, "I bet the same guy that made *Veggie Tales* is not the same one that made *South Park* [a sick, gross adult comedy that they watched at home]."

I said, "You're right." That led to a discussion about what a Christian was, and they both became one that night.

They just blessed me so much over those years.

I had so many people say to me, "What a burden they must be. Getting them every week, keeping them for a few hours, feeding them, and so on."

They blessed me more than I can ever tell you. My kids had just reached the age of moving out. These little boys were so needy, and I was so fortunate to be the one to be there for them for the few short years I could be.

Describing to Friends What the Lord Has Done

My favorite witnessing experiences have been leading friends from high school to the Lord. They saw a major change in my life after I was saved. I told them that I was changed through Jesus Christ, and they wanted what I had.

Sharing a Testimony with a Hired Man

My favorite witnessing experience happened when I hired a man to clean up at my business. While we were talking, I decided to give him a tape; but I didn't have one with me. God spoke to me, "You don't need the tape; just talk to him."

I shared my complete testimony with him. He decided to follow me home because he wanted to have a tape of my testimony.

When we got there, I got a tape from my house and took it out to where he sat in his truck. As I reached in the window of his truck to give him the tape, he said, "I have to go."

I put my hand on his shoulder and said, "I want to pray for you." I was amazed that he immediately bowed his head. I prayed, "God, melt his heart. Don't allow this man to suffer without You for thirty-eight years as I did."

I looked down and saw that he was crying. I asked, "Do you want to receive Jesus?"

He replied, "I can't." He didn't say he didn't want to; he said, "I can't."

A thought came to mind, "Loosen his tongue in the name of Jesus."

I looked down at him and said in a loud and authoritative voice, "I loosen your tongue in Jesus' name. Are you ready to be saved?"

He looked up, still crying, and said, "Yes, I am!!"

That was on Friday. On Monday, his wife called me. She said, "This was the first weekend in thirteen years that my husband wasn't drunk all weekend. Jesus set him free."

Talking to a Brother on the Telephone

My favorite witnessing experience came when I was able to help bring my younger brother to Jesus. I wrote a three-page testimony about it. We were six thousand miles apart on a cell phone when he got down on the ground outside in Florida (while I was in Alaska). He asked me what to pray to have Jesus in his life. So we prayed ….

Visiting a Dying Man

My favorite witnessing experience came through a co-worker's husband whom I had met years earlier. He was dying of cancer and was in hospice care.

Every day when I prayed or I was working, I thought of him.

I decided to visit him. Before going I called a close friend and had her pray for me to be used and that God would give me the words I needed to speak.

I was very well received by this man. I was able to pray with him and help lead him to God.

When I left, I gave him a copy of *Real Life Stories*. He was so happy to have it.

He passed away four days later, and I know he is with Jesus now.

His wife also told me that he was very peaceful after my visit.

Sharing a Testimony with a Brother in a Barn

My favorite witnessing experience occurred when I was alone with my younger brother in a pole barn. I witnessed to him by telling him my story and how God changed my life. He gave his life to God that night on January 10, 2006.

Visiting an Inmate in the County Jail

My favorite witnessing experience came when I met a man in the South Bend County Jail and I helped lead him to the Lord. After a couple of conversations, he was on fire and started a Bible study with several younger men.

Helping to Save a Sister

My favorite witnessing experience came when I led my biological sister to Christ. Jesus used me as His vessel. It was an honor for the Lord to use me as His tool to bring someone to Him.

Comforting a Co-Worker

My favorite witnessing experience came at work. The Lord put this girl in my path. For about a month she opened up her heart to me about what was going on in her life.

Then I asked her if she wanted a *Real Life Stories* book. I told her about the book and that my story is in it.

Later that day, she read the book and my story. After she read it, she was in tears: My testimony touched her heart because she was going through the same thing.

We talked about Salvation, heaven, and hell. She was very open and wanted to give her heart to God.

Sharing the Lord with My Father-in-Law

My favorite witnessing experience came with my father-in-law to whom I witnessed for many years. Before he passed away, he gave his heart to the Lord. I planted, someone harvested, and God did the work. Praise God!

Helping a Family at Day Care

My favorite witnessing experience occurred when a family that came to our day care center was saved and grew in the Lord.

Sharing the Gospel with My Wife's Uncle

My favorite witnessing experience came when I shared the Gospel of Jesus with my wife's uncle. He wanted to pray for my mother-in-law who had cancer. He wanted to pray to Michael, the archangel, to heal her. She told him to talk to me about prayer.

I shared that Jesus is our only power in prayer. He accepted Jesus as his personal Savior. He realized that Jesus could help him with issues in his life.

Helping Redirect a Young Man away from Destruction

My favorite witnessing experience was while I was a youth pastor at another church. I was able to lead a young man to God who was headed for destruction.

Talking to Granddaughters

My favorite witnessing experience was talking and sharing with two of my granddaughters. One is now a child of the King, although it took her being incarcerated to accept Christ. Thank you, Jesus.

As wonderful as these stories are, the survey responses reminded us that witnessing can also help those who need to rededicate their lives to the Lord. We share two stories of this sort in the next section.

Stories from Jubilee Worship Center about Witnessing That Helped Lead to Rededication

... celebrate the dedication with gladness,
both with thanksgivings and singing,
with cymbals and stringed instruments and harps.

— Nehemiah 12:27 (NKJV)

Once people are saved, it's easy to assume that Christians will just walk closer and closer to the Lord. Unfortunately, that's not the case. Temptation is always present, and rebellion against God can occur among the saved. When that happens, witnessing can help struggling people to rededicate their lives to Him.

Discussing Beliefs about Jesus at Work

My favorite witnessing experience came from talking about Jesus with Bob, a very smart person with an IQ in the 130s. Bob knew the Bible inside and out and backwards, but he had backslid. We agreed to disagree and not argue about the Word.

I worked with him for about three weeks. Every night we would talk about his family, my family, and our Lord.

Then one night he told me he was dying from lung cancer from being exposed to insulation. He would cough a lot, but still smoked.

He said he was going to get a large settlement for his wife and son when he dies.

One night while he was coughing, I felt the Lord wanted me to pray for him. So I got up, walked over to where he was sitting bent over coughing, and prayed for his healing and to stop smoking.

The next day he said that the Lord took his smoking away from him.

I talked to him some more only to find out that he did not want to be cured of the cancer he had because his death would leave his family with the large settlement.

I told him that was selfish of him.

During our talks, I invited him and his family to come to our church, but they never came.

He did say that they rededicated their lives to the Lord.

Sharing a Written Testimony with a Backslid Friend

My favorite witnessing experience came when I shared my written testimony with an estranged, backslid friend. I loved the effect that it had on her life. I feel that I was part of the outcome: She is now serving the Lord again.

Witnessing doesn't always lead to quick results. Sometimes witnessing is simply part of the battle for someone's heart. In the next section, you will read about how rewarding Christians found it to witness with unsaved family members despite these loved ones continuing to resist accepting Jesus.

Stories from Jubilee Worship Center about Witnessing to Unsaved Family Members

... I bow my knees to the Father of our Lord Jesus Christ, from whom the whole family in heaven and earth is named, ...

— Ephesians 3:14-15 (NKJV)

Even when witnessing doesn't lead to Salvation for the lost, it can bring witnesses closer to God and to their families. We hope these stories will inspire you to keep sharing your faith even if family hearts aren't being softened towards Him. Until someone draws a last breath, it's not too late to help lead them to the Lord.

Sharing *Real Life Stories* with a Daughter-in-Law and Granddaughter

My favorite witnessing experience came while driving my daughter-in-law and granddaughter. I had given my daughter-in-law a *Real Life Stories* book. I told my daughter-in-law that my testimony was in the book and on what page.

My granddaughter was with us and she read my testimony. As she did, she began to cry. She said, "Grandma, that makes me sad. I didn't know that had happened to you."

That one thing opened up the door for me to witness to my daughter-in-law and granddaughter, to tell them about how God had touched my life and brought about healing and enabled me to be a survivor. It was wonderful.

Speaking to a Brother Who Didn't Want to Listen

My favorite witnessing experience came in my family. I shared my faith with my unsaved brother. He said he didn't want to hear it, but at least I can say I tried.

An Uncle Reads a Testimony

My favorite witnessing experience came when my uncle read my testimony and called me to say that it really touched his life and that he wanted to change.

Because you want to have a good relationship with someone you will see quite often, it can be daunting to share your faith with family members. Because you may not see them again unless you want to, it can be less inhibiting to witness to strangers. In the next section, we share stories of feeling liberated through sharing faith with strangers.

Stories from Jubilee Worship Center about Witnessing to Strangers

Beloved, you do faithfully whatever you do
for the brethren and for strangers,
who have borne witness of your love before the church.
If you send them forward on their journey in a manner
worthy of God, you will do well, ...

— 3 John 1:5-6 (NKJV)

In Chapter 6, we discuss overcoming fears of strangers and public speaking that hold some Christians back from witnessing. In this section, we share eloquent testimonies about how good it feels to share your faith with strangers. Here you'll see that God often provides nice surprises for those who witness to strangers.

Looking for the Lost While Riding the Train to Class

My favorite witnessing experiences came on the train; it was my "train ministry" as my Bible study girls have dubbed it.

I would take the train for an hour to and from Chicago every day for class. Every day I would pray for God to send me someone to share my faith with, and he really did!

Just reading my Bible on the train has started numerous conversations about God. I loved not knowing who God would next bring across my path.

I can't tell you how many hurting people I've sat next to who were delighted to have a conversation rather than sit in an awkward, squished silence.

I've prayed for the people there, cried with them, invited them to church, and shared my testimony.

Sharing God in the Mall

I guess my favorite witnessing experience probably came when I was in high school. My youth group went witnessing in a mall.

We eventually got kicked out (which was awesome!), and it was exciting.

I was amazed at how many people would actually talk to you about God.

There is a huge rush after you do the smallest thing that God actually wants you do in the area of evangelism.

How sad it is that we can ride that high for years and not repeat it.

Discussing Suicidal Thoughts

My favorite witnessing experience came after a good friend called me. One of her cousins was depressed and was having suicidal thoughts because the pain she felt was unbearable. My friend asked me to tell her cousin about my experiences with depression.

I met with both of them. God and the Holy Spirit helped me with my words, and I was able to share with her that God is always there to help you if you only call out to Him and trust God with your problems. I told her that those thoughts of suicide were from someone who hated her, "the Devil."

I helped her to understand that we all have problems. Life is not easy, but with God all things are possible.

Improving Language in a Restaurant

My favorite witnessing experience was when my husband and I were having dinner with a pastor in a restaurant. A young waiter (not ours) was using some pretty bad language. It really upset me.

A little later, he was on a break sitting in a booth across from us. I excused myself and sat down in the booth across from him.

I had a *Real Life Stories* book. I opened it up and asked his name. He said, "Jimmy." So I signed it to Jimmy. I continued to talk to him and wrote a note to him in the book.

I asked Jimmy if he attended church. He said that he always worked on Sundays and needed the money.

I said that if you put God first in your life and make an effort to do His will, God could help with his work schedule.

I introduced Jimmy to the pastor and gave him the book.

I sensed an awesome presence of God while I talked with Jimmy. My prayer is that he made the necessary changes in his life.

Witnessing in the Streets for the First Time

My favorite witnessing experience was the scariest, but most exciting also. A husband and wife team showed us how to do street witnessing by using a survey about God. They prepared us for this activity through prayer, and they went with us to do it.

Explaining about Shofars to a Police Officer

My favorite witnessing experience arose when I was riding a bike down the street with a shofar in the basket. Someone saw it and called the cops saying, "There's a man on a bike with a shotgun."

When stopped, I showed the cops the shofar and told him it's a religious musical instrument. I also handed him a tract about shofars.

He asked me if I would blow it for him.

Performing Witnessing Dramas in Chile

My favorite witnessing experience came while doing dramas in Chile, seeing so many lives be touched at the same time was absolutely amazing.

Helping a Woman with Lupus at the Gym

My favorite witnessing experience was my first one. I was at the gym early one morning. An older woman shared with me that she was diagnosed with lupus and was not feeling well.

This was all God at work! I had a display set up in the gym of the *Real Life Stories* books. After fighting a little with my inner spirit,

I grabbed a book, handed it to her, and began sharing with her God's healing hand upon my life.

It was just awesome!

Performing for the Lord

My favorite witnessing experiences are when I hear the responses of the crowds we play for, hearing how God has changed their lives through our music.

Glowing at the Gas Station

My favorite witnessing experience happened at a gas station. A man started talking to me. He asked me if he knew me. I handed him the first *Real Life Stories* book and told him about the church.

He told me that when he first saw me, he saw a light glowing like he had never seen before and wanted to find out where that light was coming from.

Buying a Book at a Garage Sale

My favorite witnessing experience came at a garage sale in another state while I was visiting with my sister. At the sale I met a woman while purchasing a book by Joyce Meyer.

She told me how ill her daughter was and how she was beginning to lose her faith. My testimony is about how God is a healer. I was able to share words with her in that area. I asked for her address and sent her a *Real Life Stories* book.

Visiting a Nursing Home

My favorite witnessing experiences came when I used to visit nursing homes to spend time loving the patients, listening, and speaking words of encouragement. They were wonderful people and I loved being able to be their friend, to pray for them, and to show them God's love.

Pumping Gas and Sharing about God

My favorite witnessing experience was when I saw an older, senior couple trying to pump gas. I offered to help pump. They were thankful and offered money. I replied, "No, thanks. This is what God wanted me to do." I spent quite a while telling them how great God is and what He's done for me, and I invited them to church.

Because you may be concerned about how others you see frequently will think about you, sharing your faith with these people can feel much more awkward than speaking to strangers. In the next section, we share stories about the surprising, liberating effects of witnessing to those you know.

Stories from Jubilee Worship Center about Witnessing to Friends, Acquaintances, Customers, and Co-Workers

"Greater love has no one than this,
than to lay down one's life for his friends.
You are My friends if you do
whatever I command you."

— John 15:13-14 (NKJV)

Witnessing to people you know is an opportunity to show true caring and to draw closer to them. People can find it helpful to hear about your faith, even if they don't immediately develop faith.

Helping a Touchy Co-Worker with His Problems

My favorite witnessing experience was at work. My co-worker was having problems. I started talking to him a little bit at a time.

After a while I was amazed by his expression (this guy has anger issues and hadn't wanted to know about the Lord). Suddenly, he told me not to sugarcoat, but to tell him everything about the Lord.

What an experience that was (I was a little bit scared). Oh, yeah.

Discussing Inner Peace with People Who Knew Me before I Was a Christian

My favorite witnessing experience occurred when people who knew me in the past notice that I have inner peace even before talking to me. That opened up the lines of communication.

Smiling at Burger King Customers

My favorite witnessing experience was while I was working at Burger King. A girl used to come there all the time who had tried to commit suicide. She asked me why I smile all the time, and I told her about the Lord. She was really accepting.

Sharing a Testimony about Divorce with a Client

My favorite witnessing experience was when a client at work told me she was going through a really bad divorce. Before she left, I gave her a book (*Real Life Stories*). She was shocked that I was giving her something that could help her get through this time in her life. That made me feel really good.

Giving Pedicures at a Strip Club

My favorite witnessing experiences have happened while going to a local strip club where I used to work, giving the dancers free pedicures, and sharing Jesus with them.

Talking about Angels and Devils with a Girl I Knew

My favorite witnessing experience took place when I asked a girl if she believed in angels and devils. She said, "Yes." I asked if she believed in God, and she said, "No." That opened the door for me to witness to her.

Discussing God's Will with a Regular Customer

My favorite witnessing experience was sharing with a regular customer what I think is the role of God in his life and his mom's life as they deal with his dad who suffers from Alzheimer's disease. I told him that what they are going through will help them to help others who are going through something similar.

Sharing Faith with a New Widow

My favorite witnessing experience involved sharing my faith with a widow who had lost her husband the day before.

Being a Good Example for a Co-Worker

My favorite witnessing experiences took place over three years as I shared my faith with a girl I worked with. She never accepted the Lord, but she got to see that no matter what I came across, I never walked away from the Lord.

Counseling Married Couples

My favorite witnessing experiences have occurred when my wife and I share our testimony with couples that are hurting. God took us from contemplating divorce into being marriage counselors at JWC. It's a joy to let these couples know how we were saved together and how God enabled our marriage to become an example, a testimony, of what God can do.

Sharing Faith and Happiness in College

My favorite witnessing experience came while I was in college. I had a few new friends, and I just acted normally around them.

One day, a guy friend said, "You're different than most people. You're always happy and smiling."

Well, that gave me an open door to tell him why I'm always happy. I didn't have to push God or church in his face. He automatically knew that I was unique.

I let him know that there is a God who sent His Son to die for our sins, who gives us forgiveness, mercy, grace, and joy.

What a reason to be excited!

Are you feeling inspired to witness? We certainly hope so. Who can you witness to in the next hour? If you don't feel inspired yet, reread these stories to give your faith a further boost.

✝

In the Epilogue, we discuss what you should do after you finish reading the book now that you know why you should continually witness, the benefits you and others will receive from witnessing, and some of the ways you can be a joyful complete, continual witness.

Epilogue

When the Day of Pentecost had fully come,
they were all with one accord in one place.
And suddenly there came a sound from heaven,
as of a rushing mighty wind,
and it filled the whole house where they were sitting.
Then there appeared to them divided tongues,
as of fire, and one *sat upon each of them.*
And they were all filled with the Holy Spirit
and began to speak with other tongues,
as the Spirit gave them utterance ....
And when this sound occurred,
the multitude came together,
and were confused,
because everyone heard them speak
in his own language.

— Acts 2:1-4, 6 (NKJV)

As these verses from Acts relate, God can enable your words to be understood by anyone, even those who only know a language different than what you speak or write. Pentecost provides an important symbol of God's plan for Christians on Earth: No longer are people to be automatically divided to make it harder for them to cooperate, as occurred when God created language differences during the Tower of Babel's construction. The purposes of receiving the Holy Spirit include helping Christians support one another, to be closer to one another, and to assist lost people to repent and accept the Lord.

When you witness, the Holy Spirit governs the encounter and its impact from before the start to after the finish. As evidence, notice that you will probably be prompted by the Holy Spirit to share your faith before you witness. In addition, it was probably a prompting by the Holy Spirit that led you to want to know more about witnessing and to pick up and read this book. Praise God for His Holy Spirit!

If the Holy Spirit is prodding Christians to witness, why are a few continually witnessing while most don't do anything? One possible reason is that most Christians are ignoring the Holy Spirit's promptings. You have to be paying close attention to Him to notice all that God wants you to see, hear, touch, taste, smell, feel, and do. Any inattention can be costly. That person you were supposed to witness to and didn't notice may be someone who could help save millions of souls.

Let's consider an analogy to understand why God's promptings can be missed. Have you ever walked into a room and smelled a bad odor? You probably left the room. If you couldn't leave, something wonderful happened. After a while, you didn't notice the odor nearly as much. Our minds are good at ignoring what we don't focus on. When we don't concentrate on bad odors, they don't smell so bad. Similarly, when we don't focus on witnessing, we miss promptings to witness that God has shared with us.

Temptations and sins are distractions that regularly pull Christians away from focusing on God, leaving us blind to many things He wants us to notice and do. We, your authors, believe that part of God's purpose for witnessing is to provide us all with a delightful way to focus on Him at all times. What a blessing that is!

Expert "noses" (people who smell things for a living), by contrast, can detect fine odors quite easily by having something pleasant to smell and time to refresh their noses between smelling sessions, and by practice in focusing on every faint aspect of odor. Complete, continual witnesses similarly succeed in finding and acting on opportunities by perceiving witnessing as a magnificent gift from God, refreshing themselves through prayer and asking Him for more opportunities to witness, and becoming more experienced in paying attention to the Holy Spirit's promptings to witness.

How easy is it to be distracted? Scientists conducted an experiment in the 1950s (since repeated many times) where observers of a film were asked to keep track of how many times players on a basketball team passed the ball to one another. About a third of the film viewers usually get the right answer. Even when we are paying attention, it's tough to get the right answer.

But there was another aspect of the experiment: During the film an actor dressed up in a gorilla suit walked through the basketball players and stayed on camera for more than ten seconds. When observers were asked if they noticed anything else going on in the film, relatively few mentioned seeing someone in a gorilla suit. Most people refused to believe that there was a gorilla-suited person until the film was rerun, and they watched without trying to count passes. They laughed at themselves in disbelief. The lesson is that whatever we focus on is what we perceive. To be complete, continual witnesses, Christians need to focus on witnessing.

We, your authors, believe that God has surrounded each Christian with enough witnessing opportunities to draw attention towards Him and away from temptation and sin. We also appreciate that the Lord has made witnessing joyful, soul rewarding, and faith enhancing; every time Christians witness, they notice fewer temptations, sin less, and draw closer to Him.

Think of witnessing as being like a life preserver around your chest that's tied by a lifeline to God. That life preserver keeps your head above water in stormy seas of sinful temptation. Every time you witness, He pulls you by the lifeline closer to Him.

By contrast, people who haven't been witnessing are a lot like people who are learning to swim. These novices aren't quite sure what to do and are afraid that they will be hurt. Yet, there are instructors who can help most of these people to begin swimming happily after just a few classes.

How can a nonwitnessing Christian easily become a complete, continual witness by following good instruction? We summarize our answers to that question in the next section.

Become a Complete, Continual Witness

"Now therefore, write down this song for yourselves,
and teach it to the children of Israel;
put it in their mouths,
that this song may be a witness for Me ...."

— Deuteronomy 31:19 (NKJV)

To help you make rapid, joyful progress towards becoming a complete, continual witness, we have boiled down our advice to just eight key points:

1. **At least once a week, read the verses in Appendix A of this book that support witnessing** (Sunday will be a convenient day for many people). Reading these verses will remind you that God commands you to be a witness for Him. In addition, the verses will sharpen your focus on finding witnessing opportunities and being more sensitive to the promptings of the Holy Spirit.

2. **Pray daily that He will send you witnessing opportunities.** Your prayers will be answered, and your faith will be increased by His support of your witnessing. In addition, He will sharpen your focus on learning more ways to witness.

3. **Write your testimony and keep copies with you.** Your physical testimony will help remind you to be looking for witnessing opportunities. Keep copies at work, at home, in the car, and anywhere else you regularly go. In addition, read your testimony at least once a month to help you remember what God has done for you. Your reading will help keep your testimony fresh in your mind so you can describe it better to unsaved people.

4. **Give a copy of your testimony to everyone you know.** The best way to present your testimony is after first doing someone a service. In serving and sharing, you should be unconcerned about whether or not the recipient is saved. Your testimony can help Christians stay closer to Him while also demonstrating a good way to witness.

5. **Follow up in three days with anyone who receives your written or oral testimony and stay in touch every three days thereafter until Salvation is received or a life is rededicated**

to the Lord. Many Christians have been in church during an altar call for people to repent, receive Christ, and gain Salvation. The person leading the altar call will usually repeat the invitation to come forward several times. Why? Most lost people find it hard to respond immediately. With each repetition of the invitation, more people usually come forward.

Your follow-up serves the same purpose. If you have other witnessing tools, share those during subsequent contacts. If you don't have such tools, think about new information you could share with the unsaved person or the person who needs to rededicate her or his life. During follow-up conversations, we suggest that you provide information from Appendix E: The Importance and Power of the Resurrection.

6. **Invite lost people to join you for church services.** If they accept the invitation, offer to pick them up. If they want to drive, ask if you can ride with them. If that's not what they want to do, offer to let them follow your vehicle. Sit with them. Have a meal together after the service. In this way, you'll encourage both Salvation and regular church attendance.

7. **Try a new witnessing activity once a month.** Pray for guidance as to what new thing you should try. The more discomfort or fear you feel now, the better you will feel after trying a new way to witness. Look forward to enjoying these safe adventures for the Lord where He will teach you to trust Him.

8. **Assist those you help lead to Salvation to write their testimonies and learn to be complete, continual witnesses.** Many of those who gain Salvation will be excited about sharing this wonderful experience with family, friends, neighbors, acquaintances, and strangers. Take the new Christians through the process you followed to become a complete, continual witness so that they can gain this wonderful way to focus on the

Lord. Providing this assistance will also give you an opportunity to help disciple the newly saved person.

You may also feel called to help your church's congregation become more active in witnessing. We discuss what you can do to encourage witnessing development by that focus in the next section.

Help More of Your Church's Congregation Become Complete, Continual Witnesses

"Now, Lord, look on their threats, and
grant to Your servants that with all boldness
they may speak Your word,
by stretching out Your hand to heal, and
that signs and wonders may be done through the
name of Your holy Servant Jesus."
And when they had prayed,
the place where they were assembled together was shaken;
and they were filled with the Holy Spirit,
and they spoke the word of God with boldness.

— Acts 4:29-31 (NKJV)

After becoming a complete, continual witness, we recommend you take the following steps to help your fellow congregants do the same:

1. **Pray for guidance about what you should say to and share with your pastor.** Here are items of information that might be helpful to your pastor in evaluating ways to encourage witnessing. Pray over this list to decide what information items to share with your pastor.

   • Your written testimony
   • Your witnessing experiences
   • How witnessing has affected your faith
   • Benefits from having an in-congregation evangelist
   • Your calling (if it exists) to be that evangelist

- Allocating five minutes in each service and activity for witnessing messages
- Asking each person to prepare a written testimony
- Assisting in writing testimonies
- Printing a book of the congregation's testimonies
- Any new ministries you would like to help establish and lead
- Requesting additional offerings to pay for witnessing tools
- Organizing regular outreaches to help build witnessing confidence and experience
- Providing witnessing tools and training to other congregations
- Preparing to disciple more new Christians

2. **Know the facts about what you intend to share with your pastor.** Jubilee Worship Center and Step by Step Ministries will be happy to assist you in providing information, advice, and counsel. You can also refer to the appropriate chapters and appendixes in this book for information.

3. **Practice your discussion with someone who plays the role of your pastor.** It's best to practice with someone who knows your pastor and may be able to anticipate questions and concerns that your pastor might raise. This practice will help you see where you need to do more homework and will make you feel more comfortable in speaking to the pastor.

4. **Pray for guidance in how to ask for a meeting with your pastor.** Naturally, your pastor will be happy to speak with you, but you want to make the best possible impression. There are many ways that your good intentions to encourage witnessing can appear to be supporting activities that will not be in the best interest of your congregation. Your pastor might lack a complete understanding about what it's like to encourage a congregation to become complete, continual witnesses. With prayer,

the Holy Spirit can guide you to ask for your meeting in the right way.

5. **Meet with your pastor and find out what issues require more study.** We are sure that your pastor will have good questions and valid concerns. Offer to find out more information to enable your pastor to make a good decision about which way to lead the congregation.

6. **Keep meeting and sharing information with your pastor until there are no more questions.** Pastors are busy. It will be easy for the idea of helping everyone become complete, continual witnesses to get lost. Your initiative will help keep the subject under active consideration until a decision can be made and action taken.

7. **Volunteer to help implement anything you feel called to do.** The decision to proceed to establish a congregation-wide activity will be easier if your pastor knows that volunteer help is available. At a minimum, you may be able to play a helpful role in recruiting volunteers to help start the new programs that are needed.

8. **If you feel called to provide financial resources, offer those to the pastor.** It takes money to do more than encourage witnessing. If you can provide some of that money and are willing to ask others to do the same, your financial and fund-raising support may permit a larger and more effective program.

Having seen the dramatic results that can come when willing witnesses have access to the right tools, you may also wish to play a role in encouraging witnessing by those outside of your congregation who need those resources. In the next section, we describe steps to engage in those opportunities.

Help Christians Who Are Not in Your Congregation Gain Witnessing Tools and Knowledge

There are four things which are little on the earth,
But they are exceedingly wise:
The ants are a people not strong,
Yet they prepare their food in the summer;
The rock badgers are a feeble folk,
Yet they make their homes in the crags;
The locusts have no king,
Yet they all advance in ranks;
The spider skillfully grasps with its hands,
And it is in kings' palaces.

— Proverbs 30:24-28 (NKJV)

The opportunity to improve witnessing just begins with your congregation. Most Christians know little about Jesus' command to witness and the helpfulness of the witnessing tools we've described. Almost every witness will be more successful, confident, and active by learning about and employing these tools.

In other cases, willing witnesses lack the knowledge and financial resources to develop or acquire the tools. Willing witnesses can be helped by financial support and by teaching them how to attract offerings for witnessing tools.

You can decide to help with either or both of these needs in a variety of roles. Here are some steps to help you to be more effective in advancing the use of witnessing tools:

1. **Pray for guidance in selecting a type of need to serve.** Few people are called to help both needs and in all of the possible roles. Through prayer, your heart will be more strongly attracted to either teaching about witnessing tools or assisting with financial resources to provide the tools.

2. **Pray for guidance about how to serve the need you are called to help.** The narrower your focus, the easier it will be to understand what service the Holy Spirit is calling you to supply

and where. If you also pray at the same time about what type of need to support and type of service to provide, God's messages for you may confuse you.

3. **Pray for guidance about what role you should play in serving that need.** Let's say that you are drawn to helping people learn about using witnessing tools. There are many roles for serving that need, from recruiting volunteers to helping others learn to personally lead one-on-one live witnessing trainings with those who are learning to use new tools. What role are you called to perform?

4. **Pray for guidance in how you should find the right people to help.** If you ask for guidance, God will provide Divine connections to those He wants you to serve.

5. **Seek out opportunities at least once a month to learn more about witnessing needs beyond your congregation.** You may find your heart strings are tugged by different needs in addition to the ones you are serving. Or you may find that you would like to do more. There's a big need to provide tools and training.

6. **Thank God daily for allowing you to help other witnesses be more effective.** Your gratitude will help draw you closer to God and to receiving His guidance.

7. **Tell other complete, continual witnesses about what you are doing.** God may wish to use you to call others into increasing their witnessing activities and improving their witnessing effectiveness.

8. **Encourage people who are effective in using witnessing tools to share what they've learned.** Until all Christians know how the most effective, continually witnessing Christians use witnessing tools, many lost people will remain so.

Epilogue

✝

In closing, we would like to thank you for reading our book, taking its lessons to heart, and looking to apply what we've shared with you. We pray that your witnessing activities will prosper beyond your wildest dreams due to God's amazing love and support. May you receive so many blessings from your witnessing that you will not be able to recount them all!

Appendix A

Witnessing Scriptures

Here we have assembled some of our favorite verses about witnessing. We invite you to read, enjoy, and be inspired by these verses whenever you would like to be strengthened in your commitment to witnessing for the Lord.

Let's begin with Christ's authority over and role in Salvation:

Jesus said to him,
"I am the way, the truth, and the life.
No one comes to the Father except through Me."

— John 14:6 (NKJV)

"Behold, I stand at the door and knock.
If anyone hears My voice and opens the door,
I will come in to him and dine with him,
and he with Me."

— Revelation 3:20 (NKJV)

Now let's turn to what Jesus had to say about witnessing:

"Therefore whoever confesses Me before men,
him I will also confess
before My Father who is in heaven."

— Matthew 10:32 (NKJV)

"Go home to your friends,
and tell them what great things the Lord has done for you,
and how He has had compassion on you."

— Mark: 5:19 (NKJV)

*"The works that I do in My Father's name,
they bear witness of Me."*

— John 10:25 (NKJV)

*But when He saw the multitudes,
He was moved with compassion for them,
because they were weary and scattered,
like sheep having no shepherd.
Then He said to His disciples,
"The harvest truly* is *plentiful, but the laborers* are *few.
Therefore pray the Lord of the harvest
to send out laborers into His harvest."*

— Matthew 9:36-38 (NKJV)

*"Go therefore and make disciples
of all the nations,
baptizing them in the name of
the Father and of the Son and of the Holy Spirit, ..."*

— Matthew 28:19 (NKJV)

*He said to him the third time,
"Simon,* son *of Jonah, do you love Me?"
Peter was grieved because He said to him the third time,
"Do you love Me?"
And he said to Him, "Lord, You know all things;
You know that I love You."
Jesus said to him, "Feed My sheep."*

— John 21:17 (NKJV)

*"And he who does not take his cross
and follow after Me is not worthy of Me."*

— Matthew 10:38 (NKJV)

"More than that, blessed are *those*
who hear the word of God and keep it!"

— Luke 11:28 (NKJV)

Some might argue that Jesus was only speaking about what His apostles should do. Paul makes it clear that the command to witness moves forward to present-day Christians:

And the things that you have heard
from me among many witnesses,
commit these to faithful men
who will be able to teach others also.

— 2 Timothy 2:2 (NKJV)

Having seen that we are commanded to witness, let's look at what other guidance the Bible provides about helping facilitate Salvation. We need to appreciate that not witnessing is rejecting Jesus, and we imperil our souls when we do that.

"Greater love has no one than this,
than to lay down one's life for his friends.
You are My friends if you do
whatever I command you."

— John 15:13-14 (NKJV)

"For whoever is ashamed of Me and My words
in this adulterous and sinful generation,
of him the Son of Man also will be ashamed
when He comes in the glory of His Father with the holy angels."

— Mark 8:38 (NKJV)

Son of man, I have made thee a watchman unto the house of Israel:
therefore hear the word at my mouth,
and give them warning from me.
When I say unto the wicked, Thou shalt surely die;
and thou givest him not warning,
nor speakest to warn the wicked from his wicked way,
to save his life; the same wicked man *shall die in his iniquity;*
but his blood will I require at thine hand.

— Ezekiel 3:17-18 (KJV)

"Son of man, speak to the children of your people, and say to them:
'When I bring the sword upon a land,
and the people of the land take a man from their territory
and make him their watchman,
when he sees the sword coming upon the land,
if he blows the trumpet and warns the people,
then whoever hears the sound of the trumpet
and does not take warning,
if the sword comes and takes him away,
his blood shall be on his own *head.*
He heard the sound of the trumpet,
but did not take warning;
his blood shall be upon himself.
But he who takes warning will save his life.
But if the watchman sees the sword coming
and does not blow the trumpet,
and the people are not warned, and the sword comes
and takes any *person from among them,*
he is taken away in his iniquity;
but his blood I will require at the watchman's hand.'"

— Ezekiel 33:2-6 (NKJV)

For I am not ashamed of the gospel of Christ,
for it is the power of God to salvation for everyone who believes, ...

— Romans 1:16 (NKJV)

"I know your works, that you are neither cold nor hot.
I could wish you were cold or hot.
So then, because you are lukewarm,
and neither cold nor hot,
I will vomit you out of My mouth."

— Revelation 3:15-16 (NKJV)

What does it profit, my brethren,
if someone says he has faith but does not have works?
Can faith save him?

— James 2:14 (NKJV)

The Bible also says that you should let others know about your faith and what Jesus has done for you through your words and actions:

A true witness delivers souls, ...

— Proverbs 14:25 (NKJV)

"You are witnesses of these things."

— Luke 24:48 (NAS)

"And you also will bear witness, ..."

— John 15:27 (NKJV)

And there are also many other things that Jesus did,
which if they were written one by one,
I suppose that even the world itself
could not contain the books that would be written. Amen.

— John 21:25 (NKJV)

"But he who received seed on the good ground
is he who hears the word and understands it,
who indeed bears fruit and produces:
some a hundredfold, some sixty, some thirty."

— Matthew 13:23 (NKJV)

I will declare Your name to My brethren;
In the midst of the assembly I will praise You.

— Psalm 22:22 (NKJV)

Beloved, you do faithfully whatever you do
for the brethren and for strangers,
who have borne witness of your love before the church.
If you send them forward on their journey in a manner
worthy of God, you will do well, ...

— 3 John 1:5-6 (NKJV)

Now therefore, write down this song for yourselves,
and teach it to the children of Israel;
put it in their mouths,
that this song may be a witness for Me ....

— Deuteronomy 31:19 (NKJV)

And he departed and began to proclaim in Decapolis
all that Jesus had done for him;
and all marveled.

— Mark 5:20 (NKJV)

If we receive the witness of men,
the witness of God is greater; ....

— 1 John 5:9 (NKJV)

Finally, brethren, whatever things are true,
whatever things are *noble,*
whatever things are *just,*
whatever things are *pure,*
whatever things are *lovely,*
whatever things are *of good report,*
if there is *any virtue*
and if there is *anything praiseworthy* —
meditate on these things.

— Philippians 4:8 (NKJV)

Like the cold of snow in time of harvest
Is a faithful messenger to those who send him,
For he refreshes the soul of his masters.

— Proverbs 25:13 (NKJV)

"Let your light so shine before men,
that they may see your good works
and glorify your Father in heaven."

— Matthew 5:16 (NKJV)

I urge, then, first of all, that
requests, prayers, intercession and thanksgiving
be made for everyone — ....

1 Timothy 2:1 (NIV)

So then faith comes *by hearing, and hearing by the word of God.*

— Romans 10:17 (NKJV)

I will remember the works of the LORD;
Surely I will remember Your wonders of old.
I will also meditate on all Your work,
And talk of Your deeds.

— Psalm 77:11-12 (NKJV)

Fools, because of their transgression,
And because of their iniquities, were afflicted.
Their soul abhorred all manner of food,
And they drew near to the gates of death.
Then they cried out to the LORD in their trouble,
And He saved them out of their distresses.
He sent His word and healed them,
And delivered them *from their destructions.*
Oh, that men *would give thanks to the LORD* for *His goodness,*
And for *His wonderful works to the children of men!*
Let them sacrifice the sacrifices of thanksgiving,
And declare His works with rejoicing.

— Psalm 107:17-22 (NKJV)

But, beloved, we are confident of better things concerning you,
yes, things that accompany salvation, ...

— Hebrews 6:9 (NKJV)

Your testimonies also are *my delight*
And my counselors.

— Psalm 119:24 (NKJV)

In addition, the Lord has provided resources to make your witnessing more effective:

"And whatever you ask in My name, that I will do,
that the Father may be glorified in the Son."

— John 14:13 (NKJV)

I can do all things through Christ who strengthens me.

— Philippians 4:13 (NKJV)

Commit to the LORD whatever you do,
and your plans will succeed.

— Proverbs 16:3 (NIV)

"And they overcame him by the blood of the Lamb
and by the word of their testimony, ..."

— Revelation 12:11 (NKJV)

Therefore you do not lack any spiritual gift
as you eagerly wait for our Lord Jesus Christ to be revealed.

— 1 Corinthians 1:7 (NIV)

"But the Helper, the Holy Spirit,
whom the Father will send in My name,
He will teach you all things,
and bring to your remembrance
all things that I said to you."

— John 14:26 (NKJV)

"Now, Lord, look on their threats, and
grant to Your servants that with all boldness
they may speak Your word,
by stretching out Your hand to heal, and
that signs and wonders may be done through the
name of Your holy Servant Jesus."
And when they had prayed,
the place where they were assembled together was shaken;
and they were filled with the Holy Spirit,
and they spoke the word of God with boldness.

— Acts 4:29-31 (NKJV)

"Now go; I will help you speak
and will teach you what to say."

— Exodus 4:12 (NIV)

... and most of the brethren in the Lord,
having become confident by my chains,
are much more bold to speak the word without fear.

— Philippians 1:14 (NKJV)

Put on the whole armor of God,
that you may be able to stand against the wiles of the devil.
For we do not wrestle against flesh and blood,
but against principalities, against powers,
against the rulers of the darkness of this age,
against spiritual hosts *of wickedness in the heavenly* places.

— Ephesians 6:11-12 (NKJV)

And take the helmet of salvation, and the sword of the Spirit,
which is the word of God;
praying always with all prayer and supplication in the Spirit,
being watchful to this end with all perseverance
and supplication for all the saints —

and for me, that utterance may be given to me,
that I may open my mouth boldly to make known the mystery of the gospel, ...
that in it I may speak boldly, as I ought to speak.

— Ephesians 6:17-20 (NKJV)

And he gave some, apostles; and some, prophets;
and some, evangelists; and some, pastors and teachers;
For the perfecting of the saints, for the work of the ministry,
for the edifying of the body of Christ: ....

Ephesians 4:11-12 (KJV)

... the testimony of our conscience
that we conducted ourselves in the world
in simplicity and godly sincerity,
not with fleshly wisdom
but by the grace of God, and more abundantly toward you.

— 2 Corinthians 1:12 (NKJV)

The call to witness is a higher one, one that must be followed despite any difficulties:

But you be watchful in all things, endure afflictions,
do the work of an evangelist, fulfill your ministry.

— 2 Timothy 4:5 (NKJV)

... just as I also please all men *in all* things, *not seeking my own profit,*
but the profit *of many, that they may be saved.*

— 1 Corinthians 10:33 (NKJV)

Therefore we also, since we are surrounded by so great a cloud of witnesses,
let us lay aside every weight, and the sin which so easily ensnares us,
and let us run with endurance the race that is set before us, ...

— Hebrews 12:1 (NKJV)

"Whoever desires to come after Me,
let him deny himself, and take up his cross,
and follow Me."

— Mark 8:34 (NKJV)

"I did not come to bring peace but a sword.
For I have come to 'set a man against his father,
a daughter against her mother, and
a daughter-in-law against her mother-in-law'; *and*
'a man's enemies will be those of his own household.'
He who loves father or mother more than Me is not worthy of Me.
And he who loves son or daughter more than Me is not worthy of Me."

— Matthew 10:34-37 (NKJV)

"And whoever will not receive you,
when you go out of that city,
shake off the very dust from your feet as a testimony against them."

— Luke 9:5 (NKJV)

Personal benefits follow for those who are obedient in witnessing:

The fruit of the righteous is a tree of life,
And he who wins souls is wise.

— Proverbs 11:30 (NKJV)

Cast your bread upon the waters,
For you will find it after many days.

— Ecclesiastes 11:1 (NKJV)

Let all the inhabitants of the world stand in awe of Him.

—Psalm 33:8 (NKJV)

Blessed are those who have learned to acclaim you,
who walk in the light of your presence,
O LORD.

— Psalm 89:15 (NIV)

So then neither he who plants is anything, nor he who waters,
but God who gives the increase.
Now he who plants and he who waters are one,
and each one will receive his own reward
according to his own labor.
For we are God's fellow workers;
you are God's field, you are *God's building.*

— 1 Corinthians 3:7-9 (NKJV)

For we ourselves were also once foolish, disobedient, deceived,
serving various lusts and pleasures,
living in malice and envy,
hateful and hating one another.
But when the kindness and the love of God
our Savior toward man appeared,
not by works of righteousness which we have done,
but according to His mercy He saved us,
through the washing of regeneration
and renewing of the Holy Spirit,
whom He poured out onto us abundantly
through Jesus Christ our Savior,
that having been justified by His grace

*we should become heirs
according to the hope of eternal life.
This is a faithful saying,
and these things I want you to affirm constantly,
that those who have believed in God should be careful
to maintain good works.
These things are good and profitable to men.*

— Titus 3:3-8 (NKJV)

God also wants us to encourage others to witness:

*Therefore encourage one another
and build up one another,
just as you also are doing.*

— 1 Thessalonians 5:11 (NAS)

*"But I have prayed for you,
that your faith should not fail;
and when you have returned to* Me,
strengthen your brethren."

— Luke 22:32 (NKJV)

*Therefore we ought to support such men,
so that we may be fellow workers with the truth.*

— 3 John 1:8 (NAS)

Appendix B

Authors' Testimonies

Bishop Dale P. Combs's Testimony

A Godly Heritage and Legacy

For many are called, but few are *chosen.*

— Matthew 22:14 (NKJV)

Tracing my spiritual journey is a daunting task. Looking back I see three stages of my life where God has been involved: my childhood, adolescence, and adult life. I can recall significant people, events, and decisions that aided in developing my attitude towards God and ministry, both positively and negatively. My involvement in ministry today is a direct result of those influences. As with any journey, one must continue on until the destination is reached. The Bible states (in Psalm 37:23, NKJV),

> The steps of a *good* man are ordered by the LORD,
> And He delights in his way.

Childhood

Being the eldest of four brothers and the son of a minister created a childhood filled with excitement and many challenges. Reflecting on my childhood, I can see the role family played in shaping my life.

My father not only pastored the church, but also served as a Crew Chief for the United States Air Force. He spent many hours away from home ministering to the needs of others and serving his country. This left little time at home. It seemed there was always someone who needed the services of his calling.

My father's service to his country resulted in numerous moves to new locations. This left little time to develop friendships outside the home resulting in my brothers and I spending much of our free time playing, arguing, and sometimes fighting with each other. The only certainty we had was each other; after all we were family.

While stationed in Michigan, my father pioneered a new church work. In the early 1960s pioneering a church meant at times converting the living room of a small house into a church where we would worship. I can remember sitting in wooden seats in the front row of the church and being warned not to talk during the service or else there would be repercussions for my negative behavior. I would sit and listen to my father as he preached God's Word. Even at such a young age, I remember being moved by his preaching. It seemed to stir something deep within me; it was here I realized God was beginning to shape my life.

We lived in Michigan for a couple of years and then moved to the state of New York. While in New York I had the opportunity to spend some time with my uncle. He, like my dad, was a minister. He pastored a church in Niagara Falls.

During one summer visit, Uncle Dan took me to summer camp. I was only six years old and too young to be there, but because he was the Camp Coordinator special privileges were extended to me. I had no idea what was in store for me.

Each evening we attended a church service. During one of the services, the minister shared with us the need for Salvation. The message of Jesus dying on the cross for my sins was not unfamiliar to me; my dad had preached it many times before.

However, that night, I realized that I had never asked Jesus to forgive me of my sins and to live in my heart. As I listened to the minister, I watched other children begin to cry as they heard the story of the crucifixion of Christ. It wasn't long before I too began to cry, a wave of emotion flooded my heart.

The minister called for all those who would like to accept Jesus as their Savior to come forward. I stood up and walked the sawdust aisle until I came to a makeshift altar. It was there I knelt and asked for Jesus to forgive me of my sins and come into my heart. A rush of joy filled my young heart. At that moment, I knew I was forgiven. My life would never be the same.

Children are not always taken seriously. People tend to think you're cute; they smile politely when you talk with them, pat your head, and send you on your way.

I began to see that I was different from many of my childhood friends. While they were out riding their bicycles and playing hide and seek, I would call them over to my house. There on the front porch at 18 Geneva Street, Rochester, New York, I would open my Bible and without hesitation I would begin preaching to them.

At first, the kids thought it was funny to see someone their age acting like a preacher. They would come just to poke fun at me until I read from the book of Revelation. I shared that Jesus was coming one day to rapture the Christians and once they were gone, God would pour out his wrath. They didn't laugh any more. In fact, their curiosity drew them into the Word. I remember spending much of our playtime having church. I had the opportunity to lead some of them to Salvation and enjoyed their company at our church. God was showing me the importance that the Apostle Paul's words to Timothy would be to my life when he said (in 1 Timothy 4:12, NKJV), "Let no one despise your youth, but be an example to the believers in word, in conduct, in love, in spirit, in faith, in purity." Entering my teen years, I realized that there was a big difference between being a Christian as a teen rather than as a child.

Adolescence

In the early seventies my dad had loaded us up in the family station wagon, and we moved to Indiana. We arrived late in the night after traveling nonstop from Rochester. My brothers and I were all sleeping and we woke as we pulled up to the front of the church.

At first glance, the church seemed uninviting. It was old and worn. I felt my heart beat faster as one of the elders met us, walked us around to the alley, opened the side door, and let us in. This was it, our new home. There we were standing in the small living room. The musty smell almost took my breath away. The kitchen barely had enough room for a table and chairs let alone a stove and refrigerator. It had only two small bedrooms. How were all four brothers to sleep in this tiny space with only one closet?

My first thought was, "Where's the bathroom?" and as if he could read my mind, the elder said, "The bathroom is in the basement of the church. You have to share it with the congregation." My brothers and I rushed to see it.

If you've ever been in a church when all the lights are off, you know the scary feelings you get as you walk the dark corridors. I must confess that church basements offer their own eerie feel, especially if you have never been there before.

We slowly walked down the concrete steps, clinging to each other as we groped in the darkness trying to find a light switch. As our eyes adjusted to the light, we walked through the door of the bathroom.

There it was! A simple stall had been constructed by a member of the congregation, comprised of a concrete floor with a drain, a shower head, and pressboard walls. This would be our family shower for the next three and one-half years. I always heard that a pastor was to be humble, but in my opinion this was taking it to the extremes.

Despite my personal objections, we moved in and began the ministry there. Dad worked a secular job during the week, and he preached on the weekend. Mom did her best to keep the house in order.

The inadequate amount of living space forced my brothers and me to sleep in one room together. Our sleeping arrangements were simple: four to a bed, two at the head and two at the foot. The winter months were the worst. Our bedroom would have snow falling in on us. Due to the furnace being inadequate to heat our makeshift home, we slept with every available blanket we could find. In fact, my younger brother David would put on his wool hat, gloves, and long underwear just to stay warm at night

Along with the shortage of heat, food was in short supply as well. I remember one day coming home from school when Dean, the second oldest, and I were hungry for a snack. We looked everywhere for something to eat. The only thing we could find was a few stale cookies in the cookie jar. They would have made better door stops than food.

234

We ran water over them to make them soft because there was no milk in the fridge.

What I did not know at the time was my dad and mom would be on their knees praying for God to supply the need. It would not be long before there was a knock on the door. When I answered it, no one was there but a stack of groceries like I had not seen before. God did supply because he heard the prayers of a righteous man and woman.

During this time I really was not impressed with ministry. In fact, I told myself when I got old enough I would become a good layman in my dad's congregation, get a great job, and support him so he would not have to feel like he was letting his family down.

I decided since I loved the game of football I would join the City League team. I did and became a starter on defense. I made some friends with the guys on the team, but I realized the simplicity of my childhood Christianity was beginning to diminish as the trying times of adolescent adjustment set in.

Like many teenage boys I wanted to be popular. Being part of the football team opened the door to spiritual challenges that I would have to overcome. Trying to be popular and maintain Christian values is not as easy as it sounds. Being a Christian for me meant that I was to keep myself from things that were considered worldly. So when I was asked to go to parties with the guys, I had to say no! Yet inside I wanted desperately to fit in. I sensed the inward struggle of spiritual warfare.

My father had developed a reputation for being a minister who knew how to troubleshoot a church. This meant he could go to a congregation that was in trouble, bring it out of whatever mess it was in, and reestablish the work.

We moved to the city of Griffith, Indiana, so dad could assist this church and reestablish the work. Honestly, I was quite excited about coming to Griffith. I met a young man by the name of Butch Fortner who introduced me to the school and his friends. It was nice to have someone who could help you get acquainted with a new school. I've never been intimidated by new surroundings. I always did what I felt was necessary so I could move on to the next phase in my life.

My sophomore year would truly be a defining moment in my life. Since it was my childhood dream to become a professional football player, I knew I had to join the high school football team. I was used to being on the starting team, so I went all out for everything I did during practice hoping the coach would notice me and place me on the starting junior varsity team and eventually move me in to a varsity position.

Summer practice was extremely difficult. Since the summer heat was unbearable in the middle of the day, our practice times were early in the morning and again in the late afternoon as the sun was setting. During our regular morning practice the defensive coordinator had us working on tackling drills. We moved to the "Tacklematic," a machine designed to improve tackling skills. Each team member took his turn. I watched as each player did what Coach said.

When I approached the starting position, Coach yelled, "You better not move your head to the side, son! Put your body into it and take it like a man!"

As the release handle was pulled, I stood waiting for the impact of the tackle dummy to come to me. The voice of my coach was resonating in my ears. I dipped my head ever so slightly and "Bam!" Perhaps you have heard the expression, "He got his bell rung!" Well that's exactly what happened to me. It was as if a giant gong had gone off in my head. The next thing I remember, they were picking me up off the ground. I had been knocked unconscious. Coach came to see how I was, looked me over and said, "Shake it off, son" and back to practice we went.

Later that night my neck was so sore that I could not move my head. I tried to sleep that night but the pain was unbearable. I got up the next day and went to school; however, I could not move my head. One of my teachers noticed that I was in pain and suggested that I go to the school nurse, which I did. She called my mom and we drove to the hospital. After x-rays were taken, they sent me home and told my mother that I needed to see my family doctor. The following day I went to see him. He stated that I had muscle spasms and I would be fine in a few days. I just needed to take it easy.

A couple weeks went by and my mother received a call from the doctor's office. When mom answered it, I could tell by the look on her face the news frightened her. They wanted me at the hospital immediately. The doctor stated that I had broken my neck.

I arrived at the hospital and was admitted to a room and placed in traction. When the neurosurgeon spoke to my parents, he shared that I was very fortunate to be walking. The diagnosis was very clear. I had crushed the left side of the vertebra in my neck. The slightest move could sever my spinal nerves and I would be paralyzed from the neck down. As the doctor was scheduling the surgery, my parents called the church family to prayer. That was all we knew to do; when you're in need, you pray!

While in the hospital I had asked God to heal me before I would have to go in for surgery. It was during this prayer I promised God I would no longer pursue a future in football. Instead, I would do whatever He asked of my life. Within ten days God performed a miracle in my life. No surgery!

I was released from the hospital and decided to get serious about my relationship with God. I was in pursuit of His will for my life. As I prayed and read the Scriptures daily, I sensed the drawing near of His presence.

I had formed a band with my brothers and some friends from the church. We would sing for church youth groups. While at a service at the Portage Church of God, I sensed a strong urgency to pray. As I was praying, God began dealing with my heart. I remember hearing a voice speak to me as if the person was kneeling next to me. In a soft voice I heard, "I want you to preach My Word." I knew God was speaking to me. I stood before the group of young people, announced that I had been asked by God to preach His Word and that I accepted this charge.

Arriving home that evening my brother raced into the house and told my father what had happened to me at the service. Dad called me in his room and asked if I knew for sure what had happened. I explained to him that I received the call to preach God's Word. I could see the reluctant but joyful look on his face. He reached out to me and prayed a blessing over my life.

My dad believed in me. He taught me how to study the Word. He shared techniques in sermon preparation and how to deliver the message. He even gave me the opportunity to preach my first sermon.

Adulthood

Knowing the importance a college education can have on ministry, I enrolled in Bible college. This proved to be quite challenging and expensive. After my first semester the financial burden was weighing heavily on my parents so I came home, worked, and attended school part-time. Much of my time was spent doing ministry. I met my wife Lisa while I was the youth instructor. Within a few months we married, and school seemed a distant second on my list of things to do.

Marriage changes everything. It makes things complicated. For me it would seem that school and ministry were fading from view. However, my wife was a woman of prayer. Her desire was to marry a preacher, and she wouldn't settle for anything less. I can say without fear that my wife was the instrument God used to remind me of the calling God placed in my life. Her encouragement and patience enabled me to continue my pursuit of the ministry.

We attended the Ministerial Internship Program together. This program assisted young couples interested in ministry. From there we served as youth pastors at the Michigan City Church of God. While there, I further defined my calling. A year later we served as associate pastors of the Lake Station Church of God. While serving in this capacity, God again spoke to my heart. "You will pastor this church," He said. We served under the leadership of Reverend D. L. Rehmel who taught me the ministry of servanthood.

While working full-time and pursuing my call, an opportunity opened for Lisa and me to move to Lafayette, Indiana, and serve in our first pastorate. For two and one-half years, we served and learned to depend on the same God who influenced my childhood and adolescent years.

By the age of thirty, God brought me back to the place He said I would pastor which is now renamed Jubilee Worship Center. Over twenty-one years have gone by. While my leadership roles have changed, the influence of my past directly influences my present. I continue to serve the congregation at Jubilee Worship Center and will do so until the Lord says otherwise. This ministry has provided opportunities to go into foreign countries and minister the Gospel (something that I always desired to do). I have been to South America on three occasions and have seen many souls won to the Kingdom of God.

Today I serve in a variety of capacities. For over twelve years I have served with four law enforcement agencies as their Chaplain and Reserve Police Officer. This has given me a world view of ministry. I was called to go to New York City one month after the World Trade Center attack. The World Trade Center attack caused me to reevaluate my life then and after.

While I have made many accomplishments, the one thing that I had not been able to do was finish my education. I sensed a clear directive in my heart to complete what I had started so many years ago. I know that I still have much to learn but I also have much to give. I graduated in the spring of 2009 and am now working on a graduate degree.

Tragedy Meets Grace and Mercy

One of the most traumatic events of my life occurred in March 2007. I received a phone call from my father, and I immediately knew something was wrong.

To my dismay I heard these words, "Your mom has a mass on her spine and they think it is cancer."

Following the conversation with dad, I prayed for God to move, as I am a firm believer in the power of prayer and God's ability to heal.

I packed up the family and we traveled to Florida to be with my mom as she went to the oncologist. Sitting in the conference room with all my brothers and their families, we heard the prognosis: Mom had Adenocarcianoma, which is a small cell cancer.

The doctor shared that it started in her lung (which had developed about two years earlier and was not diagnosed because her symptoms looked like a common cold or a reaction to medication). Now it had moved into her spine.

Devastated, we held on to each other, but mom just took it in stride. The doctor shared that it was not operable and that there was no cure. With radiation and chemo the cancer's progression would slow, and we should enjoy at least the year and perhaps two before the cancer would totally invade her body.

I confess to you that I was dumbfounded by the news, yet hopeful. God is still the worker of miracles.

Over the next couple of months things just seemed to get worse. Mom never complained; she just went forward.

Living so far from her made life so difficult. I dreaded the phone ringing. The thoughts of life without my mom were at times so heavy that I did not even want to preach. Yet every time I stood before the people of God, the Holy Spirit would breathe new life into the message and lives were transformed by the power of the Scriptures.

My vacation was scheduled for May when my wife and I would celebrate our twenty-seventh wedding anniversary. We made preparations to see my family then. I knew this would be the last time I would see my mom alive.

We arrived late Monday evening and walked into her room. To my surprise she had been waiting up for us to get there. She sat there with her red ball cap on and with a chuckle she raised it and said, "I have something to show you. I'm bald." She just laughed and laughed about that. We shared and prayed together and left her as she fell asleep for the night.

The next morning my dad called for us to come as soon as we could; mom had taken a turn for the worse. When we arrived she was unable to get in and out of the bed without help. She had lost the use of her legs because the tumor was pressing the nerve that controlled the motor function of her legs. My brother and I helped get her back into the bed and that would be the last time she would get up.

She slept for hours and at times we thought she was gone. Then she would wake up and sing the song, "His Eye Is on the Sparrow and I Know He's Watching over Me." By late Wednesday all she could say was "Sparrow."

On Thursday (about sixty days from her diagnosis) with all the family at her bedside and prayers and songs lifted up, she was with the Lord. "How precious is the death of His saints."

At the time of this writing, it will just be a year on May 24th and the first Mother's Day without my mom. I cannot help but give thanks to the Lord for the Godly heritage I have and the legacy my mom gave to me. It was always her desire to win lost people. She always questioned if her life as a believer ever touched people.

Her going home service proved that she was truly a woman of faith and a bright witness for Christ. There is not enough time or space here to share all that her life meant and how so many people were changed because of the life she lived before them. All I will say is, what a legacy. I am truly blessed. I have a good heritage. It is a heritage that I will continue to pass on to my children and grandchildren.

Conclusion

While tracing my journey has been daunting, I know that it is not over. There are many significant people, events, and decisions that have influenced my life. Advancing my education continues to be a step towards fulfilling God's purpose for my life.

There will be more events, more people, and more decisions as I continue my journey. I guess I agree with those who say, "You never stop learning or growing."

At this present time I am pursuing my master's degree in communication and leadership.

Our church celebrated fifty years of ministry on July 20, 2008. To God Be the Glory, Great Things He Has Done! We continue to reach out to the lost, and wherever God opens a door we will go through it!

Lisa Combs's Testimony

What Do You Want to Be?

If you abide in Me, and My words abide in you,
you will ask what you desire, and it shall be done for you.

— John 15:7 (NKJV)

Have you ever been asked this simple question: What do you want to be when you grow up? I think that all of us at some point have pondered this.

My question is somewhat similar: What do you want to be now? It demands the same amount of pondering.

Many of us give up on our hopes and dreams due to unforeseen circumstances in our lives. Some have always had a recurring question of what life would be like if only different choices had been made after listening to well-meaning parents or other actions taken such as finishing college.

You as well as I know that looking back with regret (or even remorse) does not change the present situation. However, such thoughts about the past may haunt us and keep harmful doors open that should be closed.

What can you do instead? Read on, my friend.

Adolescence for me was a wonderful experience. You are not going to read about any abuses or addictions.

I was raised in a Christian home. Let me explain what I mean by Christian: It means to be like Christ.

My sisters and I were shielded from the evils of this world to the very best of our parents' ability. We were taken to church and encouraged to be active participants in all activities. I never heard my parents speak disrespectfully of any of our pastors, government leaders, or school officials. They were honest and usually taken advantage of because of their generosity. My sister and I were encouraged to pursue our dreams and aspirations with much support, love, and acceptance.

I did venture from the teaching of my parents for a few short years and became acquainted with all the traps that present themselves to young people. Thank God for praying parents and other Christians who called my name in their prayers.

My heart and life were returned to Christ in 1976 while I was in the ninth grade at Edison High School. That's when I began pursuing what I wanted to be: It was with much joy and appreciation that I decided then I wanted to become a preacher's wife. I not only wanted to serve my Lord, I also wanted to serve the one He called to serve His people. It is a most honorable position, one in which I feel most unworthy, not to mention inadequate. However, that is what I always wanted to do and who I am today.

My life is not one of remorse, regret, or "what ifs." My past has never haunted me. I am what I always wanted to be: That makes my life full, complete, and happy. It is a life filled with certainty because I know that Jesus Christ placed me where I am today. I have peace that passes all understanding, even in times of difficulty. My future actions are destined to succeed, as guaranteed by the blood of my risen Savior.

Since you are still with me, I assume that your life lacks completeness, peace, and certainty. You may need to remove regrets and remorse. You may be weighed down by questions like:

—Where did I go wrong?
—How did I get off track?
—Is it too late for me?
—How can my life be one of peace in a world where uncertainty reigns?

There are no answers to these questions without Christ. Through a genuine relationship with Christ answers come, and the unconnected pieces of a life's puzzle begin to fit together. Hope in every circumstance is renewed.

Jesus is the answer: You can be what He wants you to be, whether you are grown up or not! It is a mysterious phenomenon that takes place . . . one that cannot be explained, but which can be experienced. Jesus somehow and someway makes all things new and okay.

Here's one more question for you: What do you want to be when you grow up? Do you want to be a Christian or not? If you choose to be a Christian, you choose eternal life.

If I can be of any assistance to you, I am the senior pastor's wife at Jubilee Worship Center. I would love to meet you and hear about all the wonderful things Christ has done for you.

Jim Barbarossa's Testimony

"Free Gift"

"Repent, for the kingdom of heaven is at hand."

— Matthew 4:17 (NKJV)

Many years ago, my wife and I settled down to raise a family. My wife met some great people at the church where we were married, and I believe this was the start of my receiving the "Free Gift" that I want to tell you about.

Over the years our family grew. We had four wonderful children, a fantastic marriage, financial success, and many good friends. Sounds good, doesn't it? Even though it was good, I had many questions:

— Why am I here?
— What is life about?
— Is it possible to live just to die?
— What good is financial success when we must die?
— Why do it?
— Why even be here?
— Why do I feel so confused?
— What is the answer?
— Why, when I have so much, do I have a feeling of emptiness?

For nineteen years, I strongly believed that my family was the only thing that mattered and I set out to provide for my family with everything the world had to offer. Almost everything I did was geared to provide for my family and generations of family to come.

Also, during this period of time, I searched high and low, trying many things, to fill the emptiness or void I felt: playing softball with the guys and drinking after the games; playing racquetball and drinking after the games; buying campers, snowmobiles, new cars, houses, etc. I tried working extra hours to make more money, buying more worldly possessions, starting a business, investing in and buying real estate, etc., etc., etc. All of these things gave me a very short-lived pleasure or happiness that would not last! It would leave as quickly as it came.

Fortunately for my family, while I was providing for their worldly lives, my wife, Carla, was building the foundation for our eternal lives.

I have always believed there was a God and I would occasionally pray when things were so far out of my control that I could not fix them. A few things come to mind that caused me to pray — like when my daughter was only weeks old, we had to put her in the hospital, and I feared for her life; also, when my son lay in the hospital with a staph infection; and when my wife was very sick with an infection in her blood system, and the doctor told me that my wife only had a 50/50 chance of survival. The most recent time was when a friend called for our support when his father was very ill. Carla went to help our friend while I stayed home with the kids.

As I laid there in bed that morning, I told God that I felt my friend's father was still needed in this world and that there was much good he could do by teaching God's Word to people like me who still needed help. I asked God to please save my friend's father and to give him the opportunity to help others like myself. In return, I promised to try to follow his path, starting with attending church that coming Sunday.

The following Sunday, I attended church with my wife and it was a very peaceful feeling. The people at church all seemed so happy and full of life that it made me want to return the next Sunday.

As the service was ending on my second visit, I felt very relaxed and was in no hurry to leave. After searching for the answers to my earlier questions, I came to the conclusion that we could not possibly live just to die. There was no other answer or reasoning to my problems and questions other than believing in God and having enough faith to accept His Son, Jesus Christ, in my life, so I did!

The love I saw in all the people "hit me" and it was like nothing else I have ever felt in my life. At that time I was not sure if it was Jesus filling the empty place in my heart or just all the love of the people reaching out to me, but whatever it was, I hoped it would never stop. And, if I could have one prayer answered, it would be that all

245

God's people have the opportunity to share the same experiences that I have come to enjoy, need, and want.

Looking back, I know that the Lord was with me every step of the way, and the path He was leading me down was to teach me about the values of the world and temporary happiness versus complete and total joy and the values of the Lord.

The Lord blessed me and my family by enabling us to make the right decisions in regard to my investments. I have always based my decisions on what I called my "gut feeling," but now I know it was my inner spirit leading me to worldly prosperity so that I would some day be able to testify that the things of the world are temporary and that worldly happiness will slip away very quickly.

Even though I was blessed with prosperity before being blessed as a Christian, being a Christian means more to me than anything the world has to offer. Recently, my wife and I were approached by a lady we did not know and she asked us to pray for her heart problems. She said she could see that we were Christians. Being recognized as a Christian was one of the best moments in my life.

In 1990 I had to quit my job of almost twenty years due to a rare blood disease. The doctors did not know what caused it and said they could do nothing for me. In January of 1994 the Lord told me He was going to heal me of that rare blood disease. In March of 1994, I took the same blood test that had led to the diagnosis that I had the rare disease. This time the results were negative! My blood had been cleansed by the Blood of My Savior. By His stripes I was healed. Praise God!

Up to this point, everything you have read occurred fourteen years ago. Today, I am still healed. My blood is normal. To the glory of God, I have shared this story of God's healing power all over the world.

God has called and sent me as an equipping evangelist to the Body of Christ (the church) to speak into and bring change in four specific areas:

1. To identify, release, and establish the Ephesians Chapter 4 gift of the equipping evangelist in churches around the world.

2. To call the 97 percent of Christians who refuse to share their faith to repent and then to train and equip them to witness for Christ.
3. To raise up and equip an army of shofar (the ram's horn originally used by the Israelites) blowers around the world.
4. To teach Christians how to handle their finances according to God's plan, not the world's plan.

At the writing of this book, Carla and I have been married thirty-four years. We now have four children and six grandchildren.

If you have any questions or problems I had, don't try to weather the storm on your own; come in out of the rain and let the Son of God, Jesus, meet your every need. Let Him lead you and guide you, through the Holy Spirit, from now to eternity. Since I accepted Jesus as my Savior, the empty place in my heart has been permanently filled with the love of Jesus Christ, the Holy Spirit, and God, our Father.

God can meet your every need, and will if you do your part. I urge you to read God's Word daily, pray daily, praise the Lord's name daily, and go to church every time the door is open.

"If ye abide in me, and my words abide in you, ye shall ask what ye will, and it shall be done unto you." John 15:7 (KJV)

Receive the "Free Gift."
May God bless you.

Carla Barbarossa's Testimony

I Just Wanted to Feel Accepted

"But he who does the truth comes to the light,
that his deeds might be clearly seen,
that they have been done in God."

— John 3:21 (NKJV)

I grew up in a small town in Pennsylvania. I can always remember being in church. In fact, at age thirteen, I was saved at church.

I liked going to church. I always felt it was the right thing to do. I also liked feeling accepted and being part of a group. I had a good-girl image, and I wanted to live up to that. So being a good girl meant going to church.

The world also had some things to offer. So, if cigarettes meant being popular, I tried cigarettes. If drinking could get me accepted, I tried drinking. There was always that fear of letting someone down. That someone was first of all God, then my family.

My father worked in a car factory, and my mother was a housewife. I had an older sister and a younger brother. My father was very strict, so I definitely did not want to get caught.

I had an aunt who lived in another town about twelve miles away. My sister and I used to love to stay at her house. My aunt and uncle would let us stay a couple of weeks in the summer or the whole summer. They would spoil us and we loved it.

The summer I turned thirteen, I was staying at my aunt's when I met Jim. We liked each other and hung out together over the summer. When school started back up, we broke it off. Two years later, Jim called to invite me to a post-prom picnic. I went, and we started dating. Dating was difficult because we went to different schools. We saw each other on weekends and when there was no school.

Then we made a big mistake. We became sexually active. I remember at first I didn't want to do it. I was so mad at myself when I gave in. I knew I couldn't take it back. We had to sneak around to be together because once we started, we couldn't stop.

In 1972 I was fifteen years old. My dad had been diagnosed with cancer. On September 23, 1972, my father died of cancer at the age of forty-one.

Jim and I continued to date, and in 1973 we got engaged. Jim was two years older than me, and in 1973 he graduated from high school. He was enrolled at a computer school in Pittsburgh. He had relatives who lived in Indiana, and they were working at different steel mills. They raved about how much money they were making. So Jim decided to go to Indiana for the summer and make some money. Once he got to Indiana, he liked it and decided to stay.

After he was out there for awhile, he got homesick and wanted for us to get married sooner. I wanted to finish high school. I had one year left. He asked me to marry him and said I could finish school in Indiana. I was scared. I didn't know what to do. I gave in and said yes.

Over the next year, there were a lot of emotions about getting married because I was saved and he was not, although I had been pretty wishy-washy about being a Christian. Jim found a church in Indiana that would marry us. That was hard, not only because I was saved and he was not, but also because we came from two different faiths.

We were married on June 22, 1974. Before we got married, I said that I would pray and believe, and that in a "short while" Jim would be saved. That short while took nineteen years!

A couple of years after we got married, I got serious about being a Christian. I still wanted to be that good girl and do the right things. I am glad that I never got addicted to the alcohol or the cigarettes. I would smoke and drink on and off to try to fit in, but I always felt guilty. Eventually, with the help of God, I quit smoking and drinking and never went back to them.

Jim, on the other hand, was a drinker and a smoker. He went out with his friends a lot. Sometimes he wouldn't come home until four or five in the morning.

We started a family after we were married seven months. I did go to school in Indiana, and I graduated.

I became focused on the children and continued praying for Jim to get saved. Jim and I had four children: one daughter and three sons. I raised them in church. Jim never kept his family from going to church. I praise God for that. At times it was hard, because I didn't think he would ever get saved.

I remember once in 1980 when he went out drinking and didn't come home for two days. After that, he quit drinking and smoking. It was amazing, but he still didn't get saved. The church I was attending started standing and agreeing with me for Jim to be saved.

There were times when I would get on his case about being saved, and I knew I was just pushing him away. I tried to reach him by my lifestyle. I did that by being the kind of wife and mother that God wanted me to be. That helped me to see that I didn't need to find man's approval any more. I only needed to have God's approval.

Finally, on March 21, 1993, Jim was saved. Praise God. I do praise God for saving my husband, and for getting me on track.

The hardest part of the story is that I committed all of these sins I have described after I was saved. That bothers me so much, especially the premarital sex.

I did repent, and I know I was forgiven because 1 John 1:9 (NKJV) says *"If we confess our sins, He is faithful and just to forgive us our sins, and to cleanse us from all unrighteousness."* I kept feeling guilty until I allowed Jesus to completely set me free.

I was forgiven, but Satan tried to convince me that I wasn't. Satan is a liar.

Two years after we were married, I was baptized in the Holy Spirit, and it felt like God opened up my head and poured love through me. That really ushered me to a place of wanting to be set apart for God. It was a process that brought me to where I am today.

Life is full and complete with Jesus as my Savior. I do not want to live without Him. It is only because of Him that I am where I am. He is my everything. I love You, Jesus. I thank You, Jesus. I praise You, Jesus.

Donald Mitchell's Testimony

He Will Lift You Up

Humble yourselves in the sight of the Lord,
and He will lift you up.

— James 4:10 (NKJV)

Let me share with you how I became a Christian so you'll know where I'm coming from with regard to encouraging you to become a complete, continual witness and to improve the quality of your witnessing. My great grandmother read the Bible every day so there was a long commitment to the Lord in our family. As a youngster, my mother regularly took me to Sunday school. It was my least favorite activity; sleeping was much preferred. I did enjoy listening to sermons, but it was frowned on to take youngsters to the adult services where those sermons were given.

If I pretended to be asleep, mom would sometimes let me sleep in on Sundays. I was pretty good at pretending, so I soon was the biggest backslider in my Sunday school grade. Fortunately, it was an evangelical church so my classmates were always cooking up schemes to get me to attend again. Because of my high opinion of myself, I would always return if invited to play my clarinet for the congregation.

By the time I turned thirteen, I was pretty full of myself. There wasn't much room for God in there alongside my exaggerated opinion of myself. One day while my family was away for a drive, I felt really sick. By the time they got home, I was delirious. Within an hour I was in the hospital where I would stay for two weeks as I barely survived a bad case of double pneumonia.

My physician, Dr. Helmsley, was a dedicated Christian and worried about my soul because my life was in jeopardy. He talked to me about God, Jesus, and the Holy Spirit twice a day when he stopped by to check on me. After I recovered, he took my mom and me to a tent revival meeting.

Having recovered from the illness, I soon pushed God out of my life again. During the next year, I was, instead, very caught up in athletics. When I was in ninth grade, I desperately wanted to make a contribution to our junior high track team, which had a remote chance of winning the big meet. Our coach, Mr. Layman, told each of us exactly what had to be accomplished for the team to win. I was determined to do my part. I had to come in first!

But that wasn't likely to happen. Based on past performances, there were at least two people who could out leap me in the standing broad jump, my main event. To make such a jump you stand on a slightly raised, tilted board and spring forward as far as you can into a sand-filled pit. After two of the three jumping rounds, I knew it was hopeless. I was in sixth place and four of the competitors' jumps were longer than I had ever gone before. I also didn't like the board we were using.

Remembering that we should call on God when we need help, I thought of praying ... but what I wanted was so trivial in God's terms that I didn't think it was worthy of prayer. So I decided to make God an offer instead: "Dear God, help me win this event, and I'm yours forever." After all, if He came through, any doubts I had about God would be dispelled.

I got onto the broad-jump board and felt very calm. I did my routine and took off into the air. Suddenly, I felt light as a feather with a large, gentle hand lifting under me. I was dropped softly at the end of the pit. I had outleaped everyone, and gone more than six inches past my best jump ever. I couldn't believe it. Then I remembered my promise to God, thanked Him, repented my sins, accepted Jesus as my Lord and Savior, and ran off to tell everyone on the team.

Even more remarkable, I was the only person on the team who performed up to the plan. Knowing what had to be done had probably given us performance anxiety, and people underperformed because they didn't believe they could do what the team needed. I also suspect that God wanted to make a point with me that I needed Him.

After a few days, I started to think that perhaps I'd just developed a new broad-jump technique and God didn't have a role at all. God soon dispelled that thought by making sure that my jumps for the rest of my life were much shorter than I had jumped when He lifted me up.

Since then, God has been speaking to me on a regular basis. I've learned to pay attention and act promptly. When I pursue my own ideas, things don't go so well. When I follow His orders, things work out great. That's my secret to high performance, and I just wanted to share it with you so you could benefit, too. He knows the answers, even when you and I don't ... which is most of the time.

I didn't always listen as well as I should, but God would always do something to get my attention. I rededicated my life to Jesus in 1995 and have enjoyed great peace since then.

Having been told by God to start the 400 Year Project (demonstrating how everyone in the world could make improvements twenty times faster than normal) in 1995, I continued to receive instructions. In 2005, for example, God told me to start explaining to people how to live their lives by gaining more joy from what they already have.

In the summer of 2006, I began to see how the 400 Year Project could be brought to a successful conclusion (as I reported in *Adventures of an Optimist*, Mitchell and Company Press, 2007). Realizing that perhaps I had devoted too much of my attention to this one challenge, I began to seek ways to rebalance my life. One of those rebalancing methods was to spend more time communing with God through prayer, Scriptural studies, attending services, and listening to the still, small voice within.

For several years I had been enjoying the devotionals sent to me daily over the Internet by evangelist Bill Keller. One of those devotionals speared me like an arrow that summer. The evangelist reminded his readers that our responsibility as believers is to share our faith with others through our example and sharing the Bible. Not feeling well equipped to do more than try to be a good example, I began to pray about what else I should be doing.

The next day, my answer came: I was to launch a global contest to locate the most effective ways that souls were being saved and be sure that information was shared widely. This sharing would be a blessing for those who wished to fulfill the Great Commission to spread the good news of Jesus as commanded in Matthew 28:18-20 (NKJV):

> And Jesus came and spoke to them, saying, "All authority has been given to Me in heaven and on earth. Go therefore and make disciples of all the nations, baptizing them in the name of the Father and of the Son and of the Holy Spirit, teaching them to observe all things that I have commanded you; and lo, I am with you always, *even* to the end of the age."

Fortunately, I had been studying for several years about how such contests had been run by secular organizations to generate improvements. I decided to announce the contest in my spirituality blog, http://www.livespirituallybetterthanabillionaire.blogspot.com.

I didn't want to presume that someone already had good answers or ways to find such answers. To stimulate good ideas to arise sooner, I decided to offer free e-books of *The 2,000 Percent Solution* (Authors Choice Press, Reprint Edition, 2003) and *The 2,000 Percent Solution Workbook* (iUniverse, 2005) to anyone who enrolled in the contest. In pursuing this task, I recalled many conversations with Peter Drucker about how sharing secular knowledge with pastors had been helpful to the development of some Protestant megachurches.

I also wanted to share whatever else I could to help make the contest a success. As a prize, I offered the chance to be included in one of two books about great ways to help save more souls. I would coauthor both books and cover the launch expenses, and the proceeds would go to support the best ideas. Presumably winning such a contest might also help with getting publicity, attracting volunteers, and gaining donations. My assumption was that most people who are great at helping save souls have been working on that rather than writing about what they do and seeking publicity to alert others to the opportunity. My experience in writing, producing, and promoting such books could possibly be of help to such effective leaders.

I doubt if many people could have been more daunted than I by the task. I felt like my role, at best, was to be a conduit for God's will. At worst, I might insert myself in ways that harmed the process. I couldn't quote Scripture at the time, hadn't attended a Bible college, and often found myself with more to learn about my faith than knowledge of it. But I do have lots of faith and, as a result, felt confident that God would find a way for His will to succeed regardless of my blunders.

God blessed me greatly through this contest. Many valuable entries were provided. One stood out above the rest. The pastor of a church in Hobart, Indiana, Jubilee Worship Center (JWC), Bishop Dale P. Combs, and his wife, Lisa Combs, had teamed with two congregation members, Jim and Carla Barbarossa, to provide regular in-house evangelist services. As a result, most members of the church had written their testimonies, which were published in a book, *Real Life*

Stories, and congregation members had become very active in sharing their faith and personal testimonies based on being encouraged to do so during five minutes of each service and activity. Tens of thousands of the books and many more copies of individual testimonies were distributed in conjunction with this witnessing.

Jim and Carla wore other hats for Jesus, as founders of Step By Step Ministries in Porter, Indiana. In that role, they shared what they had learned about encouraging witnessing with evangelists and pastors around the world. Abroad, the JWC methods and tools proved to be highly effective in attracting the unsaved and many thousands of souls accepted Christ as their Savior. As this book is being written, master evangelists in several lands are taking these teachings to still other countries to spread these methods and tools into many hundreds more congregations.

It was clear to me that widespread use of what JWC and Step By Step Ministries were doing could lead many millions of people to have a chance to hear the Good News of Jesus Christ who otherwise would not by inspiring ordinary Christians to be more active and effective in witnessing. I feel most blessed to have this opportunity to assist in sharing the story in this book.

I will next be coauthoring a book about many other blessed ways of helping spread the Gospel that will feature different methods of bringing Jesus Christ to those who need His peace. I thank God for giving me this portion of His Great Commission as my assignment. I look forward to His next orders sent to me in a still, small voice.

Appendix C

Selected Testimonies from *Real Life Stories*

Here are some of over ninety-plus moving and instructive testimonies written by members of Jubilee Worship Center (JWC) and shared around the world through tracts and copies of *Real Life Stories*, which contains testimonies from JWC members. In these testimonies you learn about problems and their solutions through faith in Jesus Christ. Perhaps you'll find a testimony that matches a problem you have had or have now.

If you would like to read more of the book, you can access the complete current edition of *Real Life Stories* at http://www.step-by-step.org.

CHAPTER 1
Don't Give Up. Look Up!

Don't Give Up. Look Up!
I have been hurt.
I have seen my mom hurt.
I have seen my brothers hurt.
Family life has been hard,
but I have learned you don't give up.
You look up! You look up to the One ....

The greatest thing that I have ever done was accept Christ into my heart. I have been in church since I was about five years old. I thank God for that.

I have never gotten drunk, smoked, or had sex. I really thank God for that. I may not be able to help people with those kinds of situations, but I haven't had the best family life. What I have learned to do may be able to help you. **I don't give up. I look up!**

My parents divorced when I was three or four. My mom, my brothers, and I left. We stayed with my uncle. It didn't really affect me then because I was young, but it affects me now. My mom met a guy when I was four. He is now my mom's husband. They moved in with each other a lot of times. What I mean by that is we jumped from different houses. We moved here and there. Everything was okay. My step-dad wasn't mean. My dad just wasn't around. I didn't understand why he didn't want to come and see me and my brothers.

I have two older brothers. My older brother was a teenager, and he knew that my dad would not change. He still believes that, but I know one person, the only person that can change my dad. My dad would show up every once in a while and think everything was okay. It was okay until I moved to Valpo, and all my friends had two parents. Before that my mom had bought her own house, and my two brothers and I lived there.

My mom's boyfriend at the time would come over. He didn't like my older brother at all. He would tell my mom things that my brother did, and my mom and my brother would fight. My brother would leave and not come back for awhile. I would cry because I didn't want to see my brother go. At this time, my brother would get in trouble with the law, but **I didn't give up, I looked up**, and God always comforted my mom and my brother through those times.

During this time, I would tell my dad how I really felt. I would tell him that I needed him around. We would get in fights, and I would cry all the time. One day, I realized that fighting with my dad would not help, but **I didn't give up, I looked up**. I prayed and asked God to help me talk to my dad and not fight. Now my dad and I don't fight a lot, but every once in awhile we will get into it. Things got a little better with my dad, but things with my step-dad went downhill.

My older brother went into the Army, so my step-dad didn't have him to yell at. He would pick on my other brother instead. By this time, he and my mom were already married. It hurt me to see my brother hurt because we were so close. I always told my brother that it was the devil. It was not a battle between flesh and blood. It was a battle of the spirit. My step-dad would yell at my mom about my brother. That would upset her. There I was, right in the middle of it. I would cry and pray at night sometimes, just asking God to help change him. I still pray for that now.

One day my mom had to go to the hospital. She was in there for three or four days. She wasn't supposed to go home, but she called her doctor and told him she was leaving. She was still in pain. The day she got home was the day my step-dad kicked my brother out. That's when things went bad. We were all upset. It hurt me to realize that I didn't have my brother there all the time. It hurt to see my mom hurt.

Now that he is gone, my step-dad tries to say things to me. I know that it is the devil, and it is our spirits that are at battle. The only thing that I do is show my step-dad God's love. It's the only thing I can do. You are probably wondering how my mom and I stayed through all of this. The answer is Jesus Christ. He would give us peace, comfort, grace, and love when we needed it.

My step-dad and dad have not accepted Christ into their hearts yet. Not a day goes by that I don't pray for their Salvation. Even though things are still tough, **I don't give up. I just look up.** I look up to the One....

Who cared so much that He gave His only Son for you and me, so that we can have everlasting life.

Don't be one of those people who say I have time. Do you really? You don't know what will happen tomorrow. Accept Christ now, and have everlasting life. Let Him take that hurt and pain away in your life like He took it away in my life.

—Jessica

CHAPTER 20
I Couldn't Feel A Thing

I couldn't feel a thing. My heart was cold as ice and was in no jeopardy of ever melting. I believed that you could trust no one and to keep your enemies real close so you could get them before they got you. Lustful desires and deeds were my specialty. I treated men like I believed they treated women, use them, abuse them, and lose them. You could have told me that my parents had died, and I wouldn't have shed a tear. All of this anger and hate at the tender age of nineteen, and it consumed my life for three years.

I woke up one morning from a horrible dream. I was twenty-one now and nothing in my life had changed. But this dream was the most horrifying dream I had ever had. It was a dream about me and I was being chased, chased by what my mind had conjured up as the devil, and when I woke up, it was right before he had grabbed onto the heel of my foot. I had never been that scared in my life. But after a few days I let it go to the back of my mind, never getting the true meaning of the dream or even caring if I did or not. I kept on living my life as before, a nonpracticing Catholic, refusing to go to church because of disagreeing with man-made rules incorporated by the church. I believed in God, just not in practicing my faith at the time.

About a month later I met a man who would later be my husband and ex-husband. He went to church and invited me to go. I agreed, mainly out of curiosity, not that I felt I needed any spiritual uplifting. He was younger so I was with the youth group that first time on a Wednesday evening service. I was nervous only because I didn't know what to expect. Here I am, not living a moral life, and I am in church. Are the walls about to come crashing in? Once the service started, I started to shake a little, a feeling had come over me that I had never experienced in my whole life. I started to cry. I hadn't cried for anything in the past three years. What was going on? I felt for the first time in three years! I actually had emotions, which I thought I had pushed down so deep that they would never come up again. God was calling out to me and for the first time I was letting Him in. I was saved and baptized not long after, and experienced a wonderful year of growing and learning in the Lord.

Then I started to backslide. I got married and had a beautiful child, but my married life was a torment for me. It was a torment because it wasn't a marriage devoted to God. I got divorced and called on God to give me the strength I needed to carry on with my child alone. He blessed me with the strength and more. He blessed me abundantly with a church in which I could grow and live right, with the support of people who live for God fully. They don't care what you did in the past because they know everyone isn't perfect. They don't judge you. They take you into their arms and love you like God intended His people to love each other.

I understand what my dream meant all those years ago. It was God reaching out to me and letting me know that if I didn't make a change in my life soon, I would be giving myself a permanent residence in Hell. I pray everyday now for God to open my ears, eyes, and heart so that I will always be able to hear from God in whatever way He needs me to. I once thought my life was a game. I had to be on top by whatever means possible, not caring who I had to hurt or what I had to do to get there. I had no emotions and had no moral standards, even though I knew what was right and wrong. It didn't matter. I did whatever brought me pleasure. I know now, that life was the wrong life to lead, and for someone who didn't have emotions, I was leading the saddest life of all. I live my life for God now. Even though everyday may bring some kind of trial or tribulation, I am thankful because I know God is working in me. Don't think that there is no one to understand you or this isn't for real. God is for real and through Him all things are possible.

—Michelle

CHAPTER 33
Arrested for Attempted Murder!

Arrested for ATTEMPTED MURDER!
Alcohol, drugs, anger, and rage took me
to a place I never wanted to go ....

I started doing drugs while in high school. An older brother turned me on to marijuana. I was having an identity crisis, and the drugs seemed to help. I coasted through my classes and graduated. Then I went to college. It was there that I discovered I could sell this to other kids and make money!

It was also there that I discovered the bad side of drugs. During the Easter holiday, a couple of us stayed in the dorm. The dean caught us in full party mode with beer, wine, and reefer!

I decided to come home and go to I.U. Indiana University told me that due to my incomplete semester, I would just be an advanced freshman. I said no way and went to work in the mills, selling marijuana to supplement my income.

Another brother and I were renting out the basement apartment in my parents' home. One day, one of our drug customers couldn't find us, so he asked my mom if she had any weed to sell! After that, some guys came and robbed us at gunpoint. I knew then that I had to get that kind of lifestyle away from my parents. It was the Holy Spirit convincing me then!

Later on that year, I got hired at the Post Office. God was making a way for me to get out of that lifestyle. The security of a steady job, and a constant tugging at my spirit to be righteous, helped me to stop dealing. I was still using though. I tried cocaine and liked it. Then I started smoking it. Big trouble. I met a "coke-man" who would front me any amount I wanted. I was still working, but I was working for my habit. Bills went unpaid, and my temper was flaring. I was a mess.

It was around this time that I met my wife. We dated, then got married, and then divorced. She went through all these things that I did. Once, while trying to get back together, we went out – drinking, drugging, and arguing. The argument got out of hand, and her sister's husband got out of the car. They had been arguing too. He said he would walk home, so she told me to get out too. Then he took off in a rage. I got out and couldn't find him, so I was by myself. By this time, I was in a rage! I got a couple of rides to the state line. I was really wet and furious. When I got back to Gary to her house, I made a very foolish move. I let the rage in me build and I hit my wife in the head with a sledge hammer. I knew instantly that I was wrong. I took her to the hospital. Her dad pulled a gun on me, and told me to get out of there.

When I first went to jail, the Lord instructed me to read His Word. I know this is what everyone does when they first go to jail, "Jailhouse Religion." But this was different. God told me that He would take care of me. I felt that I was completely unworthy of His loving kindness! He provided a jailer for me that was from my neighborhood. This jailer watched over me, uplifted me, and told me that he knew I was a good person. At this time, I definitely did not feel like a "good person"!

My wife was in the hospital, in critical condition. My two sons were without a mom and dad. I felt like I was losing everything. When I got out, I vowed that I would set things straight. While sitting at home, unable to go to work, unable to go see my wife, and unable to see my kids, the Lord sent a saint by. This young man knocked at my door. I looked out and saw a young white boy. I knew he was a "Bible Thumper." Normally I would just ignore these guys and they would go away. This time the Lord had made me ready. This young man was out being obedient, trying to save souls! He asked me if I knew Christ as my Savior.

I told him he should run from me, and that I was an awful man who had almost killed my wife. He said that Jesus loved me and would forgive me if I just asked Him to. I surrendered to the Lord and let Him fill me. This young man's sincere prayer and determination won me over.

The Lord already had me reading my Bible while I was off. Things began to change. Vickie's health was improving. (Though at one time, word was that she had passed.) She was slowly coming around each day and getting stronger. One of her family members arranged for me to see my sons! After three weeks, Vickie got out. She came to see me. That just broke my heart. Here was this woman that I just hurt so bad standing at my doorway. She told me that she still loved me and forgave me. I felt so unworthy of her love. I vowed that I would never ever fight with my wife again. With God's help, I have kept that vow since 1986. We reconciled, broke up again, got back together, broke up again, got back together, just going through a cycle. We both got back into drugs, reefer, and coke. Then one day, it just clicked. God had not saved us both just to fall back into sin!

My wife and kids started going to church regularly. I was sitting at home watching football, smoking joints, drinking beer. But I could see the change in her! She quit smoking cigarettes and reefer! She changed her whole lifestyle. I realized she was setting a better example than me. I had gotten everything back, but still felt a void. I had backslidden. I realized that I had better get right with God. He was the One that had saved me, not me! I made up my mind to go to church with my family. Since that time, God has set me free of drugs, drinking and anger.

Friend, if you are dealing with any of these same problems I had, you need help. You can't fix it. Man can't fix it. Only God can help you.

—David

CHAPTER 37
Life Started Off Great

Life started off great,
but at only thirteen years old, I wanted it all to be over ....

At the age of thirteen, I wanted it all to be over. Repressed memories of being molested became unrepressed. I felt worthless and dirty. I hated myself. I became depressed, and life kept spiraling downward. At fourteen, I started using self-inflicted wounds to release my anger and pain. I became interested in satanism and witchcraft. At fifteen, I was drinking heavily and became suicidal. This continued for another year and a half. On top of this, I poured my problems on top of one another. Sex was not the answer I was looking for either. At seventeen, I was a mess. It seemed like this life was about to end. Then, at the perfect time, a door opened. God called me to Him. I realized what I was looking for and needed all along was in the scarred face and hands of Jesus! My Savior took me out of nearly five years of depression and hurt. I finally chose to serve Him.

If I could hand it all over to Jesus, you can too. You're never too bad to come to Jesus. He takes us from the world broken, and makes us whole! So what's stopping you?

Come to Jesus today. Call on Jesus, and allow Him to help you.

—Erin

CHAPTER 42
Work All Day, Party All Night

Work all day, party all night.
Day after day, month after month.
Then, I thought,
there had to be more to life than this.
I don't want do to this any more.
I want more out of life.
What's missing?

I was twenty-six years old, living what I thought was a normal life. I would go to work, and then I would go out every night to party with my husband. My husband was an alcoholic. It didn't seem to bother me much until I had decided I didn't want to live that life anymore. I felt there had to be more to life than this.

One day, a lady came into the office where I worked and handed me a New Testament Bible. Since I never had a Bible, I was glad to get it.

I was brought up in a Catholic church, and I faithfully went to church every Sunday. However, I really didn't have a deep under-standing of who Jesus was. I started to read the Bible, and it was as if I understood every word. It was like Jesus was speaking to me. I couldn't put it down. I would read it every chance I could.

I noticed that during this time, I started to change. My attitude started changing, and my husband started changing. My husband told me he didn't want to drink anymore. With that news, I wanted to know more and more about God.

In September of 1984, my husband, while he was drunk, went to a small church and asked the pastor to pray for him. On that very night, he was delivered from alcoholism. I knew then how real God was, and I knew Jesus had to be a part of my life.

On Thanksgiving Day in 1984, while watching a Christian station, I prayed the sinner's prayer with the preacher and gave my life to the Lord.

God has not stopped blessing me and changing me since! Glory!!! Do you want more out of life? Do you want Eternal Life?

—Lupe

CHAPTER 49
Who Has The Final Answer?

Who has the final answer?
Are incurable diseases always incurable?
Is the doctor's diagnosis <u>always</u> the final word? NO!
There is a higher authority.

In 1995, I was diagnosed with an incurable disease (Miniere's disease). The doctor said I would be on medication for the rest of my life. He also said I would have to wear patches behind my ear. One patch only lasted twenty-four hours! The medication was extremely expensive. At that time, I was a widow raising four children. I said, "My God, how can I do this?"

Then I began to pray and ask the Lord for healing. During a revival, the evangelist asked for people to come forward and be healed. I went forward and God healed me instantly. To this day, I have never had another attack of that terrible disease.

In order to be saved, you need to tell the Lord that you are sorry for your sins and ask Him to forgive you and come into your heart. Then promise to serve Him for the rest of your life. Jesus wants to care for you and supply your needs.

Friend, if you have a need today, God is your only hope. Allow God to help by receiving his Son, Jesus Christ, as your Savior and Healer today.

—Mary

CHAPTER 50
The Marijuana Test

The marijuana test. When the joint comes to me, what should I do? I grew up in a nice Christian home. We went to church pretty much whenever the doors were open for services. I was taught from the start, "Stay away from drugs and alcohol." I heard it from my parents, I heard it from the Sunday school teacher, I heard it from the pastor, and I heard it from the teachers at school.

Many of life's tests come to us when we are teenagers. The test I'm talking about now is the "Marijuana Test." Some of the neighborhood guys and I were just hanging out. They were the guys I played sports with, camped out with, and made forts with. We were all pretty much like family. We were all in a circle just talking and having a good time. One of the guys took out a joint and lit it. By this time, I knew they were all into smoking pot, but this was the first time they had ever done it in front of me. "Hey, this is some good stuff. It came from Mexico. You guys want some?" the first guy said. All the other guys said, "Yeah, bring it on friend."

I didn't say anything. When it came to me, I didn't know what to do. I sat there thinking, "Should I smoke it? Should I just suck it into my mouth and not inhale? Should I just tell the guys that I have to go home now?"

The second guy in the circle took the joint, put it up to his lips, took a big hit, held it in for as long as he could, then exhaled. "Dude, this is good stuff," he said. The joint was getting closer and closer to me. The third guy went. The fourth, fifth, and sixth guys went.

Then the big moment came. The joint was passed to me. By that time, I was very nervous. I took the joint from my friend, held it between my forefinger and thumb, and passed it in front of me to the next guy. "Wow, that wasn't hard," I thought. The guys made fun of me and said a few remarks, but I passed the "Marijuana Test."

Now, when I talk to those guys, they still say to me, "I wish I could have been like you and said 'No.' I really respect you for what you believe."

I am far from perfect. I have made mistakes, but I have been able to stay away from some very bad things in life. I have been able to say "No" and to stay away from trouble because my parents, church, and most importantly, because of Jesus Christ. I accepted Jesus into my heart when I was a young boy. It doesn't matter what age you are, what kind of things you have done, or who you have hurt. Jesus Christ will accept you the way you are. "For all have sinned, and come short of the glory of God." — Romans 3:23 (KJV).

It's simple. Talk to Jesus. Tell Him you are sorry for the sins you have committed. Ask Him to come and live in your heart and be your personal Savior. Do it now.

—Russ

CHAPTER 56
I Was Dead on Arrival

I was dead on arrival.
I heard a voice say: "Welcome home, my child."
Have you found your home?

"I was born sixteen years old and a mom." That's what I tell people.

I was born in Georgia, but at age three, my family and I moved to Illinois. I only remember bits and pieces of my childhood. (I have the ability to forget the things I don't want to remember.)

While growing up, both my parents worked. So I, being the oldest of five children, had to take on the responsibility of babysitting, housekeeping, and cooking. I was always the one to blame when things didn't go right or when my siblings didn't do things, and when they didn't do them right.

My father was an alcoholic, which made my mother the strong one in our family. She was also the one who was with us most of the time. However, my mother was physically, verbally, and mentally abusive towards me, which caused me to do a lot of rebelling.

I ran away from home on several occasions and was raped at the age of twelve by a slightly retarded boy who lived in our building.

When I was sixteen and a senior in high school, we moved to Indiana. At that time, I didn't know anyone in my class, but I soon met a boy, and we dated. I had been told that I was an embarrassment to my family, and just before I turned eighteen, I found out I was pregnant and became even more of a disgrace.

My boyfriend and I married and had a baby boy. But I soon learned that my husband liked the wild life. He got involved with some people from the Mafia, with drugs, and with other women.

At the time, I was working at the steel mill and had several friends who told me that I didn't need him or that kind of lifestyle. When my son was two, and I was twenty-one, I divorced my husband. I asked God to let me keep my job until I had raised my son. He did that and so much more, yet that wasn't enough for me.

Now, I was looking for something and someone to love me. I was introduced to alcohol, then drugs, men, and sex. In 1981, I was introduced to another man, and we married a year later in 1982. Soon after that, I learned that he loved to drink and party. I began drinking more, trying to keep up with him to keep peace, but that didn't work. We tried church, but neither of us was into it. We began arguing more frequently. He started beating me every time I opened my mouth, and I opened it a lot. Finally, after two years, I divorced him.

By this time in my life, my father's addiction to alcohol had taken his life. He died of cancer in 1988. My father had taken care of me and my son and had become a very big part of my life. When he died, I felt as though a huge part of me had died too.

My son was now twelve years old, and I learned that he was into the drug scene. I tried to stop him, but I couldn't. I fell into a deep depression, and my doctor prescribed Valium, which I later overdosed on.

When I overdosed, something made me call my doctor and tell him what I had done. Since I wasn't home alone, my doctor told me to get to the hospital. When I came to, he told me I was dead when I arrived at the hospital. He said I should thank God I was alive because that was the only reason I was living.

When I look back over my life, I know now that God is the only reason I am alive today. After my father died in 1988, I admitted that I had a drinking problem and started to attend AA meetings.

It wasn't until then that my son's problems finally caught my attention. Not only was he into drugs, he was also in trouble with the law. Everything that he had done and was doing finally surfaced. I was beside myself. I didn't know what to do or who to call.

At the time, my son had been attending youth meetings at a local church. He would often tell me all about them and the people there. So, one day I talked to the youth pastor, and he told me it might help my son if I went to church.

So, one Sunday evening I went. When I walked into the sanctuary, I could see people moving around and talking. But I didn't hear any noise. Then a voice spoke to me. It was a man's voice. He said, "Welcome home, my child."

I looked around to see who was talking to me; no one was there, but I could hear all the noise in the sanctuary and the music playing. I let this pass. I knew from experience that alcoholics hallucinate.

I sat with the only person I knew there, a friend of my son. A lady came to introduce herself to me and welcome me. They had fellowship after the service that night, and the lady invited me to join. I did. Before I went home that night, I had given her my phone numbers at home and at work. I thought that the people I had met were the nicest and friendliest people I had ever met. I felt good for the first time in a long time.

She called me the next day at work and invited me to her house. I said yes. She and her children made me feel like I had known them all my life. They made me feel like family. To this day, they are my family.

I kept going to this church with these people who really seemed to like me and made me feel like I was a part of their lives. I wanted to belong, and I wanted what they had. I wanted to be happy like they were. I finally gave my life to God in 1988.

It wasn't easy to let go of my being in control. There were times when I didn't want to because there were things I had to give up and change. I don't like change.

My son did go to jail. That was very hard for me. I blamed myself. What kind of role model had I been? I did try to teach him right from wrong, and he knew that he was doing wrong.

By this time, we had a new pastor. I was comfortable enough in church now to go to him. He said he was there for us day or night. I called on him day and night. He stood by me and my son all the way. He went with me to court each time I needed him to. The first time was real hard for me. My son had never been without me. I still saw him as my little boy.

On our way home the first time, God spoke to me again. I had been in church enough by now to know it was God. He put me at peace. He told me He has always been in control and always will be. All I had to do was trust Him.

I thought that would be easy, but it wasn't. I still liked to take control of things. My son has been in and out of jail three times now. The last time, I made up my mind that I was going to obey God. I was going to let Him be in control. It still hurt when my son went to jail again, but God put his arms around me and held me. This time I surrendered it all to Him, and let Him take charge. I no longer felt defeated. I started really applying God's Word to my life and holding Him to His promises.

Today, my son is not in jail and is trying to build a good life for himself. He is struggling, but I remind him every chance I get that he needs to let God in and let God be his pilot. While I was going through all of this, I did not face it alone. Not only did I have God; I had a church family to walk with me also. These are the greatest people on earth. I thank God every day for them.

In 1989, I was introduced to a young man, who I thought was a real geek. He was much younger than me, yet he seemed much older. He helped me move one day, and we talked a lot about what he wanted. He wanted to get married and settle down. I started praying for God to send him the right girl to be his wife.

One time during prayer, God spoke to me. He told me He had chosen a wife for this young man. When we didn't see who she was, I kept praying. This man and I grew to be very good friends. God spoke to me a second time while I was in prayer. He seemed to speak with more sternness. He said, "I have chosen him a bride, now go." I kept thinking, what is He talking about?

In May of 1990, I married this man. We are still married today, almost thirteen years later. For awhile, I was afraid of what people would think. I knew him inside and out. To me, the age difference could have meant disaster. We have both had a lot of growing to do, but we have done so with God in our lives. I don't think it would have worked without God.

When I started church, I told God I wanted Him to work on me and get me right. I didn't want a man in my life unless he was chosen by God. I thank God everyday for my life, my son, my husband, and my church. I remember where I came from starting at the age of sixteen. I don't want to go down those same roads ever again. I promised myself that I would only follow God. HE IS MY SAVIOR! I know I am here today because even when I wasn't with God, He was with me.

Friend, today God is here for you. God can and wants to heal all of your hurts. Maybe you were raped, verbally abused, physically abused, hooked on drugs, hooked on alcohol, divorced, or have faced a number of problems and hurts. Your past really doesn't matter. From this point, it is your future that counts. God has a wonderful plan for your life. Call on Him right now, and allow Him to help you.

—Carolyn

Chapter 61
Was I Too Bad?

Was I too bad? Are you too bad?
After ten days, I found out I was not too bad for ....

I was born sixth in birth order. My father left my mother to start a new life with another woman. With no support from my father, we found ourselves hungry and financially strapped. My mother sought employment as a waitress at the local truck stop. This put a heavy responsibility on the older children, as they were left at home to care for us younger children.

Things went from bad to unbelievable as my mom met a man who soon became the father of my two baby brothers and the monster whom we came to fear. My early memories of him were of him beating my mother bloody, being stabbed with forks at the dinner table, being beat myself, and being forced to hold pinching bugs for his entertainment. There seemed to be no end to his cruelty.

One morning, I was awakened to the news that our mommy was hit and killed by a drunk driver. We went through her funeral and burial, and then the separation of our family took place. My stepfather took his two sons, and my grandmother took my four older sisters. Due to her age, limited space, and finances, she was unable to keep all six of us. My sister and I were put into foster care.

The social worker took my sister and me to the home of a wonderful couple. Their home was a beautiful redwood house, which sat proudly on a hill, nestled in by mature oak trees. Our foster parents provided love, compassion, instruction, discipline, and home-cooked meals. My foster mom said the first time she saw us, she knew she wanted us to stay.

Things were definitely looking up. My sister was now eight, and I was six. We began to settle into our new life and were looking forward to our upcoming adoption. Suddenly this sense of peace and security was shaken when our (foster) mom was diagnosed with terminal cancer. Since the adoption was not yet finalized, my family became concerned that this news could spoil the adoption proceeding. My mother began praying that they would be allowed to adopt us and that she would live long enough to raise us. God heard and said yes to my mom's prayers, and our adoption was finalized. Although her days were spent living with cancer and diabetes, she lived long enough to raise us.

We had parents who genuinely loved us. Unfortunately, as hard as my parents tried to protect me, I became the victim of sexual abuse. This set me up for a lot of hardships in my life. At twelve years old, I started smoking cigarettes. By the age of fourteen, I was drinking, and at fifteen I started smoking pot, which led to harder drugs. By seventeen, I was married to an abusive alcoholic and had my first child.

Somehow, I made it through all of these experiences, and I came to a place where I began calling out to God. "God, if You're there, or if I haven't been too bad, let me know." I cried out this prayer for ten days. On the tenth day, I looked towards heaven and said, "God, I believe You're there. I must have been too bad." A sadness came over me because I knew there was no hope.

That evening, I received a phone call from a friend's father. He said, "Lisa, for ten days God has been telling me to call you." I was ecstatic because I knew this was more than a coincidence. I went with him to a Full Gospel Businessmen's meeting, and at the end of the meeting, I prayed and asked God to forgive me and to become Lord of my life. At that moment, something wonderful happened. A change took place in me. My sadness left, and I became happier than I had ever been in my life.

Twenty-five years have gone by since that day. I have remarried and just celebrated my nineteenth wedding anniversary. I have raised three wonderful children and have experienced an ever growing relationship with God. I have found that He has given us His written Word, the Bible. His Word is true and dependable. I have found out that God restores. He's been doing this from the beginning. When Adam and Eve sinned and their relationship with God was messed up, God made a way by Jesus coming to Earth, dying for our sins, and being raised again. Through this, He restored our relationship with Him.

God has restored my purity, my finances, and even my education. I have found that He desires to spend time with us, and as we do, He uses our conversation (prayers) to do miracles not only in our lives, but also in the lives of others. I have experienced love, joy, peace, hope, and restoration. My words seem too few and inadequate to express what I have experienced and gained. I pray that God's Holy Spirit will bring you into this same type of relationship with Him.

—Lisa

CHAPTER 62
Something Fantastic Happened to Me

Something fantastic happened to me,
and I want to share it with you.
Please let me tell you an amazing story.

When I was fifty-four years old, I was bent out of shape, physically and mentally. I had arthritis so bad that I had to waddle just to walk forward. The only way I could get out of bed was to fall out and crawl to a chair and pull myself up. Mentally, I was a vegetable. I felt as if I had but six months to live. I was as low as a man could get and still be alive. I desperately needed a miracle and received it. It came when I asked Jesus into my heart and turned my life over to Him. He instantly saved my soul. Almost immediately 98 percent of the pain left my body. My face was wrinkle free, and I could stand up straight for the first time in many years.

Someone asked why I suddenly looked years younger. Up to the time Jesus changed me, people would remark that I was the oldest looking fifty-four-year-old man they had ever seen; that I looked more like a ninety-year-old.

Maybe, right now you are in pain and need a friend to talk to, someone to sympathize with you, someone to bear your burdens, someone to love you, someone who will never leave you or forsake you. If you will call out to Jesus with sincerity, He will come into your heart, and renew your mind, body, soul and Spirit.

After you have called out to Jesus, start reading the Bible everyday, and pray everyday. The benefits will amaze you. You will enjoy better health and more love and compassion for others when you begin to line your life up with the Word of God. You will have all this and more than you can possibly imagine.

Romans 12:1 and 2 says, "And so dear brothers, I plead with you to give your bodies to God. Let them be a living sacrifice, Holy, the kind he can accept." When you think what He has done for you, is this too much to ask? Don't copy the behavior and customs of this world, be a new and different person with all freshness in all you do and think. Then you will learn from your own experiences how His ways will really satisfy you.

I love you, but Jesus loves you even more.

—Ray

CHAPTER 67
I Worried About Everything

I worried about everything.
I needed something in my life.
It seemed like all I knew how to do was worry. Until ....

I had attended church, however I never really knew God in His fullness. I spent all my time worrying about things.

One evening, my aunt invited me to her church for a revival. I remember the preacher was really anointed and the invitation was given to receive Christ. I don't know how I got there, but when I finally got my composure back, I realized I was at the altar crying out to God.

That night, fifty-four years ago, was life changing. I began to take my worries to God. Immediately, relief began to flood my soul. Through prayer and studying the Bible, I found out that God wanted me to give Him all my worries. I also found out He didn't just want me to give Him all my worries, He wanted me to give Him all my needs too.

There have been some rocky times along the way. God will hear and answer our prayers, and He has been very faithful to me.

I had prayed for a good Christian husband for many years, and God sent one my way. We raised two wonderful daughters, who are in the ministry along with their husbands. We have four grandchildren, all of whom are in church and serving the Lord. I feel so blessed.

That night, fifty-four years ago, changed my life completely. I can't imagine any other way of life other than life with God. I have so many experiences of healings and miracles I could tell you about.

The wonderful life of giving your all to God will cause you to miss out on NOTHING, and I have found nothing that can compare to the way God can fill our every day. The best part is ... He wants to do it for you! He is life to anyone that will accept Jesus, His Son. It is so simple, and it is worth it. One day with God is greater than a thousand without Him. I would take one day and give up the thousand. It would be worth it all.

This is from my heart. My hope is that it will help you to know life can be great with Jesus in your heart. Don't hesitate to begin a great life now. You will have some setbacks along the way, but you will know and feel God right beside you every step of the way, leading you through. My prayers go out with this testimony, that you will receive this abundant life.

If you need help dealing with worry, or with anything else, call on the One that has been faithful to me for over 54 years. He will never leave you or forsake you.

—Deloris

Chapter 91
Married, Divorced, and Viet Nam — All By Age Twenty

Growing up in a family with eight siblings and a Christian mom, that meant we all went to church twice on Sunday, once on Wednesday, once on Friday for young people's meeting (Roy was the youth leader), and seven days a week when a tent revival was in town.

My mother lost two sons, Roy at eighteen years old from a cerebral hemorrhage and Rodney dying later from brain cancer at thirty-one. It almost drove my mother crazy, but she held on with the Grace of Jesus Christ to see her through.

By the time I reached the age of twenty, I had been married to a girl from my brother Rodney's church, divorced, and had been to Viet Nam and came home and was ready to party! Forget about church, I had other things to do like drugs, booze, and wrecking cars, running into cop cars, and driving through train gates. Boy was I having fun – so I thought. Ha! Ha!

After about three years of that kind of living, I met my soon-to-be wife, Sue, who I boondoggled into marrying me. That will be thirty-three years ago on July 6, 2007. Thank you Jesus for my wife. (I don't think she always thought that though.) Through the years before my mom's death, I would always call my mom or other saved family members to pray for me, my wife and children, and also for work and other problems.

You see, I knew God wouldn't hear my prayers. I wasn't a Christian, so I went around the back door for what I needed. By doing it that way, I knew it worked for me, and I sometimes got the help we needed. The Holy Spirit would always question me about where my family and myself were going to spend eternity. At almost every free moment on or off work, He would pose the question. Day after day, year after year, never any peace of mind. I'd always think to myself if my family's not going to Heaven, then I don't want to go either. Well that worked for years, but after a while things just kept getting worse. My mother died and she begged me on her deathbed to accept Jesus, but I would not do it. Then a year later, my dad passed away.

I came home from work after a really bad day feeling down, needing help. So I went upstairs and laid in our bed. I got on the phone to my brother Jack (to use the back door method again). He's the CEO of HopeForce.org. They work with the Salvation Army to help out when disaster strikes. I told him about my day and while he was praying for me, Jack asked if I wanted to accept Jesus. Well, I broke down and started crying and couldn't stop crying long enough to say the sinner's prayer. I asked Jack if I could just think the words and he said, "NO. You have to profess Jesus as your Savior with YOUR mouth." I finally stopped crying long enough to profess Jesus as my Lord and Savior. THANK YOU, JESUS!!!

That night the phone rang off the hook. Nick finally came to Jesus. What a shocker to everybody in our family. I always knew I wanted to come to Jesus. I just didn't know when. I always feared going to Hell, because Hell is real and forever.

My brother Clarence and his wife Mary called from Streamwood, Illinois to say they were coming down that Saturday to spend the night. They knew of a church here in Hobart, Indiana, called Jubilee Worship Center. Their pastor knew Bishop Combs. I went with Clarence and Mary for Sunday services at Jubilee Worship Center. I was enjoying the service and at one point, the pastor asked anyone who needed prayer to come up on the platform. So I ran up there along with about a dozen other people. Then Pastor Combs said he was going to pray a special anointing on whoever wanted it, but if you stayed for this, you better take it serious or leave. As I was praying with God trying to figure out what to do, I told God I came to You with ALL OR NOTHING and I was staying. While God and I were working this out with the thought of ALL OR NOTHING running through my mind, the pastor walked up to me and said, "YOU'RE A NEW LAMB OF GOD," and guess what else he said to me. (Now remember I had never seen Pastor Combs before in my life.) He said just what God and I were talking about. He told me, "ALL OR NOTHING," and laid his hands on me. I could not stand up. My knees buckled and down I went. As I laid on the floor, I knew that there was a God for sure. There's no way the pastor knew what God and I were talking and thinking about. God had let Pastor Combs into our conversation. WOW, what a feeling I had and still have every time I think about how good God is.

Well, that is my story how I came to the Lord!! But I have one more short story to tell you how God spoke to me that same night and told me that I was HOME, LIKE A LOST LAMB AND HOME AT JUBILEE WORSHIP CENTER. The next time God spoke to me was the following Sunday night on the way to church. He told me to watch my tongue. I didn't have a clue what God meant. (I'm sure my wife could tell you what he meant.)

Thank you for reading my story, and I'd beg you like my mom begged me on her deathbed to come to the Lord if I thought it would work, but I know that's not how God works. In closing, I just want you to think about where your family and you will spend eternity. Who knows? Maybe today will be your day to accept Jesus Christ into your life.

—Nick

CHAPTER 92
I Sold Drugs

I had a brain tumor.
I had a motorcycle accident.
I asked for help, and ....

At the age of five, I was going to church every Sunday with my family. Soon we were going Sunday morning, Sunday night, and Wednesday night. My family was on that path until I was thirteen. Then, my parents' relationship started to fail. We started going to church less and less. As the year went by, we stopped going completely.

Over the next couple of years, I started hanging out with the wrong crowd. At the age of fourteen, I got into a gang. I ran the streets and sold drugs every day for four years. I met a girl whom I wanted to marry. I quit hanging out on the streets, but I continued selling drugs. We had children, and I was trying to support my family. I had no education to get a job, so I tried to work by selling drugs to support them.

When I was twenty-four, my kids started going to a day care at a church called Jubilee Worship Center. One Sunday, I decided to take my child to church. We went to Jubilee, and I felt like I was at home. I started going off and on for a few months. Then, I started to pray for God to change my life. I was tired of the life of selling drugs, and my family was falling apart.

At the age of twenty-five, the doctors found a tumor on my brain. My family had moved out of our home. I had to spend twelve days in the hospital for observation. When I got out of the hospital, I stayed with my mom. I went back to church that Sunday. The pastor prayed for me. I had surgery that Monday, and I felt better than I had in a long time.

I decided to move back to Portage, so I could go back to work. I stayed with a friend. I started going to church every Sunday, still praying to be changed more by God. I went for a ride on my motorcycle, and I wrecked. My foot was broken in four places, but I knew God would help me through this like he helped me through my tumor. I went back to church on Sunday morning. I am now going to church on Sunday morning, Sunday night, and Wednesday night. God has blessed me with a job that pays double what I had been making, and I am working on getting my family back in church. My motto is, "Just trust in God, and He will provide."

—Chris

Appendix D

Jubilee Worship Center
Salvation and Witnessing Contributors

The authors would like to express their gratitude to all those from Jubilee Worship Center who shared their experiences with Salvation and witnessing for this book. To recognize and thank these people, each one is listed below. Please pray for these worthy Christians as they seek to do the Lord's work.

Ismael Alicea
Lori Alicea
Daniel Allen
Jodi Allen
Anonymous (1)
Illiana Arocho
Patty Arocho

Darrell Bailey
Evelyn Bailey
Christine Ball
Carla Barbarossa
Jim Barbarossa
Jim Barbarossa, Jr.
Joy Barbarossa
Connie Bergner
Ryan Bergner
Carolyn Brown
Cindy Buck

Arcangel Camacho
Lynne Camacho
Sara Cardona
Elsie Chavez

Guy Chavez
Bishop Dale P. Combs
Dale T. Combs
Lisa Combs
Bob Contreraz
Martina Contreraz
Mary Crosier
Robert Crosier
Edward Crundwell
Bill Cumbee
Erin Cumbee
Kyle Cumbee
Mary Beth Cumbee

Guido Dabney, Sr.
Willie Mae Dabney
Kay Davis
Jackie DeBold
Steve DeBold
Erik DelValle
Priscilla DelValle
Tim Dickens
Valerie Dickens

Lupe Dickerson
Shannon Doherty

Crystal Espinosa
Dialy Espinosa
Stephanie Espinosa
David Evans, Sr.

Angela Fortenbury
Eric Fortenbury

Charlie Gabbard
Carey Gaddis
Tom Gaddis
Jennifer Gallagher
Robert Gallagher
Antonia Garcia
Jessica Garcia
Mary Lou Glenz
Noel Gorgas
Tanya Gorgas
Susan Griffith
Patricia Grissom
Tom Grissom

Rafael Hernandez, Jr.
Amanda Hritz
Andy Hritz
Debbie Hritz
Mona Hursey

Eric Israel
Rosetta Israel

Pam Jones

Michael King
Patricia King

Lois LaFevre
Jeremy Lawless
Michelle Lawless
James Lindsey
Jasmine Lindsey
Marla Lindsey
Fernando Lopez, Jr.
Irene Lopez
Nellie Lopez

Jacob Maddock
Moses Marrero
Sally Marrero
Contreraz Martina
Frank Martir
Anita Mayfield
Dewey Mayfield
Joe Mayfield
Marla Mayfield
Vanessa Mayfield
Carolyn Mills
Nick Minton
Miranda Moore

Kevin Nash
Sherri Nash
Michelle Negron
Theresa Nickelson
Rhonda Norris

Dalisha Otero
Michelle Otero
Richard Otero

Taylor Otero
Tracy Otero

Misty Ramirez
Evie Reid
Audrey Reno
Doug Reno
Gary Rich
Ruby Robbins
Cesar Ruiz
Selma Ruiz

Chris Saffrahn
Ed Saffrahn
Whitney Sanchez
Evelyn Scott
John Scott
Patricia Seeba
Josiah Sherrow
Pat Sherrow

Russ Sherrow
Marie Sweeney

James Taylor, Sr.
Alvin Thomason
Iris Torres
Ivan Torres

Bobby Underwood
Deloris Underwood

Kathy Vaughan
Mike Vaughan

Pauline Ward
Audra Watson
Gervaise Weaver
Zelma White

Lisa Zottneck

Appendix E

The Importance and Power of the Resurrection

Aaron Wentz

First preached at Calvary Chapel in the City, Boston, Massachusetts, April 19, 2009

Moreover, brethren, I declare to you the gospel
which I preached to you,
which also you received and in which you stand,
by which also you are saved, if you hold fast
that word which I preached to you —
unless you believed in vain.
For I delivered to you first of all that which I also received:
that Christ died for our sins according to the Scriptures,
and that He was buried, and
that He rose again the third day according to the Scriptures,
and that He was seen by Cephas, then by the twelve.
After that He was seen by over five hundred brethren at once,
of whom the greater part remain to the present,
but some have fallen asleep.
After that He was seen by James, then by all the apostles.
Then last of all He was seen by me also,
as by one born out of due time.

— 1 Corinthians 15:1-8 (NKJV)

If you were a guest on the *Larry King Live* show, and he looked at you square in the eyes and he asked the hard questions such as: "What about the Muslims? What about the Jews? Are they going to hell? Are you telling me you have the only way, the only truth? What do you think about that?" If he looked at you square in the eyes and asked you those hard questions, would you be able to answer them?

Most Christians in America don't know how to answer those questions. The first typical response is "Larry, this is just what I believe ...."

You can believe that the Earth is flat and cows fly, but it doesn't make it true. In America, we think that if we believe something, it makes it true. But again, you can believe cows fly and that the Earth is flat; but your belief doesn't make it true.

The Christian faith is: Because what God says is always true; therefore, I believe it. Do you see the distinction there? Because something is true, therefore you believe it .... Not because I believe it; therefore, it's true. And the latter viewpoint is what the world is using today.

A second way people would answer a hard question is to tell how Jesus has changed their lives and what Jesus means to them. I do believe that is a valid response. At my church last Sunday for the Easter service we had three people stand up and give their Salvation testimony.

But here's one problem with such testimonies: All you have to do is get a Mormon, a Jew, a Hindu, a Muslim, and put them in the room with an evangelical Christian, and, guess what, their faiths have changed their lives, too! So what makes your belief any better?

See, you can tell someone how God has changed your life, but in the Muslim and Buddhist and Hindu worlds, their god has changed their lives as well.

But what's missing in all these elements is the truth. As evangelicals, we have to remember there is Truth with a capital T. You may have your truth, your friends may have their truth, people in your college or school or work may have their truth, but are their truths true, with a capital T?

Let's get back to being on the *Larry King* show. What should you tell Larry King? There is only one answer you should give. And the wonderful thing about is, it's only two words: *the resurrection*! Jesus Christ's resurrection is the answer to all of those questions. It's the answer to every question Larry King would ask you.

Where in the Bible do we find the importance of the resurrection? 1 Corinthians 15 is one of the most important chapters on the power and importance of the resurrection. What exactly is the Christian message found there?

In 1 Corinthians 15:1 the Apostle Paul says, "... I declare to you the gospel ...." Mark it. Write it down. Get it there in your mind. There is one Gospel. People might use the word gospel and have different meanings when they say the word gospel, but there is only one Gospel. Paul is declaring here in black and white very clearly what is the Gospel.

I declare to you; I remind you of the Gospel. Get it into your heart; there's only one Message. People all around the world are laying down their lives for this very Message. Why lay down your life for something that is not true or that you're not firm on? If there's one Message that we need to know for certain and have deep in our hearts, that we're going to be able to take a stand on, it's the Gospel.

And I think there are many reasons why so many popular evangelical preachers come onto the *Larry King* show and can't answer his questions. Here's one possibility: Maybe it's because they don't know the Gospel.

Have you thought of that? How can someone go on the air with Larry King and not talk about the Gospel, fudge on the Gospel, and not take a stand on the Gospel? Maybe they don't know It!

I know pastors who have been saved after being in the ministry. I know missionaries who have been saved after being in the ministry. I know people who have been saved in Bible college. I think it's possible that people who go on *Larry King* don't know the Gospel. Maybe it's not firm in their own hearts.

Now look at what it says in verse 2, "by which also you are saved, ..." This is the Message by which people are saved. This is the Message of how people cross over from darkness to light, from death to eternal life. There is the one Message to believe; there is one Message to take hold of. There are not many Messages; there is one Message.

It is sad to think that you could scoop up a bunch of evangelicals and put them in a room and ask, "What is the Gospel?" and they would probably have many different answers to what is the Gospel.

Paul goes on to say this "… if you hold fast …." Many people who say they know the Lord also say they believe in the Gospel. But eventually, if someone falls away and holds onto a different message, obviously their faith was in vain. They didn't actually believe it themselves.

Paul goes on to say in verses 3 and 4 "… that Christ died for our sins according to the Scriptures, and that He was buried, and that He rose again on the third day according to the Scriptures." That is the Gospel.

You can go to many book stores and get Gospel tracts, and most have the resurrection missing from their tracts. I just picked up a Gospel tract from a popular denomination here in America, and it was missing the cross and the resurrection. It talked about belief in Jesus, receiving Jesus, repenting; but it had nothing of the Gospel.

I was on YouTube recently trying to find a good video that I could download to give out to friends, and I found a cool video with a surfer walking along the ocean sharing Christ. Unfortunately, it was missing the resurrection.

When we do training for adults in our ministry, the one thing that most adults leave out is the resurrection. Recently, I bought a DVD for our ministry, and I watched it with our staff. I asked them what was missing from this video, and they scratched their heads. When I told them, they said, "Ah … the resurrection."

I called the guy who made the DVD and told him that the cross was preached but the DVD missed having even one mention of the resurrection. His reply was, "You know, you're the first one who ever caught that." They sold this DVD to a popular ministry, it's been translated into 20 languages, and they tell me I'm the first one to call and say it's missing the resurrection? Later, the guy goes on to say it's really not that important. He was embarrassed. Wouldn't you be if you spent a big budget on this DVD, translated it into 20 different languages, and some young guy calls up from Boston and says the resurrection is missing from *your Gospel presentation*?

287

The resurrection is so important because this is the Message that we proclaim, by which we are saved: that Christ died, He was buried, and then rose from the dead. We are very cross-centered people and we don't forget the cross, hopefully; but the resurrection, that's a different story. I think it's because we may not always understand why the resurrection is so important.

The Credibility of the Resurrection

... He rose again the third day according to the Scriptures,
and that He was seen by Cephas, then by the twelve.
After that He was seen by over five hundred brethren at once,
of whom the greater part remain to the present,
but some have fallen asleep.
After that He was seen by James, then by all the apostles.
Then last of all He was seen by me also,
as by one born out of due time.

— 1 Corinthians 15:4-8 (NKJV)

Early Christian Belief in the Resurrection

Before Paul talks about the importance of the resurrection, he first talks about the credibility of the resurrection. In verse 3, there is a phrase that is often overlooked which is a very important point in the credibility of the resurrection: "For I delivered to you first of all that which I also received ...." What Paul is saying in verses 3 and 8 ("Then last of all He was seen by me also, as by one born out of due time.") is in essence: "I'm writing to you, Corinthians, to tell you that the Gospel was passed along and taught to me as one who was saved late."

Some resurrection skeptics say the resurrection developed into a myth. They argue that as Christianity began to progress, supposedly old wives tales and rumors about Jesus' death and missing body began to develop. Many skeptics believe that as time went on, Jesus was turned into a god and a story was made up that He rose from the dead.

Let's look at the historical evidence for the resurrection. The book of 1 Corinthians was written between 50 and 55 A.D. The remaining parts of the New Testament were written later on in the first century.

So if Christ was resurrected, buried, and ascended to heaven in about 33 A.D., and 1 Corinthians was written in 55 A.D., you're talking about only a slightly more than 20-year span between which Christ rose from the dead and ascended, and the letter of 1 Corinthians was written. So in about a little more than a 20-year time span, not a 100-year time span, we have the Message of the early church that was passed on to the Apostle Paul, which was that Christ died, was buried, and that He rose from the dead.

So to think that Christianity or the resurrection was made up later on doesn't fit the historical record. Again, the earliest New Testament book is saying what the church believed then: This is what the church taught Paul; this is what they believed, they preached, and they passed on to Paul, and that Paul then understood as a newcomer into the faith, a late-comer in a sense. The Gospel was described in 55 A.D. that Christ died, He was buried, and that He rose from the dead.

Many people think that this is a creed. You may be familiar with the Apostles' Creed (which says that Jesus rose from the dead on the third day), and the Nycian Creed (which also says that Jesus rose on the third day). Many scholars think that these creeds are based on creeds of the early church as those Christians shared what the foundation of their faith was. Because the New Testament books were not yet written, the first creed began to serve almost like Scripture as early Christians began to record the formations of their faith.

Secondly, Paul says this in verses 5 and 6 "… that He was seen by Cephas, then by the twelve. After that He was seen by over five hundred brethren at once …."

We live in a world in which science, of course, is supreme. If you can't prove it by science, it's not valid.

But we know that in a court of law it is very hard to prove something scientifically. Once you leave the present and look at the past, science is less helpful because it is based on observations in the present. Go back a year, a month, a week, even a day, and you're no longer dealing with pure science because science deals with observations in the present.

So in a court of law, what do they do to prosecute someone? The best thing they can do in a court of law during the present is to ask an eyewitness. If you have one, that's good. If you have 10 or more eyewitnesses all saying the same thing, most likely the case is closed.

With the eyewitness accounts of the resurrection, the Bible is saying that Jesus didn't die and rise again in a closet. It wasn't a secret. In verses 5 and 6 we read that Jesus was seen by his disciples and by over 500 other people. Jesus' disciples touched the nail-scarred hands and ate with Him. At the end of verse 6, Paul says that some of the disciples still remain (are still alive). Paul means: "If you don't think Jesus has risen, go ask them." The eyewitnesses were still there; the apostles were still around. The Corinthians were being challenged by Paul about the resurrection: Go ask the witnesses if Christ has risen.

Why Begin Christianity in Jerusalem?

At the end of verse 6, Paul says that "some have fallen asleep," meaning that some have died. Of course, some of these people died a natural death, and we know from history that most or many of the New Testament Christians were persecuted for their faith or even died for their faith.

If Jesus Christ didn't die and rise from the dead, why would the early Christians begin their movement in Jerusalem?

If the whole thing was a fraud and you want to succeed in fooling people, don't start Christianity in Jerusalem. It would be wiser to go to India to start your own little cult in a village promoting a guy named Jesus who did all these miracles and rose from the dead. No one there could find out that you were lying.

It doesn't make any sense to think that Christianity is bogus on the basis of the resurrection if the leaders started their movement in the city by which he was killed.

Why did they kill Jesus? Because they wanted to get rid of Christians. If you kill their leader, they believed that Christianity would diminish or die.

But when Jesus died, His followers started preaching in Jerusalem — not indoors secretly, but out in the open air, outdoors in front of the very people who killed Jesus and watched Him die, saying that Jesus was risen from the dead. Now if Christianity is not credible, it doesn't make any sense to begin the movement in the city where everyone would know that your belief in His resurrection is bogus.

Who Would Die for a Known Lie?

Early Christianity began on the basis that the tomb of Jesus was empty as described by people who were convinced He had appeared to them personally. Because of their great zealousness, they began to preach publicly. The early Pharisees and religious leaders could not stop them. We also know that many of early apostles were not only jailed or persecuted, but that many of them were killed for their beliefs such as Paul, John, and Peter.

Most historians believe the tomb was empty because if it wasn't, Christianity would have ceased immediately. Unbelievers would have scoffed by saying, "Jesus is risen from the dead? Of course not, his body is right here in the grave where it always has been."

But, of course, history did not unfold such events. Most people say if the tomb was empty that there are only two good options: either the disciples stole the body or the Pharisees stole the body.

Why would the Pharisees or religious leaders take the body of Jesus? They killed Jesus to destroy Him and His movement. If they take the body, they're giving more fuel to the Christians who can then say "Our Leader rose from the dead."

Maybe the disciples took the body. Think about the terrorist attacks on 9/11 in terms of a willingness of believers to die for a cause. What happened on 9/11 is the most important, most quintessential recent example of how people, when they really believe something, will go to the extreme and even lay down their lives for something. Those terrorists laid down their lives for their belief, in their extreme Islamic faith, that if they were to martyr themselves, they would go right to Paradise.

People often say, "People die for what they believe all the time." We can point to those extremist Muslim men as people who gave their lives for *what they believed to be the truth.*

But here is the difference with the early Christians: If the disciples took the body, then began preaching, being persecuted and then dying for their belief in the resurrection, *they would be dying, not for what they knew to be the truth, but for what they knew was a lie.* Do you see the difference?

Is there any historical evidence that people die for what they know is a lie? No. People die for what they believe is the truth. Even in the Jonestown mass suicide, people died for what they believed to be the truth ... not for a known lie.

There is credibility in the resurrection because of the persecution the early Christians faced and suffered from. Many people when given this simple argument, (and I've seen it at universities, graduate-level places, on the street) go "hmmm." It is a very powerful argument.

I actually think that in God's sovereignty He allowed the disciples to be persecuted and die just so that the resurrection would be seen as credible. There is great evidence among scholars and just in the Biblical accounts themselves for the credibility of the resurrection. Listen to what the Oxford professor, Roman historian, and scholar, Thomas Arnold (who wrote a multiple-volume history of Rome), had to say in *Christian Life, Its Hopes, Its Fears, and Its Close: Sermons,* Third Edition (B. Fellowes, London, 1845), "Sermon II: The Sign of the Prophet Jonah", pp. 15-16:

> *I have been used for many years to study the history of other times, and to examine and weigh the evidence of those who have written about them; and I know of no one fact in the history of mankind, which is proved by better and fuller evidence of every sort to the understanding of a fair enquirer, than the great sign which God has given us, that Christ died and rose again from the dead ....*
>
> *But where the evidence of other facts ends, that of our great sign of Christ crucified and Christ risen may be said only to*

begin. I might convince your understandings, as my own has been convinced long since, that the fact is proved according to the best rules of testimony; — but if our belief rest here, we do not know the full richness, the abundant and overflowing light of our Christian faith. The evidence of Christ's apostles, preserved to us in their writings, is very strong, very full, very irresistible; hear it fairly, and we cannot believe that Christ is not risen. But the evidence of Christ's Spirit is much more strong, more full, more penetrating our whole nature.

Paul's Testimony

So let's move on to verse 8. Paul says that Jesus appeared to him as one who was "born out of due time." By that, Paul meant that he was one of the last leaders of the early church in 55 A.D. to have been converted: He was saved late in comparison to the other disciples. As one who formerly persecuted the church, Paul essentially said (and I paraphrase verses 9-10) "I'm going to work harder. I'm going to make up for lost time. I'm going to make sure that my life isn't wasted. I'm going to work harder than other people."

And that's what Paul did. He traveled all around the world. He was persecuted, beaten, shipwrecked, and laid down his life for this belief that the resurrection was true, that Jesus appeared to him and called him into the ministry. And in verse 11 it says at the end "... so we preach and so you believed."

Are You Saved?

If you have believed a different gospel, it's very important to know that you may not be saved. People today come to Jesus for many different reasons: "God, my marriage is broken"; "God, I need a job"; "God, I'm lonely"; "God, make me happy." God can help us with those things, but that's not the Gospel.

I know many people who God helps to find a job. All of a sudden they feel closer to God, and they feel like God has accepted them. They walk around thinking they are right with God, and they're not.

If you possibly think Jesus is here only to meet your felt needs, unfortunately that is not the right message. THE Gospel is about us being reconciled with God. God is good and holy, and we are not. We cannot approach God in our own selves for we are sinners. We have broken God's laws and have become lawbreakers and sinners in His eyes. We cannot approach God in our own righteousness.

When God sees you, He does not see a man or a woman who has been good enough to go to heaven. We have not been good enough because we have sinned. The punishment for our sin is death.

So when Christ came, what did He do? He actually took our judgment, our death penalty, for us. He literally died my death; He took my punishment, an innocent God-man taking my place, dying for my sins, being buried, and then rising from the dead, proving that He is victorious over sin and death.

And we come to God, through Jesus Christ, for the purpose of Salvation. By this I mean, have you ever come to God and said, "God, I have disobeyed you; I have led a rebellious life; I have lived a selfish life; and the only way I can come to you and have a right relationship with you is that I need to confess that I am a sinner, that I need your forgiveness"?

If you've never truly come to God personally as a sinner to find forgiveness, you may not be saved. You may have believed in vain. And now I'll move on to the importance of the resurrection.

The Importance of the Resurrection

Now if Christ is preached that He has been raised from the dead,
how do some among you say
that there is no resurrection of the dead?
But if there is no resurrection of the dead,
then Christ is not risen.
And if Christ is not risen,
then our preaching is empty
and your faith is also empty.

— 1 Corinthians 15:12-14 (NKJV)

In verses 12-14 of 1 Corinthians 15, some translations use the phrase "in vain" meaning that if Christ has not risen, the Bible says your worship service, your prayers, your Bible reading are nothing and empty. You're praying to someone who doesn't exist. You're talking to and worshipping someone who is not alive. It's all a farce. It's all phony. If Christ has not been risen, then our prayer life, our worship, our Bible reading, it's all in vain.

Think of it this way: If the resurrection is not true, everything that Jesus taught essentially was a lie. Jesus said that He had the same authority as God. Who is God? God has authority over life and death (Deuteronomy 30:15-19). If Jesus said He had the same authority as God, God who has authority over life and death, and Jesus is defeated by death, it means everything that Jesus taught was a lie. *If that's the case, as followers of Jesus everything we hold to is a lie.* Everything we follow is a lie.

Also, Jesus said that He is the resurrection and the life, and whoever believes in Him will live even though he dies. If Jesus didn't rise from the dead and still live, we don't have a resurrected life in Him; we won't have eternal life; and we're not going to heaven.

If Jesus can't overcome death, you can't overcome death. You have no power. You have no hope. We have no hope for the future. We're not going to heaven. It's all a lie.

Here's another thought: We believe that Jesus was perfect and sinless. But if Jesus didn't rise from the dead, then He wasn't perfect.

Think of it this way: Death is the punishment for sinners; therefore, if Christ stayed dead, it would mean that He got what was justly due to Him.

But if He was raised from the dead, it would prove that the death He died was for others, not because of His own sin. When people die, it is the consequence of their sin. If Jesus died and stayed dead, it would mean He was a sinner.

But if He rose from the dead, then Jesus didn't die for His own sin as a sinner. He died on behalf of us as the perfect God-man who died for our sins and rose from the dead.

Do you ever like being called a liar? If Jesus didn't rise from the dead, then the last time you witnessed to somebody you were promoting lies. According to verse 15, if the resurrection isn't true, there is no life after death, heaven isn't real, and Jesus Himself was a liar. If Jesus was a liar and we follow Jesus, then we are no different.

Let's consider verse 16: "For if *the* dead do not rise, then Christ is not risen." As Christians we believe that we have been saved and rescued from our sins. That's important because we have broken the commandments of God: We have lied, stolen, cheated, committed adultery, or murdered in our hearts. We have come to Jesus for forgiveness, and Christians believe they are saved. However, you can't call on someone who is dead. The Bible says, "For *'whoever calls on the name of the LORD shall be saved.'*" (Romans 10:13, NKJV).

At some point in your life, hopefully, you have said, "Jesus, come into my life; save me, a sinner." But you can't call on someone who is dead. Dead people don't answer you, so you're still in your sins. You're no better off than where you were 10 or 20 years ago. You're not saved.

However, if Jesus has risen, if He was resurrected from the dead, if He has conquered sin and death, then we do call upon a risen Savior and that is our hope. That is our belief: that Someone who rescued us is present and alive — He is resurrected.

But if He's dead, He can't save us. We're still in our sins. That's what verse 17 tells us.

In verse 18 it says those who have fallen asleep are lost as well if Christ has not risen. "Fallen asleep" is another way of saying people have died.

We all know people who have died: moms and dads, grandmas and grandpas. We have the hope that one day we're going to see these people again. We're going to see mom and dad, grandma and grandpa, whoever has fallen asleep or died in Christ.

If the resurrection isn't true, there's no life after death. There's no hope. Then all those people that you hoped to see someday, you're not going to see them. They're dead. There's no hope, you're not going to see them at all. They're lost forever.

If Jesus did not rise from the dead, then not only are we liars, believing a false message, but we are wasting our lives! We've got one life to live, and we're out talking about Jesus, singing about Jesus, worshiping Jesus, and it's all a lie. You know some people look at us and say "Man, you're sad." They think what we're doing is a lie, it's phony, it's made up, it's a fairy tale. They look at us and they laugh at us, it's made up. Paul is saying in verse 19, "They're right!" If it is all a lie, we should be pitied. "Poor Christians, gosh, I wish they'd get a life. I wish they'd grow up."

At the end of 1 Corinthians 15 Paul basically says, "I'm walking around, animals are trying to eat me, I'm getting shipwrecked, and if it's all not true, forget it! Eat, drink, and be merry. Go for it. Go nuts. This is the only life you've got. Forget it. Go to town, party, and do whatever you want because this is the only life you've got!"

There's a popular skeptic out today who is writing books against the Bible. He graduated from my school, Moody Bible Institute, and has now become an atheist. What does an atheist have to live for? This is what he said, "Now that I've turned atheist I eat better food and drink better wine." That's about as good as it gets for human beings. If the resurrection is not true, eat better food, drink better wine, get into lots of debt on your credit card, and go to town. There really is no hope. Once you die, that's it.

So we can see that the resurrection is very, very important. It is the foundation of our faith. It is everything. We do not have a Gospel if the resurrection is not included and is not preached.

The Power of the Resurrection

The last enemy that *will be destroyed* is *death.*
For "He has put all things under His feet."
But when He says, "all things are put under Him,"
it is *evident that He who put all things under Him is excepted.*

— 1 Corinthians 15:26-27 (NKJV)

Once a guy came up to me on the street after I was done preaching and said, "Look, I'm going to tell you one more thing before I go: There have been other resurrections!" And he walked off.

Yes, Jesus raised Lazarus from the dead in John 11. But poor Lazarus. Why? He only lived to die again.

In verse 20, it says that Jesus is the first fruit of the resurrection: That's the Jewish way of saying He's the best, He's the greatest, He is supreme over all other resurrections. Why? When Christ rose from the dead, He didn't die again. He ascended into heaven.

The ascension is important because the ascension of Christ is Jesus Christ proclaiming in essence, "I no longer am going to die again. I have defeated death forever. Death has no hold on me at all. I am totally victorious over death." And the ascension also validates everything He taught, everything He believed, everything He preached, so we know that everything He stood for and died for is true. God, the Father, was blessing Him and ascending Him into heaven, showing He was victorious over sin and death. He is the first fruit. His is the greatest of all resurrections. Christ is risen, and that's our hope.

In verse 21, we read that Christ is victorious over our greatest enemy, death ("For since by man *came* death, by Man also *came* the resurrection of the dead." — NKJV). And it's so sad when I go to colleges and the new atheism is proclaimed: "Oh we're not afraid of death. That's a part of life, naturalism. Everybody dies. That's a part of life, and I'm not afraid of death anymore." It's so sad to hear young people say they're not as afraid of death as they used to be because death is part of life. It's our culture's belief now. "Death is a part of life. You've got to accept it," people think.

And the Bible is saying, "No, don't accept it. Don't believe it. Don't think that way. Death is an enemy! Death is terrible. Death is tragic. Death is the worst thing in life, and Jesus has overcome death." As Christians our message is: "We know Someone who has overcome death."

I don't know about you, but I've looked death square in the eyes. I've seen people die. I've looked into the caskets of people who have died. It's not good. It's not normal. It's not natural. It's the effect of sin. It's the effect of evil on this world.

And Jesus came into the world, looked at death square in the eye, grabbed it by the throat, and overcame it. He was victorious over death. He is our Savior; He is our resurrected King. That's what we proclaim, and how sad it is that we evangelicals don't even preach the resurrection that is our hope and glory.

Proof for Life after Death

I have been crucified with Christ;
it is no longer I who live, but Christ lives in me;
and the life *which I now live in the flesh*
I live by faith in the Son of God,
who loved me and gave Himself for me.

— Galatians 2:20 (NKJV)

Let me ask you a question: Is there any proof that there is life after death? Yes. Christ died, and He rose again. We know when it occurred in time, in history, with objectivity. It's not subjective.

Do you believe in reincarnation? Can you prove that reincarnation occurs? Can you prove that your Uncle Sam is now a cow walking down the street in Calcutta?

I don't mean to rude but that's what some believe: That their Uncle Sam is reincarnated as a cow, a bug, a whatever. They believe that if you are good, you're reincarnated to something good. If you lived a bad life, you're reincarnated to something bad such as a cow, a bug, or something like that.

But can you prove that? No, it's just a belief.

Can we prove the resurrection? Yes! It happened in history, at a set time, was recorded, has been studied by historians, can be researched through eyewitness accounts, and credited by the death and persecution of the apostles. We have evidence, we have hope, we have objectivity that what we believe is not just what I believe, it's not just my opinion.

We need to ask non-Christians: "Do you believe in life after death?" They will say, "Sure." The next question needs to be, "Is there any proof?" They will sadly say, "No." At that point we need to share our Message: "I've got proof. Christ died and was raised from the dead; therefore, we know that there's life after death. Jesus said, 'I am the resurrection and the life. He who believes in Me, though he may die, he shall live. And whoever lives and believes in Me shall never die ....'" (John 11:25-26, NKJV).

In 2003, my sister was hit by a drunk driver. She was newly married, driving from New Jersey to Michigan. She and her new husband were on the cell phone saying, "Mom, I'll be home soon" and then she was hit by a drunk driver. That day she died. The day I was told about my sister and her fatal car crash, my tears of sadness instantly turned to tears of joy because she was a believer. I automatically had hope. My thought wasn't "I'm never going to see her again." Instead, our whole family had hope that she was in heaven and that we would see her again. We have something good to hold on to.

Lastly, in 1 Corinthians 15:55 the Apostle Paul says, *"O Death, where is your sting? O Hades, where is your victory?"* (NKJV). One commentary said it's Paul mocking death, laughing at death, looking death square in the eye and saying, "You have no hold on me anymore! You have no power. I don't fear you anymore! Where is your victory? Where is your sting? You have no power over me. Jesus is my resurrected hope! I have no fear of you anymore!" This is our Message as Christians. This is our hope!

Aaron Wentz is a graduate of Moody Bible Institute with a B.A. degree in Evangelism/Discipleship and is currently the Boston Branch Director of Open Air Campaigners (OAC), www.oacusa.org. The goal of OAC Boston is to reach Americans and internationals with the Gospel and bring them into fellowship with local evangelical churches. This is accomplished by going out into the streets, universities and subways, publicly proclaiming the Gospel as Jesus and the Apostle Paul did in the New Testament. After the message, people sometimes stay to ask questions and engage in conversation. Gospel material is given out, including an address for follow-up.

Aaron Wentz's Testimony

Place Your Life in His Hands

Therefore, if anyone is in Christ,
he is a new creation; ...."

— 2 Corinthians 5:17 (NIV)

Hello, my name is Aaron Wentz. I was born and raised in Flint, Michigan. My parents loved music and were music teachers. Around the age of 12, I fell in love with music, especially the drums and percussion.

By the end of the year in eighth grade, I was full of dreams and knew what I wanted to do for a living and where I wanted to go to college. Because of my dreams, I became a very driven person in the realm of music. Most people take up music because it's fun. I took up music because I wanted to be a professional and even become famous. In many ways, drums became my god. I lived and breathed music. I would sit in front of the TV for hours and study musicians.

However, by the time I was a junior in high school, my drive to be the best drove me into the ground. I lost my ability to play because of the swelling in my arms from playing too much. For ten months I couldn't play. Not being able to practice meant I couldn't get as ready as I would like for my college auditions. All this stress began to break me down day after day.

Towards the end of my senior year in high school, my mom gave me a book on prayer as way to help me out. I read a chapter on giving things up to God and letting Him handle our problems. Now, as a child, my parents raised me as a Christian. Therefore, I did believe in the Bible as God's Word and that God was real. The only problem was that I didn't really know how to have a relationship with Him. I thought that being religious or being good was the ticket to heaven. I found out I had the wrong views of how to be accepted by God.

Because of the rebellion in our hearts towards God and others, God is not happy with our lives. The rebellious choices we make are called sin. Sin actually keeps us out of heaven. Because God is a good God, He has to punish sinners. This is why people go to hell. The good news is that God sent Jesus, the Son of God, to take our punishment on Himself so we could go free. God could have left us in our sins, but, instead, He loved us so much that Jesus died on the Cross and rose from the dead to pay our sin debt, a debt we could never pay ourselves.

The night I read the chapter on prayer, God worked in my heart. I realized that I couldn't reach Him through religion but only through Jesus Christ. So, paraphrasing the words at the end of my testimony, I placed my life in the hands of Jesus and asked Him to take over. My prayer went something like this, "Dear God, I have made a mess of my life. I know Jesus is Lord and died for all my sins and rebellion. Please save me and come into my life and take over. My life is Yours. Amen." After I said that, I went to bed hoping that something might change.

When I woke up, and in the days to follow, I truly was changed by God. I felt clean and as if a weight was lifted off my shoulders. I later found out that I was born again. Jesus said in the book of John, chapter 3, verse 3, that a person must be born again to enter the Kingdom of God. So, praise God, in May of 1992, I was born again and forgiven of all my sins. And now, I choose to live for Jesus and tell others about Him.

To provide Northwest Indiana a church where
both seekers and believers from any background
or cultural difference can experience the Love
and Power of God through corporate Worship,
Praise, and Ministry. To train them from New
Birth to a growing maturity in Christ to be an
active participant in the Harvest.
"A Place Of New Beginnings"

Jubilee Worship Center
415 North Hobart Road
Hobart, IN 46342
(219) 947.0301
JubileeWorshipCenter.com

Step by Step Ministries

Jim and Carla Barbarossa are equipping Evangelists that have been sent out to the world wide church and are available to advise your church, your organization or you as an individual as to the best resources we have to help you to implement the strategies that God has shown us.

You can see our evangelism products at our web site www.step-by-step.org, you can email questions to Jim at jim@step-by-step.org or you can call Jim to personally guide you as to what would best meet your needs at 219 787 9933.

Please keep in mind that Jim travels and teaches on these subjects internationally and may not be able to take your call immediately but he will get back to you as soon as he can.

Jim is committed to helping pastors of local churches to raise up strong witnessing congregations by helping to identify and raise up an in house evangelist and a team of fire starters to equip the saints to share Jesus. Once these things are in place Jim is only a phone call away and will partner with you to help you to build a strong witnessing church.

If you would like to help Step by Step Ministries continue its mission:

1. To establish the gift of equipping the evangelist in local churches around the world.

2. To call the 97% of Christians that refuse to share their faith to repent and then teach them how.

3. To plant tract, tape and CD distribution centers around the world to supply evangelism tools to local people to reach the lost.

For every $220 we sow into the nation of Pakistan we are able to produce 1000 CDs or audio tapes. For every 1000 CDs or audio tapes given to the lost we are seeing 500 people come to Jesus. The tract, tape and CD distribution centers is very very good soil.

Please send your love gift to:

Step by Step Ministries
815 S. Babcock Road
Porter, Indiana 46304

Phone 219-787-9933
Fax 219-787-8033
www.step-by-step.org
jim@step-by-step.org